T0256582

Data Analysis and Related Applications 3

Big Data, Artificial Intelligence
and Data Analysis Set

coordinated by
Jacques Janssen

Volume 11

Data Analysis and Related Applications 3

Theory and Practice – New Approaches

Edited by

Yiannis Dimotikalis
Christos H. Skiadas

WILEY

First published 2024 in Great Britain and the United States by ISTE Ltd and John Wiley & Sons, Inc.

ISTE Ltd
27-37 St George's Road
London SW19 4EU
UK

www.iste.co.uk

John Wiley & Sons, Inc.
111 River Street
Hoboken, NJ 07030
USA

www.wiley.com

Library of Congress Control Number: 2023949006

British Library Cataloguing-in-Publication Data
A CIP record for this book is available from the British Library
ISBN 978-1-78630-962-4

Contents

Chapter 6. Restricted Minimum Density Power Divergence Estimator for Step-stress ALT with Nondestructive One-shot Devices

Narayanaswamy BALAKRISHNAN, María JAENADA and Leandro PARDO

Chapter 7. Properties of American Options Under a Semi-Markov Modulated Black-Scholes Model

Kouki TAKADA, Marko DIMITROV, Lu JIN and Ying NI

Chapter 8. Numerical Studies of Implied Volatility Expansions Under the Gatheral Model

Mohammed ALBUHAYRI, Marko DIMITROV, Ying NI and Anatoliy MALYARENKO

Chapter 15. A Dynamic Neural Network Model for Accurate Recognition of Masked Faces

Chapter 16. An Action-based Monitoring Tool for Processes Subject to Multiple Quality Shifts

**Chapter 17. Phi Divergence and Consistent Estimation for
Stochastic Block Model**   243
Cyprien FERRARIS

Part 1

Data Analysis Classification

Walking into the Digital Era: Comparison of the European Union Countries in the Last Decade

This study allows us to understand how European Union countries are more or less prepared for confronting the digital era. In particular, we aim to understand whether the least developed countries are close or fairly distant from the others. For this study, data for some variables associated with digital skills, digital economy and digital society have been collected from the Eurostat database during the period 2010–2020. To analyze the data, we applied a double principal component analysis.

These results allow us to identify the differences and similarities between countries and indicators from 2010–2020, and, more precisely, to study the countries' evolution trends and the evolution of the relations between the different indicators.

1.1. Introduction

This study allows us to understand how the countries in the European Union are more or less prepared for confronting the digital era. People and societies have to deal with these new challenges not only to gain knowledge but also to promote growth, development and opportunities for everyone. In particular, it is interesting to see whether the least developed countries are close or relatively distant from the others in this route, in order to develop new strategies and to overcome detected fragilities.

Chapter written by Fernanda Otilia FIGUEIREDO and Adelaide FIGUEIREDO.

For a color version of all the figures in this chapter, see www.iste.co.uk/dimotikalis/data3.zip.

G1: Activity and employment status of individuals
V1 – % employed persons in the universe of active persons with ICT education
V2 – % males in the universe of employed persons with ICT education
V3 – % persons with tertiary education among employed persons with ICT education
V4 – % persons aged 15–34 among the employed persons with ICT education
G2: Internet at households with population aged 16–74 years
V5 – % households with Internet access
V6 – % households with broadband Internet connection
G3: Internet use by individuals
V7 – % individuals with daily Internet access in the last three months before the survey
V8 – % individuals with Internet use in the last three months before the survey
V9 – % individuals with Internet use in the last 12 months before the survey
V10 – % individuals with Internet use more than a year ago before the survey
V11 – % individuals who have never used Internet before the survey
G4: Online purchase by individuals
V12 – % individuals with last online purchase in the last three months before the survey
V13 – % individuals with last online purchase in the last 12 months before the survey
G5: Reasons of the individuals for using Internet
V14 – % individuals using Internet for finding information about goods and services
V15 – % individuals using Internet for looking for a job or sending a job application
V16 – % individuals using Internet for selling goods and services
G6: Enterprises use for selling (having e-commerce)
V17 – % enterprises with e-commerce sales of at least 1% turnover
G7: Enterprises that provided training to develop/upgrade
ICT skills, excluding enterprises of the financial sector
V18 – % small enterprises provided training to ICT/IT specialists
V19 – % medium enterprises provided training to ICT/IT specialists
V20 – % SMEs provided training to ICT/IT specialists
V21 – % large enterprises provided training to ICT/IT specialists
V22 – % small enterprises provided training to other employed persons
V23 – % medium enterprises provided training to other employed persons
V24 – % SMEs provided training to other employed persons
V25 – % large enterprises provided training to other employed persons
V26 – % small enterprises provided training to their personnel
V27 – % medium enterprises provided training to their personnel
V28 – % SMEs provided training to their personnel
V29 – % large enterprises provided training to their personnel

Table 1.1. *Variables considered in the study grouped by topic*

1.1.1. *The dataset*

For this study, a large number of indicators associated with digital skills, digital economy and digital society (29 variables) have been considered, as well as all European countries for which we have data available (30 individuals). The data for these indicators were collected from the Eurostat database during the period 2010–2020.

The variables are grouped by topic (groups G1–G7), and are listed in Table 1.1. When we refer to ICT (Information and Communication Technology) Education, in the general sense, it means providing users with a diverse set of technological tools, definitions and resources to create, store, communicate, manage and optimize information. The database aggregates the ICT education levels into two categories: upper-secondary and post-secondary non-tertiary (levels 3 and 4), and tertiary (levels 5–8). Concerning employed persons with ICT education, they are divided by two classes of age: 15–34 and 35–74. The enterprises are classified accordingly to the number of employees and self-employed persons as follows: small (10–49), medium (50–249), SMEs (10–249) and large (250 or more).

Of course, it would be interesting to include other indicators such as the percentage of the ICT sector in GPD, the R&D personnel in the ICT sector as a percentage of total R&D personnel or the business expenditure on R&D in the ICT sector as a percentage of total R&D expenditure, for instance. However, we do not have information for all countries and years during the period.

The countries (individuals) considered in this study are presented in Table 1.2. We also further analyzed six data tables, corresponding to the years 2010, 2012, 2014, 2016, 2018 and 2020, each one with the same countries and variables. As the United Kingdom was not part of the EU in 2020, we considered the values obtained in 2019, instead of 2020, so we could still include it in the analysis.

Countries	Countries	Countries
EU27 – European Union 27	FR – France	AT – Austria
BE – Belgium	HR – Croatia	PL – Poland
BG – Bulgaria	IT – Italy	PT – Portugal
CZ – Czechia	CY – Cyprus	RO – Romania
DK – Denmark	LV – Latvia	SI – Slovenia
DE – Germany	LT – Lithuania	SK – Slovakia
EE – Estonia	LU – Luxembourg	FI – Finland
IE – Ireland	HU – Hungary	SE – Sweden
GR – Greece	MT – Malta	UK – United Kingdom
ES – Spain	NL – Netherlands	NO – Norway

Table 1.2. *Countries considered in the study*

1.1.2. *Preliminary analysis of the data*

Before proceeding with a multivariate data analysis, we carried out an exploratory analysis in order to gain insight into the data. In particular, we represented the boxplots by year and for all of the variables (not presented here) and among other conclusions, it is worth mentioning here the huge number of outliers observed in the data, and reported in Table 1.3. The countries with an * are severe outliers. Some countries appear as outliers with respect to some variables during several years of the period 2010–2020, such as GR, RO and BG: GR is a severe lower outlier in variable V1 (the percentage of employed persons in the universe of active persons with ICT education is small comparatively to the corresponding percentage in the other countries); RO and BG are lower outliers in variables V21, V25 and V29 (the percentage of large enterprises providing training in ICT skills to their personnel, specialists or other employed persons is small when compared to what happens in other countries). We also mention, for instance, DK and FI, who appear during some years of the period as upper outliers in variable V15 (with a large percentage of individuals using the Internet to look for a job or sending a job application compared to other countries), and countries such as BE and FI, who in 2020 were upper outliers in variables V19, V23 and V27 (i.e. they have a large percentage of medium enterprises providing ICT training when compared with other countries). Other details can be found in Table 1.3.

Year		Variables and associated outliers
2010	Lower	V1(GR), V3(IT), V21(RO), V29(RO)
2012	Lower	V1(ES,GR*), V21(RO), V29(RO)
	Upper	V10(CZ)
2014	Lower	V1(PT,GR*), V7(RO), V21(RO), V29(RO)
	Upper	V10(BG)
2016	Lower	V1(GR*), V2(CY), V7(RO), V21(RO),V25(BG,RO), V29(BG,RO)
	Upper	V15(DK), V17(IE)
2018	Lower	V1(GR*,IT,PT), V3(PT), V21(RO),V25(BG,RO), V29(RO)
	Upper	V26(NO)
2020	Lower	V1(GR*,ES), V2(DK), V14(IT,RO),V19(RO), V21(RO), V23(BG,RO),V25(BG,RO), V27(BG,RO), V29(RO)
	Upper	V10(BG,IT), V15(DK,FI), V19(BE),V23(FI),V27(FI)

Table 1.3. *Variables that present several outliers along the period*

After an introduction, aiming to present this study and detailed descriptions of the dataset, as well as a preliminary data analysis, this chapter is organized as follows. Section 1.2 gives a small description of the double principal component analysis method, the statistical methodology applied in this work, and also includes part of the results obtained from the application of this method to the data. The representation and interpretation of the trajectories are provided in section 1.3, and section 1.4 concludes the chapter with some final conclusions.

1.2. Double principal component analysis: a brief description

To analyze the data, we applied a double principal component analysis (DPCA), a method of multivariate data analysis introduced in Bouroche (1975) to analyze three-way data with quantitative variables. This method can be modified to allow the analysis of categorical data. See, for instance, Lera et al. (2006).

DPCA is an extension of the principal component analysis (PCA) method, and allows us to jointly analyze several data tables with information collected on the same variables and individuals, in several instants of time, for instance. In this study, we have six data tables, corresponding to the years 2010, 2012, 2014, 2016, 2018 and 2020, all with the same countries and variables.

The application of the DPCA method comprises four steps: (1) interstructure, i.e. the analysis of the global evolution of the data along the period of time; (2) analysis of the clouds of individuals; (3) intrastructure, i.e. the choice of the best common space to represent the individuals and the variables; and (4) representation and interpretation of the trajectories of the individuals and variables.

From Figure 1.1, we can observe that the years appear in chronological order along the first axis. As can be expected, there are big changes between the periods of 2010 and 2020.

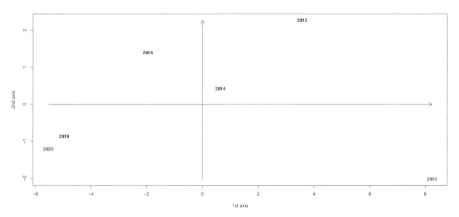

Figure 1.1. *Representation of the interstructure*

The analysis of individuals' clouds and, in particular, the percentage of explained inertia when they are projected in a subspace of a smaller dimension, lead us to select the plan of the first two principal axes obtained from the PCA of the year 2014 to represent the individuals and variables for all years. This system of principal axes minimizes the average loss of information, i.e. it globally maximizes the percentage of explained inertia. The projection of the countries and variables in this plan globally explains 76.6% of the total inertia. If we consider three axes, the percentage of the explained inertia increases to 81%, but the balance between the gain and the increase of complexity to interpret the trajectories lead us to choose only two axes. The results corresponding to the last step of the method are presented in the next section.

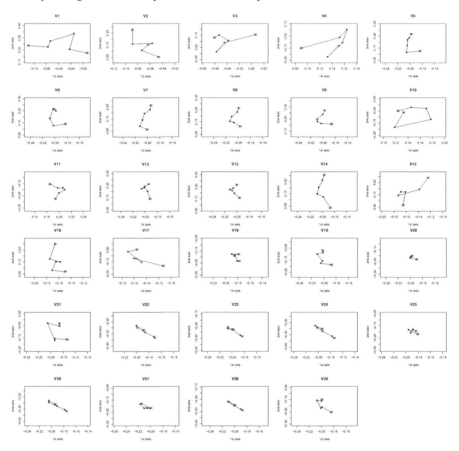

Figure 1.2. *Variables' trajectories*

1.3. Representation of the trajectories

The representation and interpretation of the trajectories is an important step in DPCA. It allows us to identify the differences and similarities between individuals (countries), and analyze the evolution of the correlations between the different variables during the 2010–2020 period. These trajectories are presented in Figures 1.2 and 1.3. All of the graphics have the same scale, i.e. the range in the first axis is the same, as well as the range in the second axis, to have comparable graphics. We have highlighted the year 2010 in red and the year 2020 in blue.

Looking at Figure 1.2, among the variables that present closed trajectories (i.e. they are variables with correlation values with the other variables stable along the period), we highlight the variables V18, V20, V25 and V27, related to the percentage of small or medium enterprises providing training in ICT skills to specialists or to their personnel employees or large enterprises who provide training to other employed persons. All of the other variables have extended trajectories, i.e. they are variables with relevant changes in their correlations with the others along the period. Among them, we highlight the variables V1, V2, V3 and V4 from group 1 (Activity and employment status of individuals), the variable V10 – % of individuals with Internet more than a year ago, the variables V15 and V16 from group 5 (Reasons for using Internet) and the variable V17 – % enterprises with e-commerce having received orders online, at least 1%.

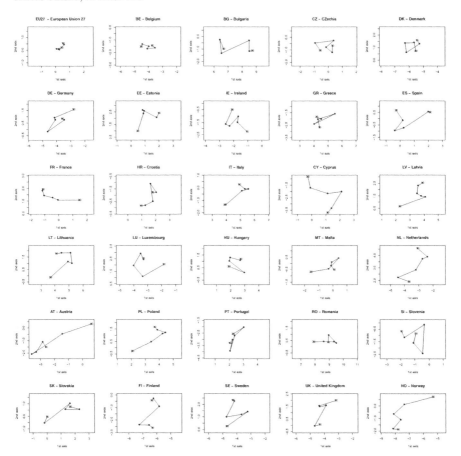

Figure 1.3. *Countries' trajectories*

As shown in Figure 1.3, in general, most of the countries present large or extended trajectories, at least along one of the axes, and in particular, we highlight the trajectories of BG, ES, FR, CY, NL, AT, PL and NO. With very closed trajectories, we highlight EU27 and BE. The countries PT and GR also exhibit some instability in their trajectories.

For the interpretation of the trajectories, we only considered the countries that contributed the most to the axes, with their trajectories represented together in Figures 1.4–1.5, and the variables correlated more so with them.

Concerning the first axis, which explains 65.3% of the total inertia, almost all of the variables have high correlations with the axis in all years, except V1, V2 and V3. Therefore, we only highlight the variables with correlations above 0.8 in absolute value. The first axis opposes the group of countries NO, FI, DK, SE, DE and BE that have large values in the variables V5–V7, V9, V12–V14 and V19–V29 and small values in variable V11, to the group of countries RO, BG, IT, GR, LT and PL that present large values in the variable V11 and small values in the others.

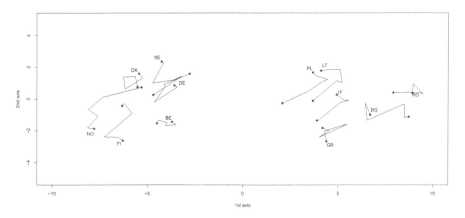

Figure 1.4. *Interpretation of trajectories in the first axis (65.3% inertia)*

The second axis only explains 11.3% of the total inertia, and few variables have significant correlations with this axis. Thus, we highlight the variables with correlations above 0.5 in absolute value. The second axis opposes the group of countries PT, HR, FI, CY, AT and BE, all of which have high values in the variables V24, V26 and V28 (years 2010, 2012 and 2014), V23–V24 (years 2010 and 2012) and small values in variable V1 (years 2010, 2012, 2014 and 2016), compared to the group of countries NL, LU, EE, LT and LV, all of which present high values in variable V1 and small values in the others.

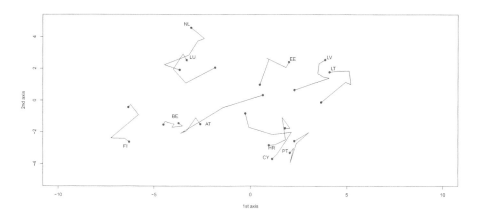

Figure 1.5. *Interpretation of trajectories in the second axis (11.3% inertia)*

1.4. Some final conclusions

The results of this study allow us to identify some existing differences or similarities between groups of European countries during the period 2010–2020 under analysis, concerning ICT skills and employment, Internet usage and digital development.

As expected, this study confirms our perception that the countries of the north and central Europe are very prepared for confronting the challenges of the digital age, since they have already greatly invested in providing training in ICT skills to their populations and how everyone is comfortable using the Internet for a variety of purposes: communication, purchase, selling, finding, and so on. Among these countries, the most similar are the following subgroups of countries: (DE and SE), (NO and DK), FI and BE.

On the other hand, the countries of the East and South of Europe are less prepared, having made little investment in ICT education and, in most of them, a large part of the population has never used the Internet. Among these countries, the closest are the subgroups (PL and LT), (IT and GR), BG and RO.

We also observe that in countries such as PT, AT, CY, HR, BE and FI, where the percentage of employed persons with ICT education is yet small, a large percentage of small and medium enterprises provide training to their personnel or to other employed persons to develop or upgrade ICT skills. The opposite happens, for instance, in the countries LT, LV, EE, LU and NL.

1.5. Acknowledgements

This work was supported by the National Funds through the Portuguese funding agency, FCT – Fundação para a Ciência e a Tecnologia, within the framework of the projects UIDB/00006/2020 (CEAUL) and LA/P/0063/2020 (INESC TEC).

1.6. References

Bouroche, J.M. (1975). Analyse des donnés ternaires : la double analyse en composantes principales. Third-cycle PhD Thesis, Université de Paris VI, Paris.

Lera, L., Pérez, R., Bouquet, A. (2006). El doble análisis em componentes principales para datos categóricos y su applicación en un estudio de migración. *Revista Columbiana de Estadística*, 29(1), 17–34.

Multivariate Kernel Discrimination Applied to Bank Loan Classification

The purpose of this chapter is to apply a kernel discriminant analysis to classify bank loans and determine which loans are at risk of default. This study begins by introducing the concept of kernel density estimation, which is a widely used non-parametric technique to obtain an estimate for the probability density function. This procedure is based on two main parameters: the kernel function and the bandwidth, the latter being the crucial parameter. The multivariate kernel density estimator is later applied to discriminant analysis to obtain kernel discrimination. This is a method that classifies observations into a predetermined number of distinct and disjointed classes. Finally, we apply multivariate kernel discriminant analysis to a sample of bank loans to determine which loans can be classified as defaulted. This model can help predict the likelihood that future loans may default.

2.1. Introduction

As the name implies, credit risk analysis is used to assess the likelihood of a borrower's repayment failure and the loss caused to the financer when default occurs. This concept greatly affects the long-term success of any bank or financial institution. In Malta, the non-performing loan ratio stood at 3% in December 2019 (Central Bank of Malta). This ratio reflects the country's credit quality of loans. Banks need to determine the probability of non-performing loans of companies to decrease the prospect of weakened liquidity. The aim of this study is to create a model that predicts whether a company will be able to pay its outstanding loan, based on several variables. To obtain such a model, we apply the multivariate kernel discriminant analysis. This technique uses kernel density estimation, as well as non-parametric discriminant analysis.

Chapter written by Mark Anthony Caruana and Gabriele Lentini.

Rosenblatt (1956), Whittle (1958), Parzen (1962) and Watson and Leadbetter (1963) studied and presented a number of results regarding univariate kernel density estimation. Moreover, Cacoullos (1966) extended Parzen's results to the multivariate case. Loftsgaarden and Quensenberry (1965) and Epanechnikov (1969) also applied multivariate non-parametric kernel density estimation.

The quality of multivariate kernel density estimation depends mainly on the choice of the bandwidth matrices. The univariate plug-in bandwidth estimator provided by Sheather and Jones (1991) was extended to the multivariate case by Wand and Jones (1993). Moreover, a number of authors, including Chacón and Duong (2010, 2012) and Horová et al. (2013), also contributed to the field of optimal bandwidth selection by applying a number of novel techniques.

Multivariate kernel density estimation has been applied to discriminant analysis. The properties of this technique feature in Murphy and Maron (1986) and Silverman (1986). Over the past several years, kernel discriminant analysis has been applied to several fields. For example, Liberati et al. (2012) and Widiharih et al. (2018) both used kernel discriminant analysis to address the problems of credit risk analysis in banking and making efficient credit granting decisions. Some further applications of kernel discriminant analysis include Hand (1983) and Chen et al. (2005) in medicine, Martin (2011) in agriculture and Farida and Aidi (2016) in education.

This section concludes by giving a brief overview of the structure of this chapter. In section 2.2, we discuss multivariate kernel density estimation. In section 2.3, we outline the properties of kernel discriminant analysis. In section 2.4, we apply these techniques to a local dataset that contains not only the data of a number of local companies but also the status of their bank loan (whether the company is in default or otherwise). Further details concerning the said dataset are provided in section 2.4. As mentioned earlier, the main aim will be to create a model which uses kernel discriminant analysis, which can identify firms that are close to bankruptcy. In this section, we split the data into the training set and test set. We train the model using the former dataset and test the model performance using the latter dataset. Section 2.5 contains some concluding remarks and suggestions for future research.

2.2. Multivariate kernel density estimation

Let p denote the total number of variables in the dataset and let n denote the total number of companies in the dataset.

Let X_i be a random variable representing the ith variable. Moreover, let X be a random vector, where $X = \left(X_1, X_2, \cdots, X_p\right)^T$ and $\mathbf{x}_n = \left(\mathbf{x}_{n1}, \mathbf{x}_{n2}, \cdots, \mathbf{x}_{np}\right)^T$ will be the vector that contains all of the observations of the nth company. Let $\mathbb{x}$ be the $n \times p$ matrix which contains all the observations of the dataset, such that:

$$\mathbb{x} = \begin{pmatrix} \mathbf{x}_{11} & \cdots & \mathbf{x}_{1p} \\ \vdots & \ddots & \vdots \\ \mathbf{x}_{n1} & \cdots & \mathbf{x}_{np} \end{pmatrix}.$$

Multivariate kernel density estimation is composed of two main components: the kernel function, which will now be denoted by K, and the bandwidth, which will now be denoted by $\mathbf{H}$. In a multivariate setting, the bandwidth is a $p \times p$ matrix, where p represents the dimension of the data, i.e. the number of variables being studied. The approach chosen for multivariate kernel density estimation highly depends on the type of bandwidth matrix considered. When $\mathbf{H}$ is taken to be diagonal, this is usually referred to as a constrained bandwidth matrix. Otherwise, it is referred to as an unconstrained bandwidth matrix. The diagonal bandwidth matrix is thus a special case of the unconstrained bandwidth matrix.

2.2.1. Kernel density estimator

For the multivariate case with a bandwidth matrix $\mathbf{H}$, the kernel density estimator is defined as follows:

$$\hat{f}(x; H, X_1, X_2, \cdots, X_n) = \frac{1}{n}\sum_{i=1}^{n} K_H(x - X_i),$$

where n represents the sample size and $K_H(x)$ is said to be the scaled kernel, which is defined as:

$$K_H(x) = |H|^{-\frac{1}{2}} K\left(H^{-\frac{1}{2}}x\right),$$

where $|H|^{-\frac{1}{2}}$ is the inverse of the square root of the determinant of the matrix $\mathbf{H}$ and $H^{-\frac{1}{2}}$ is the inverse of the matrix square root. Therefore, the kernel density estimator can be written as:

$$\hat{f}(x; H, X_1, X_2, \cdots, X_n) = \frac{1}{n|H|^{\frac{1}{2}}}\sum_{i=1}^{n} K\left(H^{-\frac{1}{2}}(x - X_i)\right),$$

where K is the multivariate kernel function. K is assumed to be the symmetric function. Furthermore, $\int_{\mathbb{R}^p} K(z)dz = 1$ and $K(z) \geq 0 \ \forall z \in \mathbb{R}^p$, implying that K satisfies the properties of a multivariate probability density function. There are various types of functions that satisfy the above-mentioned properties, which include the standard multivariate normal kernel density function and the multivariate

Epanechnikov kernel function. Similar to the univariate case, the choice of the kernel function is not crucial. However, the choice of the bandwidth matrix is extremely important.

It is important to note that the formula discussed above regarding the kernel density estimator is not affected by the choice of bandwidth matrix (constrained or unconstrained).

2.2.2. *The optimal bandwidth*

Finding the optimal bandwidth is crucial when performing kernel density estimation. This is because an incorrect bandwidth matrix will lead to either over fitting or under fitting. There are three ways to find the optimal bandwidth and these are: unbiased cross-validation (UCV), biased cross-validation (BCV) and smoothed cross-validation (SCV). These techniques can be applied to constrained and unconstrained bandwidths.

2.2.2.1. *Unbiased cross-validation*

Rudemo (Rosenblatt 1956) and Bowman (1984) discuss the method of UCV. This can be classified as a leave-one-out type cross-validation method and is defined as follows:

$$UCV(H) = \int_{\mathbb{R}^p} \hat{f}(x; H, X_1, X_2, \cdots, X_n)^2 dx - \frac{2}{n} \sum_{i=1}^{n} \hat{f}_{-i}(X_i; H, X_1, X_2, \cdots, X_n)$$

where $\hat{f}_{-i}(x; H, X_1, X_2, \cdots, X_n) = \frac{1}{n-1} \sum_{j=1, j \neq i}^{n} K_H(x - X_j)$.

Hence, the optimal bandwidth, denoted by $\widehat{H}_{UCV}$, can be obtained as follows:

$$\widehat{H}_{UCV} = argmin_{H \in \mathcal{F}} UCV(H).$$

2.2.2.2. *Biased cross-validation*

Scott and Terrell (Rudemo 1982) discuss this method of cross-validation and refer to it as BCV and is defined as follows:

$$BCV(H) = \frac{1}{n}|H|^{-\frac{1}{2}}R(K)$$
$$+ \frac{1}{4}m_2(K)^2 \left(vec^T R \left(D^{\otimes 2}\hat{f}(; H, X_1, X_2, \cdots, X_n)\right)\right)(vecH)^{\otimes 2}$$

where $R(K) = \int K^2(x)dx$, $m_2(K) = \int x^2 K(x)dx$. Moreover, $\otimes$ represents the Kronecker product.

Then, we obtain the optimal bandwidth $\widehat{H}_{BCV}$:

$$\widehat{H}_{BCV} = argmin_{H \in \mathcal{F}} BCV(H).$$

2.2.2.3. Smoothed cross-validation

The last version of cross-validation discussed is SCV.

Hall et al. (1992) discuss this technique and propose the use of a pilot kernel function, which we denote by L, and a pilot bandwidth matrix, which we denote by G, such that L and G may be different from K and H, obtaining:

$$SCV(H; G) = \frac{1}{n}|H|^{-\frac{1}{2}}R(K) + \frac{1}{n^2}\sum_{i,j=1}^{n}(\bar{K}_H * \bar{L}_G - 2K_H * \bar{L}_G + \bar{L}_G)(X_i - X_j)$$

where $\bar{K} = K * K$, $\bar{L} = L * L$ and $*$ represents the convolution operator.

The optimal bandwidth $\widehat{H}_{SCV}$ is therefore obtained as follows:

$$\widehat{H}_{SCV} = argmin_{H \in \mathcal{F}} SCV(H).$$

These three cross-validation techniques will be applied to the dataset. Moreover, we will at first assume an unconstrained bandwidth and subsequently take a constrained bandwidth. The UCV, BCV and SCV formulas for the constrained bandwidth are similar to the unconstrained case described above. The results will then be compared and contrasted, and the best result will be highlighted. We now move on to define kernel discriminant analysis.

2.3. Kernel discriminant analysis

Fix and Hodges (1951) proposed kernel discriminant analysis as a non-parametric version of discriminant analysis. Let $1, 2, \ldots, m$ denote each distinct population, where m represents the number of available populations; and let f_j denote the multivariate density function of the observations drawn from population j. Moreover, let n_j denote the number of observations obtained from population j. Finally, let π_j denote the prior probability that an observation belongs to population j.

Discriminant analysis uses Bayes theorem. If b_i denotes the event that an individual belongs to the ith population, and a denotes the event that an individual has a particular vector of observations, then Bayes theorem states that the probability of event b_i occurring, given that event a occurred is:

$$\mathbb{P}[\, b_i \mid a \,] = \frac{\mathbb{P}[\, a \mid b_i \,] \mathbb{P}[b_i]}{\sum_{j=1 \, j \neq i}^{n} \mathbb{P}[\, a \mid b_j \,] \mathbb{P}[b_j]}.$$

Therefore, by Bayes theorem, we have that the probability that an observation x belongs to the population j is defined as:

$$\mathbb{P}[\, X \in \text{Population } j \mid X = x \,] = \frac{f_j(x)\pi_j}{\sum_{i=1}^{m} f_i(x)\pi_i}.$$

An individual whose set of observations are contained in vector x_{n+1} is allocated to population j if and only if $\pi_j f_j(x_{n+1}) = \text{argmax}_{j \in \{1, \ldots, m\}} \, \pi_j f_j(x_{n+1})$. Hence, we deduce that an individual whose set of observations are contained in vector x_{n+1} is allocated to population j if and only if $\ln\left(\pi_j f_j(x_{n+1})\right) > \ln\left(\pi_i f_i(x_{n+1})\right) \, \forall i \neq j$. We can define the log-odds ratio that the point x is classified to population j rather than to population i as follows:

$$L_{ji}(x) = \ln\left(\frac{\pi_j f_j(x)}{\pi_i f_i(x)}\right)$$

Hence, the point x is allocated to population j if $L_{ji} > 0$ for all $i \neq j$. Duong (2007) suggests replacing the density functions f_j discussed above with the kernel density estimator $\hat{f}_j$. This approach involves the estimation of the density function f_j from a training dataset using kernel density estimation, and then substituting the density function with this kernel density function to obtain the kernel discriminant rule:

An individual whose set of observations are contained in vector x_{n+1} is allocated to population j given data X if and only if $\pi_j \hat{f}_j(x_{n+1}) = \text{argmax}_{j \in \{1, \ldots, m\}} \, \pi_j \hat{f}_j(x_{n+1})$.

The techniques discussed in both this section and section 2.2 can now be applied to the dataset.

2.4. Applying kernel discriminant analysis to local data

2.4.1. Description of data

This dataset was originally divided into five distinct populations:

– non-impaired;

– impaired but not in default;

– default because unlikely to pay;

– default because of past due more than 90 days;

– default because both unlikely to pay and past due more than 90.

Variable number and name	Description
1) Amount in arrears	Shows the aggregate amount of principal, interest and any other fee payment that is outstanding at the reference date.
2) Credit lines limit	Shows the outstanding amount plus any unutilized credit limit that can be drawn upon by the customer.
3) Utilized balance	Shows the amount availed of from the authorized amount.
4) Outstanding balance	Shows the amount outstanding on the utilized balance at the end of the reference date, excluding any accrued interest.
5) Collateral market value of residential property	Shows the market value of the residential property that backs the exposure as per the latest valuation.
6) Collateral extendible value of residential property	Shows the collateral for the residential property which can be considered for credit risk mitigation at the reporting date.
7) Collateral market value of commercial property	Shows the market value of the commercial property which backs the exposure as per the latest valuation.
8) Collateral extendible value of commercial property	Shows the collateral for the commercial property which can be considered for credit risk mitigation at the reporting date.
9) Collateral life policy surrender value	Shows the amount of money policy holders will receive if they exit the policy before maturity. In this case, this amount is taken by the creditor to be paid for the loan.
10) Collateral cash or quasi cash	Cash or instruments that are easily converted to cash and used as collateral.
11) Collateral extendible value of other	Shows the collateral for any other types of assets not previously mentioned which can be considered for credit risk mitigation at the reporting date.
12) Specific credit risk adjustment	Shows the amount of provision against credit risk.
13) Risk-weighted assets	Shows the risk-weighted exposure amounts.
14) Interest rate	Shows the interest rate that is calculated.
15) Days past due	Shows the total number of days past due as from day 1.

Table 2.1. *Detailed description of variables*

For simplicity, it was decided to reclassify the data into two classes: the first group was labeled as "non-defaulted" and includes those loans that fall under the non-impaired population; the second was labeled as "defaulted", and includes all the remaining observations. Apart from the above-mentioned classification variable, the dataset contains 15 other quantitative variables. A detailed description of these variables can be found in Table 2.1. Each variable was given a number (which can be found in Table 2.1). This will be used to refer to a specific variable.

The dataset was divided into two sets: the training and test sets in the ratio of 70:30. When observing the training set, it was noted that 88.83% of the observations fall under the non-defaulted population. Such an imbalance in the dataset could lead to problems when using any classification technique. Indeed, the method used in this study is not immune to such problems.

To solve this issue, the dataset needs to be balanced through the creation of synthetic data. These additional data points were created through the use of a technique called the synthetic minority oversampling technique (SMOTE), as described by Chawla et al. (2002).

2.4.2. Variable selection

It is clear that not all of the variables mentioned in Table 2.1 are ideal to classify companies. Hence, the forward wrapper algorithm, discussed by Kohavi and John (1997), was used to remove variables that are not relevant. The procedure is as follows:

Algorithm: forward wrapper
1) Work out univariate kernel discrimination p times, once for every variable.
2) Work out accuracy for each model derived in step 1.
3) Select the variable whose model gives the best accuracy, and denote it as the first optimal variable.
4) Store the optimal variable in a vector named optimal.
5) Take all pairwise combinations consisting of the optimal variable with all of the other variables and, for each pair, work out the bivariate kernel discrimination and calculate accuracy.
6) Choose the pair with the highest accuracy and store the newly selected variable in the vector optimal.
7) Take all triple combinations involving the optimal two variables selected and the other variables and, for each combination, work out the multivariate kernel discrimination and calculate accuracy.
8) Choose the combination with the highest accuracy and store it in the vector optimal.
9) Repeat this process until either all remaining variables are involved or until the required number of variables is selected.

The forward wrapper algorithm and kernel discriminant analysis were applied to the training set. In particular, kernel density estimation was applied using the unconstrained and the constrained (diagonal) bandwidth matrices. Also, UCV, BCV and SCV were applied. The optimal variables for all these combinations are listed below:

1) unconstrained UCV with two variables, variables 15 and 9;

2) diagonal UCV with two variables, variables 15 and 9;

3) diagonal UCV with three variables, variables 15, 9 and 12;

4) diagonal UCV with four variables, variables 15, 9, 12 and 10;

5) unconstrained BCV with two variables, variables 15 and 9;

6) diagonal BCV with two variables, variables 15 and 9;

7) unconstrained SCV with two variables, variables 15 and 9;

8) unconstrained SCV with three variables, variables 15, 9 and 14;

9) unconstrained SCV with four variables, variables 15, 9, 14 and 12;

10) unconstrained SCV with five variables, variables 15, 9, 14, 12 and 5;

11) unconstrained SCV with six variables, variables 15, 9, 14, 12, 5 and 6;

12) diagonal SCV with two variables, variables 15 and 9;

13) diagonal SCV with three variables, variables 15, 9 and 14;

14) diagonal SCV with four variables, variables 15, 9, 14 and 12;

15) diagonal SCV with five variables, variables 15, 9, 14, 12 and 5;

16) diagonal SCV with six variables, variables 15, 9, 14, 12, 5 and 6.

Figure 2.1 shows the confusion matrices of the above-mentioned 16 kernel discriminant models.

UCV unconstrained, 2 variables: variables 15 and 9				UCV diagonal, 2 variables: variables 15 and 9			
		True				**True**	
		Non-Defaulted	Defaulted			Non-Defaulted	Defaulted
Predicted	Non-Defaulted	1487	868	Predicted	Non-Defaulted	1460	310
	Defaulted	0	470		Defaulted	27	1028

UCV diagonal, 3 variables: variables 15,9 and 12				UCV diagonal,, 4 variables: variables 15,9,12 and 10			
		True				**True**	
		Non-Defaulted	Defaulted			Non-Defaulted	Defaulted
Predicted	Non-Defaulted	1470	359	Predicted	Non-Defaulted	1486	494
	Defaulted	17	979		Defaulted	1	844

BCV unconstrained, 2 variables: variables 15 and 9				BCV diagonal,, 2 variable: variables 15 and 9			
		True				**True**	
		Non-Defaulted	Defaulted			Non-Defaulted	Defaulted
Predicted	Non-Defaulted	1468	351	Predicted	Non-Defaulted	1468	351
	Defaulted	19	987		Defaulted	19	987

SCV unconstrained, 2 variables: variables 15 and 9				SCV unconstrained, 3 variables: variables 15,9 and 14			
		True				**True**	
		Non-Defaulted	Defaulted			Non-Defaulted	Defaulted
Predicted	Non-Defaulted	1478	358	Predicted	Non-Defaulted	1483	361
	Defaulted	9	980		Defaulted	4	977

SCV unconstrained, 4 variables: variables 15,9,14 and 12				SCV unconstrained, 5 variables: variables 15,9,14,12 and 5			
		True				**True**	
		Non-Defaulted	Defaulted			Non-Defaulted	Defaulted
Predicted	Non-Defaulted	1485	384	Predicted	Non-Defaulted	1487	769
	Defaulted	2	954		Defaulted	0	569

SCV unconstrained, 6 variables: variables 15,9,14,12,5 and 6				SCV diagonal, 2 variables: variables 15 and 9			
		True				**True**	
		Non-Defaulted	Defaulted			Non-Defaulted	Defaulted
Predicted	Non-Defaulted	1487	760	Predicted	Non-Defaulted	1478	358
	Defaulted	0	578		Defaulted	9	980

SCV diagonal, 3 variables: variables 15,9 and 14				SCV diagonal, 4 variables: variables 15,9,14 and 12			
		True				**True**	
		Non-Defaulted	Defaulted			Non-Defaulted	Defaulted
Predicted	Non-Defaulted	1481	359	Predicted	Non-Defaulted	1486	385
	Defaulted	6	979		Defaulted	1	953

SCV diagonal, 5 variables: variables 15,9,14,12 and 5				SCV diagonal, 6 variables: variables 15,9,14,12,5 and 6			
		True				**True**	
		Non-Defaulted	Defaulted			Non-Defaulted	Defaulted
Predicted	Non-Defaulted	1487	783	Predicted	Non-Defaulted	1487	611
	Defaulted	0	555		Defaulted	0	727

Figure 2.1. *Confusion matrices of all of the cross-validation techniques*

A number of performance measures were applied to see which of the 16 models gave the best overall performance. The results are shown in Tables 2.2–2.4.

Measure	UCVU2	UCVD2	UCVD3	UCVD4	BCVU2	BCVD2
Accuracy	0.693	0.881	0.867	0.825	0.870	0.870
$Precision_1$	0.631	0.825	0.804	0.751	0.807	0.807
$Precision_2$	1	0.974	0.983	0.999	0.981	0.981
$Recall_1$	1	0.982	0.989	0.999	0.987	0.987
$Recall_2$	0.351	0.768	0.732	0.631	0.737	0.737
$F1_1$	0.774	0.897	0.887	0.857	0.888	0.888
$F1_2$	0.520	0.859	0.839	0.773	0.842	0.842
Cohen's Kappa	0.363	0.758	0.730	0.642	0.734	0.734

Table 2.2. *Performance measures of models 1–6*

Measure	SCVU2	SCVU3	SCVU4	SCVU5	SCVU6
Accuracy	0.870	0.871	0.863	0.728	0.731
$Precision_1$	0.805	0.804	0.795	0.659	0.662
$Precision_2$	0.991	0.996	0.998	1	1
$Recall_1$	0.994	0.997	0.999	1	1
$Recall_2$	0.732	0.730	0.713	0.425	0.432
$F1_1$	0.889	0.890	0.885	0.795	0.796
$F1_2$	0.842	0.843	0.832	0.597	0.603
Cohen's Kappa	0.736	0.737	0.722	0.438	0.445

Table 2.3. *Performance measures of models 7–11*

Measure	SCVD2	SCVD3	SCVD4	SCVD5	SCVD6
Accuracy	0.870	0.871	0.863	0.723	0.784
$Precision_1$	0.805	0.805	0.795	0.655	0.709
$Precision_2$	0.991	0.994	0.998	1	1
$Recall_1$	0.994	0.996	0.999	1	1
$Recall_2$	0.732	0.732	0.713	0.415	0.543
$F1_1$	0.889	0.890	0.885	0.792	0.830
$F1_2$	0.842	0.843	0.832	0.586	0.704
Cohen's Kappa	0.736	0.737	0.722	0.427	0.556

Table 2.4. *Performance measures of models 12–16*

In Tables 2.2–2.4, note that the optimal model is the diagonal version of unbiased cross-validation, whilst using two variables, which are variables 15 and 9 mentioned in Table 2.1. This is because a majority of the values in bold are in the column of the model that uses diagonalized UCV and two variables. These two variables are days_past_due and collateral_life_policy_surrender_value, respectively. This model is taken to be the optimal kernel discriminant model, since it has the largest values for accuracy, $Precision_1$, $Recall_2$, $F1_1$, $F1_2$ and Cohen's kappa. The bandwidth matrices for this model are:

$$\widehat{H}_{non-default} = \begin{pmatrix} 9.204281 \times 10^{-10} & 0 \\ 0 & 88803.06 \end{pmatrix},$$

$$\widehat{H}_{default} \begin{pmatrix} 200345.8 & 0 \\ 0 & 2.059234 \times 10^{-6} \end{pmatrix}.$$

The kernel discriminant analysis model was then applied to the test set, and the following results were obtained. Table 2.5 contains the confusion matrix.

		True	
		Non-defaulted	Defaulted
Predicted	Non-defaulted	628	41
	Defaulted	0	31

Table 2.5. *Confusion matrix of the optimal model applied to the test set*

Table 2.6 shows the performance measures.

Performance measure	Score
Accuracy	0.941
$Precision_1$	0.939
$Precision_2$	1
$Recall_1$	1
$Recall_2$	0.431
$F1_1$	0.969
$F1_2$	0.602
Cohen's kappa	0.576

Table 2.6. *Performance measures of the model when applied to the test set*

When looking at the performance measures, it is noted that the value for $Recall_2$ is quite low, especially when compared with the value obtained for the training set in Table 2.2 (0.768). This low value of $Recall_2$ also leads to quite a small value of the $F1_2$ score, especially when compared with the value obtained for the training set in Table 2.2 (0.859). Both these results imply that this discriminant model classifies a majority of the points as elements of the first population (non-defaulted). The value of Cohen's kappa in Table 2.6 shows that this discrimination model is moderate, since it lies in the range $0.4 \leq \kappa < 0.6$.

2.5. Conclusion

In this chapter, we applied multivariate non-parametric density estimation and discrimination through the methods of multivariate kernel density estimation and kernel discriminant analysis, respectively. These techniques were applied to a dataset provided by the Central Bank of Malta. The companies were reclassified into two classes, and the results obtained from the test set were presented and discussed. The optimal discriminant model involved two variables: *days_past_due* and *collateral_life_policy_surrender_value*, with the optimal bandwidth selection technique being the diagonal version of unbiased cross-validation. In future, the dataset will be enhanced by the addition of more data points. Moreover, other classification techniques will be applied, including neural networks, support vector machines, decision trees and random forests. The results will then be compared.

2.6. References

Bowman, A.W. (1984). An alternative method of cross-validation for the smoothing of density estimates. *Biometrika*, 71, 353–360.

Cacoullos, T. (1966). Estimation of a multivariate density. Technical report No. 40, Department of Statistics, University of Minnesota.

Chacón, J.E. and Duong. T. (2010). Multivariate plug-in bandwidth selection with unconstrained pilot bandwidth matrices. *An Official Journal of the Spanish Society of Statistics and Operations Research*, 19(2), 375–398.

Chacón, J.E. and Duong, T. (2012). Data-driven density derivative estimation, with applications to nonparametric clustering and bump hunting. *Electronic Journal of Statistics*, 7, 499–532.

Chawla, N., Bowyer, K., Hall, L., Kegelmeyer, W. (2002). SMOTE: Synthetic minority oversampling technique. *Journal of Artificial Intelligence Research*, 16, 321–357.

Chen, B., Harrison, R., Hert, J., Mpamhanga, C., Willett, P., Wilton, D. (2005). Ligand-based virtual screening using binary kernel discrimination, *Molecular Simulation*, 31(8), 597–604.

Duong, T. (2007). Kernel density estimation and kernel discriminant analysis for multivariate data in R. *Journal of Statistical Software*, 21.

Epanechnikov, V.A. (1969). Nonparametric estimation of a multivariate probability density. *Theory of Probability and its Applications*, 14, 153–158.

Farida, Y. and Aidi, M.N. (2016). Classifying students 2nd level at National Crypto Institute with vertex discriminant analysis and kernel discriminant analysis. *International Journal of Scientific & Engineering Research*, 7, 12.

Fix, E. and Hodges, J.L. (1951). An important contribution to nonparametric discriminant analysis and density estimation: Commentary on Fix and Hodges. *International Statistical Review*, 57, 233–247.

Hall, P., Marron, J.S., Park, B.U. (1992). Smoothed cross-validation. *Probability Theory and Related Fields*, 92, 1–20.

Hand, D. (1983). A comparison of two methods of discriminant analysis applied to binary data. *Biometrics*, 39(3), 683–694.

Horová, I., Koláček, J., Vopatová, K. (2013). Full bandwidth matrix selectors for gradient kernel density estimate. *Computational Statistics & Data Analysis*, 57, 364–376.

Kohavi, R. and John, G.H. (1997). Wrappers for feature selection. *Artificial Intelligence*, 97(1–2), 273–324.

Liberati, C., Camillo, F., Saporta, G. (2012). Kernel discrimination and explicative features: An operative approach. Compstat 2012, August, Limassol, Cyprus, 507–518.

Loftsgaarden, D.O. and Quesenberry, C.P. (1965). A nonparametric estimate of a multivariate density function. *Annals of Mathematical Statistics*, 36, 1049–1051.

Martin, F. (2011). An application of kernel methods to variety identification based on SSR markers genetic fingerprinting. *BMC Bioinformatics*, 12, 177.

Murphy, B.J. and Moran, M.A. (1986). Parametric and kernel density methods in discriminant analysis: Another comparison. *Computers and Mathematics with Applications*, 12A(2), 197–207.

Parzen, E. (1962). On estimation of a probability density function and the mode. *The Annals of Mathematical Statistics*, 33, 1065–1076.

Rosenblatt, M. (1956). Remarks on some nonparametric estimates of a density function. *The Annals of Mathematical Statistics*, 27, 832–837.

Rudemo, M. (1982). Empirical choice of histograms and kernel density estimators. *Scandinavian Journal of Statistics: Theory and Applications*, 9, 65–78.

Scott, D.W. and Terrell, G.R. (1987). Biased and unbiased cross-validation in density estimation. *Journal of the American Statistical Association*, 82, 400, 1131–1146.

Sheather, S.J. and Jones, M.C. (1991). A reliable data based bandwidth selection method for kernel density estimation. *Journal of the Royal Statistical Society, Series B: Methodological*, 53, 683–690.

Silverman, B.W. (1986). *Estimation for Statistics and Data Analysis*. Chapman & Hall/CRC, London.

Wand, M.P. and Jones, M.C. (1993). Comparison of smoothing parameterizations in bivariate kernel density estimation. *Journal of the American Statistical Association*, 88, 520–528.

Watson, G.S. and Leadbetter, M.R. (1963). On the estimation of the probability density. *Annals of Mathematical Statistics*, 34, 480–491.

Whittle, P. (1958). On the smoothing of probability density functions. *Journal of the Royal Statistical Society, Series B*, 20, 334–343.

Widiharih, T., Mukid, M., Mustafid (2018). Credit scoring analysis using kernel discriminant. *Journal of Physics: Conference Series*, 1025, 012124.

Introducing an Ontology of Adolescents' Digital Leisure

An ontology is a formal description of a set of concepts and relations in a given area or domain that describes the categories' objects and their inter-relations. This chapter presents an ontology that was constructed to set out the basic concepts, features, characteristics and processes that concern the online leisure time of adolescents. The ontology, as well as the respective annotation tool, offer users the ability to organize and analyze data in a well-structured and systematic manner, while simultaneously allowing concept and relational analysis to draw complex conclusions and make inferences. The terminology of the ontology has been first extracted in a semi-supervised way from a large number of scientific papers, with the aid of machine learning methodologies and a specific tool implemented for this aim, and then curated by social researchers that are experts in the field. The final ontology was developed with the use of Protégé, an open-source ontology editor. Examples of diverse data analysis using the proposed tool and the respective ontology are provided.

3.1. Introduction

An ontology is a formal description of knowledge as a set of *concepts* of a domain that describes the categories of objects and *roles* which describe the relationships between these objects. It aims to model and formalize the description of the complex entities of a domain of interest, and sometimes disambiguates the meaning of terms in the specific domain (e.g. the verb communication has a different interpretation when used by a telecommunications' organization, a

Chapter written by George FILANDRIANOS, Aggeliki KAZANI, Dimitrios PARSANOGLOU, Maria SYMEONAKI and Giorgos STAMOU.

microcontroller, and an adolescent). Formal ontological descriptions form a basis for solving numerous issues relating to computers' inability to represent human language descriptions (Biemann 2005). This inability becomes even more intense when comprehending images, audio or videos (complex multimedia information).

This is the main reason why it is currently difficult to automatically recognize high-level concepts, such as "*communication between friends*" or "*negotiation with parents*" from different types of data, especially without having a pre-annotated training set. The creation of this dataset requires several domain experts, for example, social scientists, to study the data and appropriately annotate them. In the case described above, the data may be interviews or diaries of children, where the experts must set labels to describe the information it contains, which will be concepts of a formal terminology. For example, the part: "*We have set some rules with my parents: 3 hours per day on the weekend and 2 hours on weekdays*" can be labeled as "*negotiation with parents*" by the social data analyst.

However, without the field's formal terminology, the annotations will lack formal, common understanding, therefore remaining descriptive. In this case, we have the same problem as in the automatic comprehension of natural language. For instance, how could a system process a query if the annotations are represented in a natural language? If the annotations are in natural language, then the same instances may be annotated differently among experts (for example, the same part may be annotated as "negotiation" or "regulations" or rules"). Thus, how could we search for instances of a class such as "negotiation with friends" if the annotations do not contain these terms? This issue is analogous to what happens when we store a valuable item – in this case, the expert annotations – in an inaccessible cell. An ontology will provide a systematic way to reach every annotation with the same ease. Moreover, computers would finally be able to interpret and analyze the annotations and queries in a sophisticated way if an ontology was in place and every document was marked up using it (Biemann 2005).

Knowledge must be organized in such a way that it can be easily enhanced using the already annotated data. For example, if an instance belongs to playing "*Minecraft*", "*quarrelling with friend*" and "*using tablet*", then it is easy to conclude that this child "*was playing Minecraft on the tablet while quarrelling with his friend*". Although the aforementioned class does not exist in our ontology, we can still easily capture these instances by using the information contained in the ontology. Similar queries or axioms can be defined for several classes, and automatic reasoning algorithms can be executed (Gyrard et al. 2014), helping researchers enrich their data.

Although the use of an ontology in the annotation procedure is crucial, its use is also quite complex, mainly for a novice user. Figure 3.1 shows the typical pipeline for annotating data using knowledge systems. There are three aspects in the procedure that will make things more difficult for users. The first one concerns the ontology creation, especially when there is a shift between the studied domain and the scientist's expertise. Additionally, modeling a field is a difficult and demanding process that, if carried out entirely manually, requires a large amount of effort. Next, we need to annotate the data, along with the already defined knowledge. No existing tools can support a scientist in the entire pipeline by loading different types of files simultaneously, along with an ontology, and providing a simple and intuitive method for representing annotations.

Finally, after annotating the data, experts must use a formal language to draw queries in order to analyze their data (for example, SPARQL). The aforementioned issues frequently deter scientists from using an ontology for their data analysis, especially if there is a shift in the field of expertise, whereby scientists performing the analysis are unfamiliar with these types of technologies.

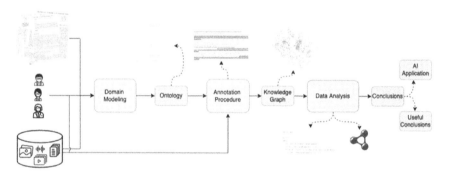

Figure 3.1. *The typical pipeline for data annotation procedure, using a formal description of knowledge, such as an ontology. For a color version of this figure, see www.iste.co.uk/dimotikalis/data3.zip*

The contributions of this chapter are manifold:

– Firstly, to create and publish the first ontology that models adolescents' digital leisure time. To the best of our knowledge, there is no other similar structure relating to this domain.

– During the ontology construction, we have developed an open-source artificial intelligence system that aims to assist experts in constructing similar structures. The system, namely *KGExtraction*[1], extracts terms from scientific literature, which will

---

1 The KGExtraction code is published on https://github.com/geofila/KGExtraction.

assist the scientific community in determining ontology concepts. KGExtraction could be used in a wide range of different domains.

– An open-source crowdsourcing platform for an end-to-end data annotation pipeline (Annotation Procedure and Data Analysis) was also created, namely *KGNotes*[2]. With KGNotes, a user can visualize an ontology, annotate different types of files simultaneously (audio, text, videos, etc.) and draw complex queries on the annotated data without the need of knowing or understanding the functioning technicalities and/or details of knowledge systems (knowledge theory, SPARQL, etc.). KGNotes aims to be a user-friendly tool that enfolds each step of the data analysis procedure (data visualization, ontology visualization, annotation procedure and querying on annotated data), for knowledge technologies to be spread and employed by unfamiliar users.

3.2. Related work

In recent years, there has been an increasing amount of literature on the development of formal knowledge description. Moreover, several methods have already been proposed, trying to model different aspects of adolescents' life. In Tacyildiz et al. (2018), an application functioning as a mobile health consultant to children or adolescents for reducing obesity is introduced. An ontology that simulates the disorders and symptoms that may be brought on by obesity was created specifically for this goal. There are also defined axioms that compute multiple measurements, such as BMI, and draw conclusions or provide suggestions. In Sermeus (2016), adolescents' depression ontology is presented, which is used to annotate data of different types (social media postings, counseling records, narratives, etc.). In a similar direction in Jung et al. (2017), an ontology that models adolescent depression is proposed that aims to provide a semantic foundation for analyzing social media data regarding this phenomenon. However, to our knowledge, there is no research and/or studies that model adolescents' digital leisure time. In this chapter, an ontology that models this field is constructed with the use of the aforementioned methodologies.

Following the literature debate, creating an ontology is a difficult and expensive process (Buitelaar et al. 2005; Al-Aswadi et al. 2020). A standard procedure for this developmental process does not yet exist. Nevertheless, the usual methodology for developing an ontology follows the structure presented in Buitelaar et al. 2005 and Al-Aswadi et al. 2020, and this approach was used here to create the proposed ontology.

---

2 The KGNotes code is published on https://github.com/ails-lab/kgnotes.

The first step is to find the terms that the ontology should model. These will be the fundamental building blocks of the ontology. They can be either simple (single-word) or complex (multi-word), and are considered as linguistic realizations of domain-specific concepts (Reimers and Gurevych 2019). Finding these terms is usually a costly procedure as it requires several experts in the field to search from multiple sources. Published studies are typically the primary source from which relevant phrases are drawn. This procedure is not completed in a single step, meaning that after the construction, it must be repeated for the ontology to remain up-to-date. To make it easier for others to understand term meaning, each term in this procedure should have a link to an appropriate definition in the literature. Thus, for each term, scientists are advised to store these connections. This process is quite complex and costly if done manually, especially if it is done simultaneously by multiple experts. To assist scientists at this stage, several methods have already been suggested in the literature. For the present ontology, a sample of a term is "Minecraft on mobile devices reshapes family dynamics" which is defined in (Balmforf and Davies 2019).

The second step is usually to find synonyms or semantic term variants in other languages for the extracted terms. This step is usually based either on additional ontologies, such as WordNet (Fellbaum 2010) or ConceptNet (Speer et al. 2017), or on systems for multilingual language encoding (Al-Aswadi et al. 2020).

Following this, the concepts that will constitute the ontology should be defined. Concepts are a group of real or fictitious, abstract or concrete terms. A formal definition of the terms (or objects) contained is recommended, even though the type of concept depends on the task. Some of the terms in this process may not fit the concepts, so they should be removed. Experts in the relevant fields can perform the above-mentioned operation manually; they can also perform it automatically using a clustering algorithm, or semi-automatically by combining various approaches. It is essential for the experts to analyze the concepts after they have been defined in order to determine the relationships between them.

These relations can be either hierarchical (e.g. hypernyms) or not (e.g. synonyms). For instance, the concept "*communicating_with_visual_friends*" is a subclass of "*communicating_with_friends*". The relationship between these concepts is hierarchical. This relationship is typically expressed as follows:

$$communicating\_with\_visual\_friends \subseteq communicating\_with\_friends$$

The final step is to define rules and axioms. We can easily enrich our data using them. For example, if an instance belongs to "playing Minecraft" or "quarrelling with friend and using tablet", then it is also an instance of a new class named "playing Minecraft on the tablet while quarrelling with his friend". The above class does not exist in our ontology; however, automated reasoning algorithms can use these axioms in order to enrich the data. It is also important to define when two classes cannot be combined in the same instance; in other words, when two classes are disjointed. A school, for example, may be named "Kennedy", but a school cannot be a person. As a result, an extensive ontology is necessary to specify the potential constraints or restrictions that cannot coexist (Elnagar et al. 2022). For instance, two disjointed classes are "*offline_video_gaming*" and "*online_video_gaming*" as both of these actions cannot be done simultaneously. This relationship is typically expressed as follows:

$$online\_video\_gaming \neq offline\_video\_gaming$$

There are three ways of constructing an ontology: manual construction; cooperative construction (needs the human intervention during the ontology constructing process), (semi-) automatic construction, and automatic construction, which has been recently developed.

Manual construction is the most common way of developing an ontology. However, it is also the most monotonous and costly way (Al-Aswadi et al. 2020). Fully automatic construction for ontologies could not be feasible at the time, especially for the whole scientific field as adolescents' leisure time (Al-Aswadi et al. 2020). Nevertheless, there is an acute need to decrease human intervention in the ontology construction process, i.e. to move from cooperative to (semi-) automatic construction methods.

For the development of the present ontology, such a method was used to assist scientists throughout the development (Buitelaar et al. 2005; Al-Aswadi et al. 2020). Of the steps presented above, the first three (terms, synonyms, concepts) are the most challenging, complicated, but also monotonous. They require experts to study a plethora of scientific papers and to extract terms defined or included in them. The number of studies is also an important decision to be made. The higher the number of papers studied, the more terms will be included in the ontology, exponentially increasing the workload for the experts. At the same time, the source of each term must be stored (also manually) to make it easier for someone else to use the ontology. Then, for each term, scientists must find similar terms or synonyms extracted from the above step or from other sources, such as other ontologies. It is easy to understand that this procedure generates a huge number of concepts that are difficult to cluster manually to create the final concepts of the ontology. The last steps, finding relations and defining rules and axioms between concepts, are also challenging, as they are very interesting for experts, and at the same time very complex for automated systems.

3.3. Ontology

The development of the presented ontology was completed to assist scientists in annotating data gathered by the Horizon2020 research program, named DigiGen. DigiGen aims to collect a significant amount of empirical data from various sources and, through them, gain knowledge concerning ICT use among children and young individuals. DigiGen data includes audios and transcripts (text) from interviews between adolescents and experts, data from communication diaries and Minecraft game sessions, data from mini-surveys, and Snapshots (i.e. images) taken using a specific app called MyView App. Since this data comes in such a wide variety of formats, it is crucial to use more sophisticated methods for data analysis. Using a formal description of knowledge for the studied field is critical to integrate and harmonize heterogeneous data from multiple sources, for example, videos, text and audio files with no difficulties.

The ontology developed is coded in Web Ontology Language (OWL) and developed by using the Protégé[3] ontology editor. Figure 3.2 shows a portion of the ontology through the editor. The ontology starts with the class "Thing" that is divided into various sub-concepts, such as *"communicating"*, *"doing_activity"*, *"gaming"*, *"spending_time_on_screen"* and *"using_digital_devices"*. These concepts model activities that an adolescent may do in their digital leisure time. Subsequently, they can be divided into sub-concepts. For example, the term communication consists of: *"communication_using_online_app"*, *"communicating_with_family"*, *"communicating_with_friend"*, *"communicating_with_schoolmate"* and *"communicating_with_stranger"*. Each of the above terms relates to their parents with the role *"subclass of"*. In addition, another semantically structured relation belonging to the classes is "OWL individual" declarations. This ontology contains various OWL individuals which have been defined by domain experts, in our case by social scientists. For instance, this part of an interview between a child and an expert: *"I use Netflix, YouTube[4]"* is an instance of both the classes: *"watching_content_on_YouTube"* and *"watching_studio_production_content_on_ Netflix"*. The developed ontology also contains semantic rules, such as the example presented above (*playing Minecraft on the tablet while quarrelling with his friend*). When these rules are executed by an automatic reasoner algorithm, it enriches our data by creating additional knowledge.

---

3 Protégé is an ontology editor and framework for creating intelligent systems, created by Stanford University and available for free download.

4 The original interview was in Greek, as was the actual instance's text in the ontology, while a translated version is presented here.

Figure 3.2. *A portion of the developed ontology in the Protégé editor*

3.4. Description of the ontology construction

The current ontology is developed in a semi-automatic way by domain experts (social and computer scientists), along with an automatic algorithm developed especially for this task, named *KGExtraction*. KGExtraction aims to alleviate scientists by finding the terms on scientific papers, saving their origins and grouping them on the ontology's final concepts. Thus, the work of a domain expert is decreased by simply inspecting the terms and concepts, and deleting those deemed unnecessary. The manual procedure would require reading all of the papers, extracting terms, storing their origin, grouping them in clusters, defining the concepts, inspecting the final terms and concepts, and deleting unnecessary terms. An outline of the terms extraction system is shown in Figure 3.3.

The basic unit of the algorithm is this keyword extraction system that extracts keywords or phrases from scientific text. This system aims to find keywords or key phrases that are semantically relevant to a document. There are already well-known and easy-to-use techniques for this task (Thushara et al. 2019). However, these methods typically use the statistical properties of the text, instead of the semantic similarity.

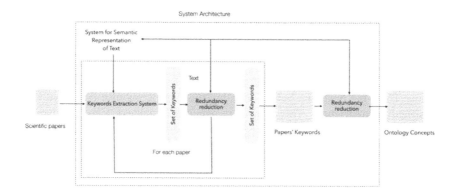

Figure 3.3. *A proposed methodology for the automatic extraction of ontology concepts. For a color version of this figure, see www.iste.co.uk/dimotikalis/data3.zip*

The proposed algorithm's first step is to find a list of potential keywords or key phrases from a single document. This extraction is based both on part of speech tagging (pos tagging) and on specific statistical properties of the document. Firstly, for each word or phrase (of a predefined maximum length), a score is calculated based on the number of occurrences in the document. Then, some of these terms are filtered, based on predefined language processing rules. For example, a single stopword cannot be an ontology term. At this point, some external rules can also be inserted, depending on the task. For example, a single adjective cannot be an adolescent's digital leisure time ontology term. However, this rule is applied only in this work, and for another ontology, this conception may be unnecessary.

The next step of this unit is to select the terms that are closer to the topic of the document. At this point, we used a state-of-the-art artificial intelligence model that can encode natural language into a fixed-size vector (encoder). By transforming both document and the candidate's term into a space of the exact dimensions, we can compare them effortlessly using well-known metrics.

Nevertheless, the coding model must ensure that semantic information is retained in the vector space. To ensure this condition, we used the pre-trained model presented in Reimers and Gurevych (2019). The model used achieves state-of-the-art results on six of the seven different datasets for semantic similarity and paraphrase identification. Specifically, it has achieved 74.53% on STS12, 77.00% on STS13, 73.18% on STS14, 81.85% on STS15, 76.82% on STS16, 79.10% on STSb and 74.29 on SICK-R dataset. The used model achieves slightly worse results from state-of-the-art only for the last dataset. The selected terms are those that are closer to the document in the vector space.

The returned terms of this step are extracted from a single paper, and there is a risk that they will be semantically close. For example, if a paper analyzes school bullying, the extracted terms may be "school bullying", "bullying at school" and "bullying between students at school". These terms are semantically close to the paper's topic, so they have been correctly selected, but they also have the same meaning. Thus, the next step before selecting the final terms of a document is the **diversification procedure**. This method is required to achieve a balance between the accuracy of keywords/key phrases and the diversity between them. **Maximal marginal relevance** (MMR) (Mao et al. 2020) is an algorithm that tries to minimize redundancy and maximize the diversity of results in text summarization tasks. Therefore, it has also been used for the selection of document extracted terms.

The above procedure is for selecting the terms of a single paper. Thus, we must run all of the papers through this algorithm and create a database of papers' terms. As multiple documents may have a common topic, this may mean that numerous exported keywords/key phrases will be semantically closed. To avoid this situation, the database is passed through the same filter to produce the final terms of the ontology. Algorithm 1, shown in Figure 3.4, sets out the general layout of the terms extraction system.

Algorithm 1: Keyword Selection System

Data: Corpus of Documents
Result: A set of Extracted Terms
$AllExtractedTerms \leftarrow []$;
foreach $d \in Documents$ **do**
    $extractedTerms \leftarrow []$;
    $Candidates \leftarrow getCandidateTerms(d)$;
    $docVector \leftarrow encode(d)$;
    foreach $term \in Candidates$ **do**
        $termVector \leftarrow encode(terms)$;
        $dist = distance(docVector, termVector)$;
        if $dist \leq thr$ **then**
            $extractedTerms \leftarrow term$
        end
    end
    $AllExtractedTerms \leftarrow MMR(extractedTerms)$
end
$AllExtractedTerms \leftarrow MMR(AllExtractedTerms)$

Figure 3.4. *Algorithm 1 depicting the general layout of the terms extraction system*

At this point, the algorithm has extracted a set of terms from a corpus of scientific literature. The next step is to cluster these terms to produce the final concepts. This is not an easy procedure at the word level. However, this is not the case in the vector space. Since each phrase has a semantic representative vector, it is easy, in that space, to form batches of terms using any clustering algorithm. In our case, we used the k-means algorithm, where the term closest to the centroid was selected as the representative concept.

3.5. Data annotation

Developing an ontology is a significant step toward studying and analyzing data in a structured and systematic manner. However, to take full advantage, the user needs to be accustomed to knowledge systems' technologies. This may not seem like a significant problem to a familiar user, but it is not the same to non-domain users. For example, how could a user read, optimize, understand and use an ontology to annotate data, if they do not know what an owl file is? How could a user study the annotated data if they do not know what SPARQL is? These technical difficulties may demotivate users, forcing them to annotate data without using the knowledge. The main implication is that since the annotation process and data analysis do not follow a formal definition of knowledge, the scientist's effort might be wasted.

To assist scientists, regardless of the domain, in applying structured knowledge to their tasks, it is critical to identify the exact areas that may affect their data analysis process. The first step is to read and visualize an ontology to grasp its structure and absorb the information it contains. This step increases the technical complexity, as it requires the installation of special software. Since this is the first step of any similar procedure, several well-known tools have already been proposed and developed for this task, such as Protégé, Neo4j[5], GraphDB[6] and Virtuoso Universal Server[7].

The succeeding step is to read the files to be annotated. Each file type must be loaded by a different program. To add an annotation, the user must copy the annotated data into the program that creates an instance of the ontology. For example, let us assume that the annotation procedure concerns a text; the annotation cannot be created using the same tool we have used to open it, such as any text editor. We must either use a particular tool that only annotates texts, or we must use two different software programs.

To alleviate the scientist's work, we have created an open-source tool that unifies every stage of this workflow into a user-friendly online platform, named KGNotes.

---

5 See: https://neo4j.com/.

6 See: https://graphdb.ontotext.com/.

7 See: https://virtuoso.openlinksw.com/.

Figure 3.5 shows the working interface of the tool for annotating a text and a video, respectively. KGNotes is able to load and visualize an ontology, load different types of files (text and videos), and annotate them using the concepts of the knowledge. Nevertheless, for every different file type, the working environment of the tool automatically changes to be intuitively easier to use. The annotations are stored in a unified way, regardless of the file type. Thus, KGNotes could search for instances of a query simultaneously for each file format.

Figure 3.5. *The working interface of KGNotes for annotating text and video, respectively. The main screen of the tool is divided into two segments. On the right, the data for the annotation is shown, while on the left is the ontology. Each ontology concept is clickable, and the user can expand it to study their subclasses. For a color version of this figure, see www.iste.co.uk/dimotikalis/data3.zip*

Readers can consult Parsanoglou et al. 2022 for a detailed description of KGNotes. In addition, KGNotes allows users to analyze the labeled data in an easy and intuitive way. For example, a user could search for annotated parts that are instances of a particular class. Also, this query could be further complicated by specifying if they want to include parts belonging to the original term's subclasses, and to which level. For example, they could search for the parts that belong to the class *"communicating"* or *"communicating with friends"* (subclass of *"communicating"*) but at the same time not to the concept *"communicating with visual friend"*, which is a subclass of the second one.

Furthermore, users could search for similar instances, regardless of the file type. We define similarity between instances as the similarity between their annotations. For example, if a part is annotated with the terms *"communicating"* and *"gaming"*, it is closer to an instance labeled with the terms *"communicating with friends"* and *"online video gaming"* than another labeled with *"watching studio production content on Netflix"*. These parts could be of any format, video or text. Through KGNotes, we could easily search for similar text parts in a video or vice versa. It is worth noting that the user does not need to have any experience with knowledge systems, such as SPARQL, to obtain these results.

3.6. Conclusions

In this study, we created an ontology that models adolescents' digital leisure. For the development of this ontology, we created an artificially intelligent algorithm for automatic concept extraction, named KGExtraction. KGExtraction can read scientific papers and extract terms contained in them that are close to their topic. This algorithm creates a collection of non-redundant terms concerning a database of scientific papers describing a domain. This ontology was used to annotate data of different types (video and text) collected by DigiGen's researchers to model adolescents' digital leisure time. For the annotation procedure and data analysis, we created an open-source online platform, named KGNotes. KGNote's purpose is to simplify the above methods and to give users unfamiliar with knowledge or data analysis technologies a user-friendly tool that integrates each step of this pipeline. KGNotes could run either online, where the users do not have to install anything to their computer, or offline, where they could download the open-source code and run a customized version for their teams (e.g. on University server).

3.7. Acknowledgments

This work was funded by the European Union's Horizon 2020 research and innovation program under the grant agreement No. 870548. Neither the European Union nor any person acting on behalf of the Commission is responsible for how the following information is used. The views expressed in this publication are the sole responsibility of the authors and do not necessarily reflect the views of the European Commission.

3.8. References

Al-Aswadi, F.N., Chan, H.Y., Gan, K.H. (2020). Automatic ontology construction from text: A review from shallow to deep learning trend. *Artificial Intelligence Review*, 53(6), 3901–3928.

Balmforf, W. and Davies, H. (2019). Mobile minecraft: Negotiated space and perceptions of play in Australian families. *Communication, Media Studies, Language & Linguistics*, 8(1), 3–21.

Biemann, C. (2005). Ontology learning from text: A survey of methods. *LDV Forum*, 20, 2.

Buitelaar, P.P., Cimiano, P., Magnini, B. (eds) (2005). Ontology learning from text: An overview. In *Ontology Learning from Text: Methods, Evaluation and Applications*. IOS Press, 123.

Elnagar, S., Yoon, V., Thomas, M.A. (2022). An automatic ontology generation framework with an organizational perspective. *arXiv preprint arXiv:2201.05910.*

Fellbaum, C. (2010). "WordNet." *Theory and Applications of Ontology: Computer Applications.* Springer, Dordrecht.

Gyrard, A., Bonnet, C., Boudaoud, K. (2014). Enrich machine-to-machine data with semantic web technologies for cross-domain applications. *IEEE World Forum on Internet of Things (WF–IoT).*

Jung, H., Park, H.A., Song, T.M. (2017). Ontology-based approach to social data sentiment analysis: Detection of adolescent depression signals. *Journal of Medical Internet Research*, 19(7), 259.

Mao, Y. et al. (2020). Multi-document summarization with maximal marginal relevance-guided reinforcement learning. *arXiv preprint arXiv:2010.00117.*

Parsanoglou, D., Mifsud, L., Ayllón, S., Brugarolas, P., Filandrianos, G., Hyggen, C., Kazani, A., Lado, S., Symeonaki, M., Andreassen, K.J. (2022). Combining innovative methodological tools to approach digital transformations in leisure among children and young people. DigiGen - working paper series, No.9. doi: 10.5281/zenodo.6492015.

Reimers, N. and Gurevych, I. (2019). Sentence-bert: Sentence embeddings using siamese bert-networks. *arXiv preprint arXiv:1908.10084.*

Sermeus, W. (2016). Development and evaluation of an adolescents' depression ontology for analyzing social data. *Nursing Informatics 2016: EHealth for All: Every Level Collaboration–From Project to Realization*, 225, 442.

Speer, R., Chin, J., Havasi, C. (2017). Conceptnet 5.5: An open multilingual graph of general knowledge. *Thirty-First AAAI Conference on Artificial Intelligence.* doi: 10.1609/aaai.v31i1.11164.

Tacyildiz, O., Ertugrul, D.C., Bitirim, Y., Akcan, N., Elci, A. (2018). Ontology-based obesity tracking system for children and adolescents. *IEEE 42nd Annual Computer Software and Applications Conference (COMPSAC).* doi: 10.1109/compsac.2018.10252.

Thushara, M.G., Mownika, T., Mangamuru, R. (2019). A comparative study on different keyword extraction algorithms. *3rd International Conference on Computing Methodologies and Communication (ICCMC).* IEEE.

4

Blackjack and the Kelly Bet: A Simulation Assessment of Selected Playing Strategies

In this chapter, we explore the efficacy of rival strategies/bet size options for playing Blackjack using Monte Carlo simulation. Strategies selected for the modeling are "Blind gambler", "Never bust" and "Imitating the dealer". Corresponding bet size choices include the Kelly bet and a number of non-Kelly alternatives.

The resulting analysis yields a wealth of insights – not least the potentially perilous nature of adopting a "pure" Kelly approach to playing the game.

4.1. Introduction

Blackjack is an enduringly popular casino game and has been for the last century (Grant and Kim 2001). Though its exact roots remain something of a mystery, it is believed to have Roman/Spanish/French origins (The World of Playing Cards 2023).

Because of the skill element involved in playing Blackjack (Chantal and Vallerand 1996), the game offers tantalizing opportunities for gamblers to gain an advantage over the casino (Fogel 2004). Indeed, according to Bond (1974), Blackjack is the only game that has the possibility of a positive expected return at the casino.

Chapter written by Jim FREEMAN and Haoyu MIAO.

Over the years, a range of **strategies** has evolved for playing Blackjack, for example, the "basic" strategy (GamblingSites 2023), the 1-3-2-6 system (Betway n.d.), the counting card strategy (Autodesk Instructables n.d.; Pinnacle 2018), etc.

Alongside these, a number of **bet size** options have emerged, including, for example, the Kelly bet, fractional Kelly bets, the minimum bet, etc.

In the study, we shall investigate the relative effectiveness of a selection of Blackjack playing strategies/bet size combinations by spreadsheet simulation. This chapter is structured as follows: sections 4.2 and 4.3 detail the **Blackjack** game modeled and the **Kelly bet,** respectively, section 4.4 provides key background information on the **simulation experiment** undertaken and section 4.5 presents an analysis and discussion of the **empirical results** obtained. **Conclusions** from the study can be found in section 4.6.

4.2. Blackjack

"Blackjack" – also known as "twenty-one" – occurs when a hand comprising two cards takes the value 21.

For this purpose, ace cards are scored 11 or 1 – depending on player preference. Correspondingly, face cards – Jack, Queen and King – are scored 10.

4.2.1. *Rules of the game*

Each player and the dealer are dealt two initial cards (Bicycle Cards 2015). The first card is face-up. The second card for the player is face-up but the dealer's second card is facedown (also known as the "hole card").

If the face-up card for the dealer is an ace or a 10, the gambler is required to glance at the second card but keeps the card facedown.

If the dealer achieves a Blackjack, the two cards are shown immediately and the dealer wins the game – unless the player also obtains a Blackjack.

When the face-up card is an ace, the dealer offers the player insurance on whether the dealer achieves a Blackjack.

After the initial two cards are dealt, the players can "hit", i.e. take another card if it is needed. This is done one card at a time. The additional cards are dealt face-up.

However, if the dealer or the player goes "bust", i.e. if the total cards value exceeds 21, the person loses by default.

The dealer, however, is required to draw cards until their hand totals 17 or more.

Descriptions of key terms used in the game are provided in Table 4.1. Correspondingly, a summary of the moves available to players is shown in Table 4.2 – and associated payment rates in Table 4.3.

Term	Description
Wager	The amount that the gambler bets. Typically, the minimum Blackjack bet in the US is $2 and £2 in the UK.
Push	Both dealer and player have the same hand value.
Bust	Either the player's or dealer's hand value exceeds 21 points.
Soft	Whenever there is an ace in the hand that can be counted as 11, it is designated a soft hand.
Hard	A hard hand in Blackjack correspondingly signifies the absence of an ace.

Table 4.1. *Terminology*

Move	Description
Stand	The player stops drawing new cards.
Hit	The player asks for an additional card.
Double down	The initial bet is doubled with the player receiving one more card.
Split	When two cards of the same value are dealt, there is the opportunity to split them and be dealt another card on each.
Insurance	If the dealer's first card is an ace, the player has the chance to buy insurance in case the dealer is able to generate a Blackjack with the facedown card. The price of the insurance is half the wager. If the dealer obtains a Blackjack, the gambler receives a double payback of the insurance.
Surrender	The player can "fold" a Blackjack hand before drawing new cards.
	When a player chooses to surrender, half of the original bet is returned to the stack, and half, forfeited to the dealer.

Table 4.2. *Player moves*

Payment rate	Description
1:1	The dealer pays the player the same amount of money as the player bets. Applicable when the total points of the player's cards are higher than that of the dealer's but neither hand is a "Blackjack".
3:2	The house provides the player with 1.5 times wager as the payment. Applicable when the player achieves a two cards "Blackjack".

Table 4.3. *Payment rates*

4.3. Kelly bet

The Kelly criterion has now become so well-established as a basis for gamblers' and investors' decisions that its use is almost taken for granted. But it has so much to recommend it: apart from maximizing the expected capital growth rate not to mention median terminal wealth (Ethier 2004), Kelly has also been found to be the best policy for attaining a target capital level in the shortest possible time (Breiman 2010).

However, there are caveats with Kelly also, namely:

– its optimality properties only hold in the very long run;

– in theory, with Kelly, the bankroll needs to be infinitely divisible (see section 4.1.1) – posing potential difficulties in situations where a minimum outlay is specified.

The Kelly bet can be defined as follows:

$$f^* = \frac{bw - l}{b} = \frac{p(b+1) - 1}{b} = \frac{\text{Edge}}{\text{Odds}}$$

where:

f^* = proportion of the current capital to wager;

b = net odds gained on the bet ("b to 1"); namely, we would receive \$b, in addition to the \$1 invested, for a successful \$1 bet (otherwise, the \$1 investment is lost);

w = probability of winning = P(Blackjack payment rate of 1 or 1.5);

$l = 1-w$ = probability of losing.

In our model, the winning probability has been taken as w = P(Blackjack payment rate of 1 or 1.5).

Note that in rounds where the edge is either zero or negative, the criterion recommends that no wager is made.

4.4. Simulation study

Loosely following the work of Keren and Wagenaar (1985), the simulation was coded in VBA (Visual Basic for Applications) to run on Microsoft Excel. Just two player moves – "hit" and "stand" – were allowed for the prototype modeling. Each simulation run – comprising 100 trials – was replicated 1,000 times.

4.4.1. *Modeling assumptions*

One dealer and one player are involved in the game.

All cards drawn are from complete decks.

The number of decks in the simulation is treated as infinite.

Each card is drawn independently and randomly.

The player's capital (bankroll) available at the beginning of a run is 1,000 currency units.

The capital is considered to be infinitely divisible.

The minimum bet size is 2 currency units.

The maximum bet size is 10,000 currency units.

The model focuses on the point scores of hands – not those of individual cards. Details of strategies and bet size alternatives simulated are summarized in Tables 4.4 and 4.5, respectively:

Strategy	Description
Blind gambler	With the "blind gambler strategy", it is assumed that the gambler has no knowledge of the rules of Blackjack, so all choices are made randomly.
Never bust	This strategy is conservative, with the player refusing to take any risk that may result in a total point score exceeding 21.
Imitating the dealer	With this strategy, the player emulates the dealer throughout. For example, the dealer never splits, doubles or surrenders, so the player forgoes these moves as well.

Table 4.4. *Playing strategies simulated*

Type of bet	Description
Kelly	See section 4.3.
Half Kelly	Instead of using the "full" Kelly proportion f* to determine the bet size, a fractional Kelly proportion αf* is employed (in this case, the α fraction is set at 0.5).
Minimum	The player simply bets the table minimum.
Doubling up (Martingale)	The gambler doubles their initial bet size every hand until they win – after which the cycle repeats itself.

Table 4.5. *Bet size options simulated*

4.5. Empirical results

Odds and edge results from the modeling are summarized by strategy in Table 4.6. Where edge values were negative – see section 4.3 – the Kelly criterion could not be applied. In effect therefore, only the "Imitating the dealer" strategy was eligible for Kelly treatment.

Strategy	Odds	Edge	Kelly criterion
Blind gambler	1.106	-0.766	N/A
Never bust	1.021	-0.0132	N/A
Imitating the dealer	1.017	0.252	0.25

Table 4.6. *Average odds and edge for each strategy*

Tables 4.7 shows the win probabilities by strategy. Clearly "Imitating the dealer" performs best here in contrast to "Blind gambler" which is – not unexpectedly – very poor.

Strategy	Outcome			Total	Win probability
	Blackjack	Other win	Lose		
Blind gambler	32	59	909	1,000	0.091
Never bust	32	409	559	1,000	0.441
Imitating the dealer	32	540	428	1,000	0.572

Table 4.7. *Win probability by strategy*

Average final bankroll results by strategy and bet size option are summarized in Table 4.8. In the case of Kelly and Half Kelly bet sizing, because neither was eligible for use with "Blind gambler" and "Never bust", the initial capital of 1,000 units did not change during the simulation.

Self-evidently, the Kelly and Half Kelly bets vastly outclass the non-Kelly alternatives when used with the "Imitating the dealer" strategy – full Kelly especially so.

Strategy	Bet size options			
	Kelly	Half Kelly	Minimum	Doubling up
Blind gambler	1,000	1,000	846.87	0
Never bust	1,000	1,000	997.08	1,450.6
Imitating the dealer	391,896.98	20,707.99	1,049.64	1,160.58

Table 4.8. *Average final bankroll by strategy and bet size option*

However, focusing on only the "Imitating the dealer" details in the table, corresponding estimated coefficients of variation are 5.55 (Kelly), 1.70 (Half Kelly), 0.02 (Minimum) and 0.58 (Doubling up). So clearly, if results in Table 4.8 are to be fully appreciated, the underlying standard errors also need to be taken into account.

4.6. Conclusions

In our simulation experiment, by far the highest return was obtained when the "Imitating the dealer" strategy was played in conjunction with the Kelly bet size.

However, the returns with the Half Kelly system – though very much lower overall – were far less volatile (the relevant coefficient of variation values differed by more than a factor of three). This phenomenon is very well-known in the literature. Hence, the growing tendency by players to turn to fractional Kelly rather than full Kelly for their bet size decisions. The question for future researchers not just for Blackjack but other applications as well, is what fraction should individual players consider using and how might this most efficiently be determined?

Finally, neither the "blind gambler" nor "never bust" strategies have anything to recommend them certainly in terms of bankroll growth – though doubling up seemed to fare better than the minimum bet alternative in the simulation.

4.7. References

Autodesk Instructables (n.d.). Card counting and ranging bet sizes in Blackjack [Online]. Available at: https://www.instructables.com/Card-Counting-and-Ranging-Bet-Sizes/ [Accessed 1 May 2022].

Betway (n.d.). Blackjack strategy 101: Using the 1-3-2-6 gambling system [Online]. Available at: https://blog.betway.com/casino/blackjack-strategy-101-using-the-1-3-2-6-gambling-system/ [Accessed 1 May 2022].

Bicycle Cards (2015). Learn to play: Blackjack [Online]. Available at: http://www.bicyclecards.com/how-to-play/blackjack/ [Accessed 1 May 2022].

Bond, N.A. (1974). Basic strategy and expectation in casino Blackjack. *Organizational Behavior and Human Performance*, 12(3), 413–428.

Breiman, L. (2010). Optimal gambling systems for favorable games. In *The Kelly Capital Growth Investment Criterion: Theory and Practice*, MacLean, L.C., Thorp, E.O., Ziemba, W.T. (eds). World Scientific Publishing, Singapore.

Chantal, Y. and Vallerand, R.J. (1996). Skill versus luck: A motivational analysis of gambling involvement. *Journal of Gambling Studies*, 12(4), 407–418.

Ethier, S.N. (2004). The Kelly system maximizes median fortune. *Journal of Applied Probability*, 41(4), 1230–1236.

Fogel, D.B. (2004). Evolving strategies in blackjack. *Proceedings of the 2004 Congress on Evolutionary Computation (IEEE Cat. No.04TH8753)*, 2, 1427–1434.

GamblingSites (2023). Blackjack strategy guide [Online]. Available at: https://www.gamblingsites.com/online-casino/games/blackjack/strategy/ [Accessed 1 May 2022].

Grant, J.E. and Kim, S.W. (2001). Demographic and clinical features of 131 adult pathological gamblers. *The Journal of Clinical Psychiatry*, 62(12), 957–962.

Keren, G.B. and Wagenaar, W.A. (1985). On the psychology of playing blackjack: Normative and descriptive considerations with implications for decision theory. *Journal of Experimental Psychology: General*, 114(2), 133–158.

Pinnacle (2018). Revisiting the Kelly Criterion Part 2: Fractional Kelly [Online]. Available at: https://www.pinnacle.com/en/betting-articles/Betting-Strategy/fractional-kelly-criterion/GBD27Z9NLJVGFLGG [Accessed 1 May 2022].

The World of Playing Cards (2023). History of blackjack [Online]. Available at: http://www.wopc.co.uk/history/blackjack/blackjack [Accessed 1 May 2022].

PART 2

Estimators

5

An Evaluation of the Efficiency of a Shape Parameter Estimator for the Log-logistic Distribution

The log-logistic distribution has been successfully used in various fields. This model is often presented with shape and scale parameters. For additional flexibility, a location parameter can be added resulting in the three-parameter or shifted log-logistic distribution. In this chapter, we will study recently introduced shape parameter estimators. Different properties of the proposed estimators were obtained and their efficiency was evaluated for finite sample sizes using simulation results.

5.1. Introduction

The log-logistic distribution is obtained through the logarithmic transformation of the logistic distribution. This model is widely used in different fields of study. It has been used for modeling failure data, lifetimes and insurance claims, among others. A random variable X has the classic or two-parameter log-logistic distribution if its distribution function (d.f.) is given by

$$F(x) = 1 - \frac{1}{1 + \left(\frac{x}{\sigma}\right)^{\alpha}} = \frac{1}{1 + \left(\frac{x}{\sigma}\right)^{-\alpha}}, \quad x > 0. \tag{5.1}$$

with α the shape parameter and σ the scale parameter. In the economic field, this probabilistic model is also known as the Fisk (1961) distribution. This is a Pareto-type distribution with the tail (or Pareto) index equal to α (Ahsanullah and Alzaatreh 2018). More precisely, we can write

$$1 - F(x) = x^{-\alpha} l(x), \tag{5.2}$$

Chapter written by Frederico CAEIRO and Ayana MATEUS.

with $l(x)$ a slowly varying function at infinity that measures the departure of F, in [5.1], to the Pareto type I d.f. $F^\star(x) = 1 - x^{-\alpha}, x > 1$. The corresponding probability density function of the log-logistic distribution is as follows:

$$f(x) = \frac{\frac{\alpha}{\sigma}\left(\frac{x}{\sigma}\right)^{\alpha-1}}{\left(1 + \left(\frac{x}{\sigma}\right)^{\alpha}\right)^2}, \quad x > 0. \tag{5.3}$$

The log-logistic model is right skewed and can take different shapes. If $\alpha \leq 1$, f is decreasing, while if $\alpha > 1$, f increases until the mode $x = \sigma\left(\frac{\alpha-1}{\alpha+1}\right)^{1/\alpha}$, then decreases. Moreover, the density function can be very similar to the log-normal density; however, it has heavier tails and the advantage of being mathematically more tractable (Singh et al. 1993). Figure 5.1 shows the probability density function of the log-logistic distribution for selected values of the shape and scale parameters.

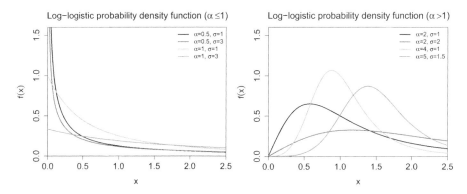

Figure 5.1. *Probability density function of the log-logistic distribution with different shape and scale parameter values. For a color version of this figure, see www.iste.co.uk/dimotikalis/data3.zip*

Since this is a heavy-tailed model, not all r-th moment, for all positive r, exists. The r-th order moments about zero only exist if $r < \alpha$ and are given by

$$E(X^r) = \sigma^r \mathrm{B}\left(1 - \frac{r}{\alpha}, 1 + \frac{r}{\alpha}\right),$$

where $\mathrm{B}(a,b) = \Gamma(a)\Gamma(b)/\Gamma(a+b)$ and $\Gamma(a) = \int_0^\infty x^{a-1}e^{-x}dx$ represent the complete beta and the complete gamma functions, respectively, and a and b are positive real values. Thus, the mean of X only exists if $\alpha > 1$. Regarding the distribution of order statistics, the density function of the i-th order statistic obtained from the random sample of size n, $X_{i:n}$, has a simple closed form. Clearly, the density function is

$$f_{X_{i:n}}(x) = \frac{\frac{\alpha}{\sigma}\left(\frac{x}{\sigma}\right)^{\alpha i - 1}}{B(i, n - i + 1)\left(1 + \left(\frac{x}{\sigma}\right)^{\alpha}\right)^{n+1}}, \quad x > 0.$$

which corresponds to a generalized beta distribution of the second kind (McDonald 1984).

Another attractive property is that the inverse of a log-logistic model is also a log-logistic model. That is, if the random variable X has a log-logistic distribution, with the shape parameter α and scale parameter σ, then $Y = \frac{1}{X}$ has a log-logistic distribution with the shape parameter α and scale parameter $1/\sigma$.

If we choose the scale parameter σ to be equal to 1, we obtain the standard log-logistic distribution. For this model, Balakrishnan et al. (1987) noted the following relation

$$xf(x) = \alpha F(x)(1 - F(x)), \quad \alpha > 0.$$

To make the log-logistic model more flexible for data modeling, an additional location parameter can be added to [5.1], yielding the three parameters or shifted log-logistic model. The d.f. is thus given by

$$F(x) = 1 - \frac{1}{1 + \left(\frac{x-\mu}{\sigma}\right)^{\alpha}} = \frac{1}{1 + \left(\frac{x-\mu}{\sigma}\right)^{-\alpha}}, \quad x > \mu. \qquad [5.4]$$

This model is also referred to as the Pareto type III distribution (see Arnold 2015). Considerable attention has been paid to the estimation of the parameters of the log-logistic model. Balakrishnan et al. (1987) derived the best linear unbiased estimators (BLUEs) for the location and scale parameters of a three-parameter log-logistic model with d.f. in [5.4]. In real life situations, the value of the shape parameter is unknown. Thus, to use the BLUEs for the location and scale, we also need to estimate the shape parameter.

Ahsanullah and Alzaatreh (2018) proposed a location invariant modification of the classical Hill estimator (1975) for the estimation of the shape parameter. This well-known estimator is often used to estimate the tail power behavior. One of its weaknesses is the bias. This problem motivated other authors to derive new estimators. Recently, Mateus and Caeiro (2022) introduced a reduced bias estimator of the shape parameter of the log-logistic model. In the present study, we will evaluate the efficiency of the aforementioned estimators of the shape parameter.

The rest of the chapter is organized as follows. Section 5.2 presents the estimators under study and summarize their asymptotic properties, including the nondegenerate asymptotic behavior. Section 5.3 contains a simulation study to assess the efficiency of the estimators and some concluding remarks.

5.2. Estimation of the shape parameter

5.2.1. *Estimators under study*

In what follows, assume that $(X_1, X_2, \ldots, X_n)$ is a sample of n independent and identically distributed random variables, with a common underlying d.f. F, given in [5.4]. All three parameters are assumed to be unknown. The corresponding sample of nondecreasing order statistics is denoted by $(X_{1:n}, X_{2:n}, \ldots, X_{n:n})$. Since the shape parameter corresponds to the tail index of the log-logistic distribution, and tail index estimator can be used to estimate the shape parameter. Most of the existing semi-parametric tail index estimators are only scale-invariant. A change in the location can modify the asymptotic behavior of the tail and the bias of the estimator (for more information, see the papers by Gomes and Oliveira (2003) and Caeiro and Gomes (2008)). The properties of the Hill estimator and the fact that the d.f. in [5.4] has a location parameter led Ahsanullah and Alzaatreh (2018) to propose the estimation of the shape parameter α with the following location-invariant Hill-type estimator:

$$\hat{\alpha}_H(k) = \frac{1}{H(k)}, \quad H(k) = \frac{1}{k} \sum_{i=1}^{k} \ln \frac{X_{n-i+1:n} - X_{1:n}}{X_{n-k:n} - X_{1:n}}, \quad 1 \le k \le n - 2.$$

[5.5]

Note that the estimator $H(k)$, in [5.5], corresponds to the Hill estimator based on the sample values, shifted by the sample minimum. In addition, the estimator $H(k)$ is a member of the class of estimators in Fraga-Alves (2001), Gomes and Oliveira (2003) and Araújo Santos et al. (2006). Regarding the choice of the parameter k, Ahsanullah and Alzaatreh (2018) proposed $k = \lfloor n/10 \rfloor$, if $n > 100$, where $\lfloor x \rfloor$ denotes the integer part of x. To reduce the mean squared error, it is advisable to work with intermediate values of k, i.e. $k = k_n \in [1, n-1]$ is assumed to be a sequence of positive integers satisfying

$$k \to \infty \quad \text{and} \quad k/n \to 0, \quad \text{as} \quad n \to \infty.$$

[5.6]

Despite the good performance of this estimator, it shares some drawbacks with the Hill estimator: high sensitivity in the choice of k and a substantial bias. These problems motivated several researchers to construct reduced bias estimators of the tail index. These reduced bias estimators have usually a stable sample path, close to the target value, which makes them less sensitive to the choice of k. We mention the first reduced bias estimators in Drees (1996) and Peng (1998) (see also the papers by Beirlant et al. (2012) and Gomes and Guillou (2015) for a general overview on bias reduction). In the context of Pareto-type tails, different authors proposed several alternative estimators for the tail index α or for the extreme value index $\xi = 1/\alpha$. Such estimators provide a reduction of bias with a small increase on the variance. Nevertheless, these estimators were able to provide a reduction in the mean squared error. Gomes et al. (2000) considered the following generalized jackknife (GJ) estimator of the extreme value index:

$$GJ(k) = MR(k) - H(k) = \frac{M^{(2)}(k)}{M^{(1)}(k)} - M^{(1)}(k), \quad k = 1, 2, \ldots, n-1,$$

[5.7]

and

$$M^{(j)}(k) := \frac{1}{k} \sum_{i=1}^{k} (\ln X_{n-i+1:n} - \ln X_{n-k:n})^j, \quad j > 0,$$ [5.8]

are the moments of order j of the log-excesses. The estimator in [5.7] is based on the Hill and the moments ratio (MR) estimators (Danielsson et al. 1996) and belongs to the class of GJ statistics introduced in Peng (1998). The estimator $GJ(k)$ is also non-invariant to changes on location, since it is based on non-invariant location statistics. For models with a non-null location parameter, it is advisable to make inference based on location invariant statistics. Mateus and Caeiro (2022) modified the generalized Jackknife statistic in [5.7] and proposed the following location invariant GJ estimator for the shape parameter of a log-logistic model:

$$\alpha^{GJ}(k) = \frac{\tilde{M}^{(1)}(k)}{\tilde{M}^{(2)}(k) - (\tilde{M}^{(1)}(k))^2}, \quad k = 1, 2, \ldots, n-2,$$ [5.9]

with

$$\tilde{M}^{(j)}(k) := \frac{1}{k} \sum_{i=1}^{k} \left(\ln \frac{X_{n-i+1:n} - X_{1:n}}{X_{n-k:n} - X_{1:n}} \right)^j, \quad j > 0,$$ [5.10]

the moments of order j of the shifted log-excesses. The same authors concluded that $\hat{\alpha}^{GJ}(k)$ has a higher asymptotic variance than $\hat{\alpha}^H(k)$. Regarding the absolute asymptotic bias, $\hat{\alpha}^{GJ}(k)$ has a null dominant component of asymptotic bias. Thus, there is a trade-off between bias and variance.

5.2.2. *Asymptotic properties of the estimators*

Some asymptotic properties are discussed in this section.

PROPOSITION 5.1 (Mateus and Caeiro 2022).– *Assume that k is an intermediate sequence of integers satisfying [5.6]. Then, the following distributional representation*

$$\hat{\alpha}^H(k) \stackrel{d}{=} \alpha \left(1 - \frac{Z_k}{\sqrt{k}} + O_p \left(\frac{\sqrt{k}}{n} \right) - \frac{k}{2n}(1 + o_p(1)) \right)$$ [5.11]

is valid, where $Z_k = \sqrt{k}\frac{1}{k}\sum_{i=1}^{k}(E_i - 1)$, *with E_i being a sequence of independent exponential random variable with the mean value equal to 1, is asymptotically standard normal.*

Moreover, if $\sqrt{k}(k/2n) \to c$, then

$$\sqrt{k}(\hat{\alpha}^H(k) - \alpha) \xrightarrow{d} N\left(-\alpha c, \alpha^2\right).$$ [5.12]

From [5.11], we conclude that the asymptotic variance of $\hat{\alpha}^H(k)$ is α^2/k and the dominant component of asymptotic bias is always negative and equal to $-\alpha k/(2n)$.

PROPOSITION 5.2.– *Assume the conditions of Proposition 5.1. Then, the following distributional representation holds:*

$$\hat{\alpha}^{GJ}(k) \stackrel{d}{=} \alpha\left(1 - \frac{\sqrt{5}Z_k^{GJ}}{\sqrt{k}} + O_p\left(\frac{\sqrt{k}}{n}\right) + o_p\left(\frac{k}{2n}\right)(1 + o_p(1))\right)$$

[5.13]

where Z_k^{GJ} is an asymptotically standard normal variable. Moreover, if $\sqrt{k}(k/2n) \to c$ then

$$\sqrt{k}(\hat{\alpha}^{GJ}(k) - \alpha) \xrightarrow{d} N\left(0, 5\alpha^2\right).$$ [5.14]

Regarding the asymptotic variances, note that we have $V(\hat{\alpha}^H(k)) < V(\hat{\alpha}^{GH}(k))$. The absolute asymptotic bias of $\hat{\alpha}^{GJ}(k)$ is null, while the absolute asymptotic bias of $\hat{\alpha}^H(k)$ is non-null and equal to $|Bias(\hat{\alpha}^H(k))| = \alpha k/2n$. Moreover, the results in [5.13] do not allow to evaluate the asymptotic value of k that minimizes the root mean squared error. To find such an optimal value, it is necessary to compute higher-order terms of the asymptotic bias. This is a topic outside the scope of this chapter.

5.3. Simulation study

In this section, we study the finite sample behavior of $\hat{\alpha}^H(k)$ and $\hat{\alpha}^{GJ}(k)$ with a simulation study, taking 5,000 samples of size n, for several selected values of n between 20 and 10,000. For this purpose, we generated samples of the log-logistic distribution with the following parameter combinations:

- $(\alpha, \mu, \sigma) = (0.25, 1, 1)$;
- $(\alpha, \mu, \sigma) = (0.75, 1, 1)$;
- $(\alpha, \mu, \sigma) = (1.25, 1, 1)$;
- $(\alpha, \mu, \sigma) = (2, 1, 1)$;
- $(\alpha, \mu, \sigma) = (3, 1, 1)$.

For each sample, the estimates of α are first computed for every k. We then compute the simulated bias,

$$Bias(\hat{\alpha}^{\bullet}(k)) = \frac{1}{5000} \sum_{i=1}^{5000} \hat{\alpha}^{\bullet}(k) - \alpha$$

and the root mean squared error (RMSE)

$$RMSE(\hat{\alpha}^{\bullet}(k)) = \frac{1}{5000} \sum_{i=1}^{5000} (\hat{\alpha}^{\bullet}(k) - \alpha)^2$$

for each k, with $\bullet$ denoting either H or GJ. We have further computed the simulated optimum level

$$\hat{k}_0^{(\bullet)} = \arg \min_k \mathrm{RMSE}[\hat{\alpha}^{\bullet}(k)], \qquad\qquad [5.15]$$

and the simulated bias and RMSE at the optimal level in [5.15]. The optimal value of k provides a benchmark of the best possible performance obtainable with each estimator of the parameter α. In practice, such an optimal value may not be achieved. Finally, the following measure of relative efficiency

$$REFF_{GJ|H} = \frac{\mathrm{RMSE}[\hat{\alpha}^H(\hat{k}_0^{(H)})]}{\mathrm{RMSE}[\hat{\alpha}^{GJ}(\hat{k}_0^{(GJ)})]} \qquad\qquad [5.16]$$

was evaluated. The higher than one this REFF indicators is, the better the GJ estimator performs comparatively with the H estimator.

REMARK 5.1.– *Since log-logistic samples were generated from a uniform random numbers in [0, 1] with the inverse transformation method, and the estimators are location and scale invariant, the simulated values of $\hat{\alpha}^H(k)$ and $\hat{\alpha}^{GJ}(k)$ are independent of the location and scale parameters μ and σ.*

The simulated values of the bias and RMSE, both computed at the simulated optimal threshold, are given in Table 5.1. The following notation will be used: $\hat{\alpha}_0^H = \hat{\alpha}^H(\hat{k}_0^{(H)})$ and $\hat{\alpha}_0^{GJ} = \hat{\alpha}^{GJ}(\hat{k}_0^{(GJ)})$. It can be easily seen that $\hat{\alpha}_0^{GJ}$ has the lowest bias when the sample size is not very small ($n \geq 100$ if $\alpha \leq 1.5$, $n \geq 500$ if $\alpha = 2$, and $n \geq 20$ if $\alpha = 3$). Similar conclusions hold for the RMSE.

The measure of the relative efficiency, $REFF_{GJ|H}$, can be found in Table 5.2. The empirical results show that the GJ estimator performs better than H estimator, except for small sample sizes.

	20	50	100	200	500	1,000	2,000	5,000	10,000
				$(\alpha, \mu, \sigma) = (0.25, 1, 1)$					
$\text{Bias}[\hat{\alpha}_0^H]$	-0.0516	-0.0414	-0.0294	-0.0250	-0.0178	-0.0130	-0.0118	-0.0092	-0.0072
$\text{Bias}[\hat{\alpha}_0^{GJ}]$	0.0943	0.0461	0.0291	0.0202	0.0133	0.0087	0.0065	0.0045	0.0031
$\text{RMSE}[\hat{\alpha}_0^H]$	0.0838	0.0630	0.0501	0.0408	0.0310	0.0251	0.0204	0.0153	0.0122
$\text{RMSE}[\hat{\alpha}_0^{GJ}]$	0.1732	0.0903	0.0603	0.0426	0.0278	0.0203	0.0151	0.0101	0.0077
				$(\alpha, \mu, \sigma) = (0.75, 1, 1)$					
$\text{Bias}[\hat{\alpha}_0^H]$	-0.1597	-0.1250	-0.0884	-0.0750	-0.0533	-0.0389	-0.0353	-0.0275	-0.0216
$\text{Bias}[\hat{\alpha}_0^{GJ}]$	0.3026	0.1417	0.0884	0.0609	0.0400	0.0262	0.0194	0.0136	0.0093
$\text{RMSE}[\hat{\alpha}_0^H]$	0.2528	0.1893	0.1503	0.1223	0.0930	0.0752	0.0612	0.0458	0.0366
$\text{RMSE}[\hat{\alpha}_0^{GJ}]$	0.5400	0.2735	0.1815	0.1280	0.0836	0.0609	0.0453	0.0303	0.0230
				$(\alpha, \mu, \sigma) = (1.25, 1, 1)$					
$\text{Bias}[\hat{\alpha}_0^H]$	-0.3014	-0.2021	-0.1535	-0.1280	-0.0898	-0.0653	-0.0591	-0.0460	-0.0360
$\text{Bias}[\hat{\alpha}_0^{GJ}]$	0.4989	0.2352	0.1476	0.1018	0.0669	0.0436	0.0323	0.0226	0.0155
$\text{RMSE}[\hat{\alpha}_0^H]$	0.4349	0.3210	0.2532	0.2052	0.1554	0.1255	0.1021	0.0763	0.0609
$\text{RMSE}[\hat{\alpha}_0^{GJ}]$	0.8949	0.4519	0.3013	0.2128	0.1391	0.1014	0.0755	0.0504	0.0383
				$(\alpha, \mu, \sigma) = (2, 1, 1)$					
$\text{Bias}[\hat{\alpha}_0^H]$	-0.5197	-0.3376	-0.2406	-0.2063	-0.1630	-0.1160	-0.0883	-0.0768	-0.0561
$\text{Bias}[\hat{\alpha}_0^{GJ}]$	0.6490	0.3015	0.1912	0.1338	0.0914	0.0695	0.0510	0.0317	0.0237
$\text{RMSE}[\hat{\alpha}_0^H]$	0.7429	0.5431	0.4271	0.3447	0.2583	0.2061	0.1672	0.1246	0.0990
$\text{RMSE}[\hat{\alpha}_0^{GJ}]$	1.2972	0.6573	0.4466	0.3195	0.2113	0.1557	0.1166	0.0785	0.0600
				$(\alpha, \mu, \sigma) = (3, 1, 1)$					
$\text{Bias}[\hat{\alpha}_0^H]$	-0.9078	-0.6218	-0.4660	-0.3566	-0.2760	-0.2202	-0.1737	-0.1269	-0.0970
$\text{Bias}[\hat{\alpha}_0^{GJ}]$	0.5516	0.1814	0.1361	0.0943	0.0629	0.0433	0.0411	0.0254	0.0174
$\text{RMSE}[\hat{\alpha}_0^H]$	1.2325	0.9148	0.7225	0.5825	0.4388	0.3492	0.2822	0.2090	0.1660
$\text{RMSE}[\hat{\alpha}_0^{GJ}]$	1.6152	0.8145	0.5604	0.4047	0.2678	0.1979	0.1493	0.1008	0.0771

Table 5.1. *Simulated values of the bias and RMSE at the simulated optimal level $\hat{k}_0^{(\bullet)}$*

n	20	50	100	200	500	1,000	2,000	5,000	10,000
α									
0.25	0.4838	0.6971	0.8305	0.9569	1.1130	1.2355	1.3504	1.5119	1.5888
0.75	0.4681	0.6920	0.8281	0.9557	1.1125	1.2354	1.3504	1.5119	1.5888
1.25	0.4860	0.7105	0.8403	0.9643	1.1172	1.2383	1.3528	1.5134	1.5898
2	0.5727	0.8263	0.9564	1.0789	1.2225	1.3236	1.4342	1.5878	1.6516
3	0.7631	1.1231	1.2893	1.4393	1.6385	1.7647	1.8900	2.0734	2.1525

Table 5.2. *Values of $REFF_{GJ|H}$, for different values of the shape parameter α*

5.4. References

Ahsanullah, M. and Alzaatreh, A. (2018). Parameter estimation for the log-logistic distribution based on order statistics. *REVSTAT – Statistical Journal*, 16, 429–443.

Araújo Santos, P., Fraga Alves, M., Gomes, M.I. (2006). Peaks over random threshold methodology for tail index and high quantile estimation. *REVSTAT – Statistical Journal*, 4(3), 227–247.

Arnold, B.C. (2015). *Pareto Distributions, Monographs on Statistics and Applied Probability*. Chapman and Hall/CRC, London.

Balakrishnan, N., Malik, H., Puthenpura, S. (1987). Best linear unbiased estimation of location and scale parameters of the log-logistic distribution. *Communications in Statistics – Theory and Methods*, 16(12), 3477–3495.

Beirlant, J., Caeiro, F., Gomes, M.I. (2012). An overview and open research topics in statistics of univariate extremes. *REVSTAT – Statistical Journal*, 10, 1, 1–31.

Caeiro, F. and Gomes, M.I. (2008). Minimum–variance reduced-bias tail index and high quantile estimation. *REVSTAT – Statistical Journal*, 6(1), 1–20.

Danielsson, J., Jansen, D.W., de Vries, C.G. (1996). The method of moments ratio estimator for the tail shape parameter. *Communications in Statistics – Theory and Methods*, 25(4), 711–720.

Drees, H. (1996). Refined pickands estimators with bias correction. *Communications in Statistics – Theory and Methods*, 25(4), 837–851.

Fisk, P.R. (1961). The graduation of income distributions. *Econometrica*, 29(2), 171–185.

Fraga-Alves, M. (2001). A location invariant Hill-type estimator. *Extremes*, 4(3), 199–217.

Gomes, M.I. and Guillou, A. (2015). Extreme value theory and statistics of univariate extremes: A review. *International Statistical Review*, 83(2), 263–292.

Gomes, M.I. and Oliveira, O. (2003). How can non-invariant statistics work in our benefit in the semi-parametric estimation of parameters of rare events. *Communications in Statistics – Simulation and Computation*, 32(4), 1005–1028.

Gomes, M.I., Martins, M.J., Neves, M. (2000). Alternatives to a semi-parametric estimator of parameters of rare events – The jackknife methodology. *Extremes*, 3(3), 207–229.

Hill, B.M. (1975). A simple general approach to inference about the tail of a distribution. *The Annals of Statistics*, 3(5), 1163–1174.

Mateus, A. and Caeiro, F. (2022). Improved shape parameter estimation for the three-parameter log-logistic distribution. *Computational and Mathematical Methods*, 8400130, 13.

McDonald, J.B. (1984). Some generalized functions for the size distribution of income. *Econometrica*, 52, 647–663.

Peng, L. (1998). Asymptotically unbiased estimators for the extreme value index. *Statistics & Probability Letters*, 38(2), 107–115.

Singh, V.P., Guo, H., Yu, F.X. (1993). Parameter estimation for 3-parameter loglogistic distribution (LLD3) by Pome. *Stochastic Hydrology and Hydraulics*, 7(3), 163–177.

6

Restricted Minimum Density Power Divergence Estimator for Step-stress ALT with Nondestructive One-shot Devices

One-shot device data represent an extreme case of interval censoring. Some kinds of one-shot units do not get destroyed when tested, and so, survival units can continue within the test, providing extra information about their lifetime. Moreover, one-shot devices may last for long times under normal operating conditions, so accelerated life tests (ALTs) may be used for inference. ALTs relate the lifetime distribution of a unit to the stress level at which it is tested via a log-linear relationship. In particular, the step-stress ALT model gradually increases the stress level at which units are submitted to at pre-fixed times during the life-testing experiment. However, when the number of units under test is small, the outlying data may greatly influence the parameter estimation. In this chapter, we develop robust restricted estimators based on the density power divergence (DPD) under linearly restricted subspaces, for nondestructive one-shot devices under the step-stress ALTs with exponential lifetime distributions. We theoretically study the asymptotic and robustness properties of the restricted estimators and we empirically illustrate such properties through a simulation study.

6.1. Introduction

One-shot devices can be only tested at some discrete inspection times, and so we can only know whether a test unit has failed or not before certain fixed times. Inference under censored data is of great interest in reliability. Indeed, many works in survival analysis deal with the problem of type I and type II censored data. In these scenarios, only a few observations are censored. One-shot devices represent the extreme case of interval censoring, where all observations are either right- or left-censored, and so they play an important role in survival analysis.

Chapter written by Narayanaswamy BALAKRISHNAN, María JAENADA and Leandro PARDO.

Real-life one-shot devices usually have large mean lifetimes under normal operating conditions, and so accelerated life test (ALT) plans may be useful to infer their reliability. ALT plans assume that the reliability of the product is related to a stress factor, and therefore they accelerate the time to failure by increasing the stress level. ALT plans can be classified into three main categories, depending on how the stress level is increased. Constant ALT plans apply different constant stress levels to different groups of devices, while step-stress and progressive ALTs progressively increase the stress level at which units are submitted, maintaining constant stress until certain times of stress change for the step-stress set-up and continuously increasing the level for the progressive one.

Generally, one-shot devices are assumed to get destroyed when tested, and so one-shot data are right and left censoring. However, the destructiveness assumption may not be necessary in many practical situations. In this chapter, we focus on these nondestructive one-shot devices and study some inference methods for analyzing their lifetime characteristics. The non-destructiveness condition allows surviving units to continue in the experiment, providing extra information about their lifetime distribution. The methods can then be applied to the experimental set-up where real-time monitoring is not available. For example, Balakrishnan et al. (2022b) assessed the effect of temperature on some electronic components.

In this context, step-stress ALTs make the best use of the nondestructive devices under tests. Indeed, increasing the stress level causes a greater number of failures in a shorter period of time, so step-stress tests are faster and require fewer sample sizes for accurate inference than constant-stress ALTs. Here, we assume that the lifetime distribution of the one-shot device at one stress level is related to the distribution at preceding stress levels by assuming that the residual life of the device depends only on the cumulative exposure it had experienced, with no memory of how this exposure was accumulated.

On the other hand, classical inferential methods for one-shot data are based on the maximum likelihood estimator (MLE), which is efficient but lacks robustness. To overcome the robustness drawback, Balakrishnan et al. (2022a) proposed robust estimators for one-shot devices based on the popular density power divergence (DPD) (Basu et al. 1998) under exponential lifetimes. They developed minimum DPD estimators (MDPPE) as well as Wald-type tests based on them, and theoretically and empirically studied their asymptotic and robustness properties. However, some inferential procedures such as Rao-type tests are based on restricted estimators. Basu et al. (2018) developed robust restricted estimators based on the DPD for general statistical models, and derived their asymptotic distribution and robustness properties. Jaenada et al. (2022) extended the theory using the Rényi pseudodistance and developed some testing procedures based on the restricted estimators. Balakrishnan et al. (2022c) developed Rao-type tests based on restricted MDPDE for nondestructive one-shot devices exponentially distributed tested under step-stress ALT. However, they did not analyze the theoretical aspects of the restricted estimators. Here, we fill the gap by examining the asymptotic behavior of the restricted MDPDE as well as its robustness properties under linearly constrained subspaces.

The rest of this chapter is organized as follows: in section 6.2, we define the restricted MDPDE, and we state its asymptotic distribution. Section 6.3 theoretically analyzes the robustness of the restricted MDPDEs through its influence function (IF). Section 6.4 gives some main applications of the restricted estimator. Finally, in section 6.5, a simulation study is carried out to evaluate the performance of the proposed estimators under different scenarios of contamination.

6.2. Minimum density power divergence estimator and restricted minimum density power divergence estimator

Consider a multiple step-stress ALT with k-ordered stress levels, $x_1 < x_2 < \cdots < x_k$, and their corresponding times of stress change $\tau_1 < \tau_2 \cdots < \tau_k$. We assume that the lifetimes of one-shot devices follow an exponential distribution, which is widely used as a simple lifetime model in engineering and physical sciences. The exponential assumption can also be applied to obtain benchmark predictions or initial estimates for more complex parametric families, containing the exponential as a special case, such as Weibull or gamma distributions.

The cumulative exposure (CE) model describes the lifetime distribution of a device as

$$
G_T(t) = \begin{cases}
G_1(t) = 1 - e^{-\lambda_1 t}, & 0 < t < \tau_1 \\
G_2(t + a_1 - \tau_1) = 1 - e^{-\lambda_2(t + a_1 - \tau_1)}, & \tau_1 \leq t < \tau_2 \\
\vdots & \vdots \\
G_k(t + a_{k-1} - \tau_{k-1}) = 1 - e^{-\lambda_k(t + a_{k-1} - \tau_{k-1})}, & \tau_{k-1} \leq t < \infty,
\end{cases}
\tag{6.1}
$$

with

$$
a_{i-1} = \frac{\sum_{l=1}^{i-1} (\tau_l - \tau_{l-1}) \lambda_l}{\lambda_i}, \quad i = 1, ..., k-1.
\tag{6.2}
$$

and

$$
\lambda_i(\boldsymbol{\theta}) = \theta_0 \exp(\theta_1 x_i), \quad i = 1, .., k,
\tag{6.3}
$$

where $\boldsymbol{\theta} = (\theta_0, \theta_1) \in \mathbb{R}^+ \times \mathbb{R} = \Theta$ is an unknown parameter vector of the model. The log-linear relation in [6.3] is frequently assumed in accelerated life test models, as it can be shown to be equivalent to the well-known inverse power law model or the Arrhenius reaction rate model.

Additionally, consider a grid of inspection times, $t_1 < t_2 < \cdots < t_L$, containing all times of stress change. The probability of failure within the interval $(t_{j-1}, t_j]$ is given by

$$\pi_j(\boldsymbol{\theta}) = G_T(t_j) - G_T(t_{j-1}), \quad j = 1, .., L, \tag{6.4}$$

and the probability of survival at the end of the experiment is $\pi_{L+1}(\boldsymbol{\theta}) = 1 - G_T(t_L)$.

Given the sample of one-shot data, $(n_1, ..., n_{L+1})$, the empirical probability vector of a multinomial model can be defined as

$$\widehat{\boldsymbol{p}} = (\frac{n_1}{N}, ..., \frac{n_{L+1}}{N}). \tag{6.5}$$

For step-stress ALT with one-shot devices under exponential lifetime distributions, the DPD between the empirical and theoretical probability vectors, defined in [6.4] and [6.5], respectively, is given by

$$d_\beta\left(\widehat{\boldsymbol{p}}, \boldsymbol{\pi}\left(\boldsymbol{\theta}\right)\right) = \sum_{j=1}^{L+1} \left(\pi_j(\boldsymbol{\theta})^{1+\beta} - \left(1 + \frac{1}{\beta}\right)\widehat{p}_j \pi_j(\boldsymbol{\theta})^\beta + \frac{1}{\beta}\widehat{p}_j^{\beta+1}\right), \tag{6.6}$$

The density DPD family represents a rich class of density-based divergences and it is indexed by a tuning parameter $\beta \geq 0$ controlling the trade-off between robustness and efficiency.

From the above, we define the MDPDE for the step-stress ALT model with one-shot devices as

$$\widehat{\boldsymbol{\theta}}^\beta = \left(\widehat{\theta}_0^\beta, \widehat{\theta}_1^\beta\right) = \arg\min_{\boldsymbol{\theta} \in \Theta} d_\beta\left(\widehat{\boldsymbol{p}}, \boldsymbol{\pi}\left(\boldsymbol{\theta}\right)\right). \tag{6.7}$$

Note that, at $\beta = 0$, the DPD coincides with the Kullback–Leibler divergence and so the MDPDE for $\beta = 0$ coincides with the MLE.

In many practical situations, it may be of interest to reduce the parameter space to values of $\boldsymbol{\theta}$, satisfying a linear constraint of the form

$$g(\boldsymbol{\theta}) = \boldsymbol{m}^T\boldsymbol{\theta} - d = 0, \tag{6.8}$$

with $\boldsymbol{m} = (m_0, m_1)^T \in \mathbb{R}^2$ and $d \in \mathbb{R}$. Accordingly, the restricted MDPDE, $\widetilde{\boldsymbol{\theta}}^\beta$, is defined by

$$\widetilde{\boldsymbol{\theta}}^\beta = \arg\min_{\boldsymbol{\theta} \in \Theta_0} d_\beta(\widehat{\boldsymbol{p}}, \boldsymbol{\pi}(\boldsymbol{\theta})). \tag{6.9}$$

Since the restricted MDPPE is a constrained minimum, its estimating equations can be written in terms of Lagrange multipliers. That is, the MDPDE restricted to the linear constraint [6.8], $\widetilde{\boldsymbol{\theta}}^\beta$, must satisfy the restricted equations

$$\boldsymbol{W}^T \boldsymbol{D}_{\boldsymbol{\pi}(\widetilde{\boldsymbol{\theta}}^\beta)}^{\beta-1} \left(\widehat{\boldsymbol{p}} - \boldsymbol{\pi}(\widetilde{\boldsymbol{\theta}}^\beta)\right) + \boldsymbol{m}\widetilde{\boldsymbol{\lambda}} = \boldsymbol{0}_2, \tag{6.10}$$

for some vector $\widetilde{\boldsymbol{\lambda}}$ of Lagrangian multipliers, where $\boldsymbol{0}_2$ is the two-dimensional null vector, $\boldsymbol{D}_{\pi(\theta)}$ denotes a $(L+1) \times (L+1)$ diagonal matrix with diagonal entries $\pi_j(\boldsymbol{\theta})$, $j = 1, ..., L+1$, and $\boldsymbol{W}$ is a $(L+1) \times 2$ matrix with rows $\boldsymbol{w}_j = \boldsymbol{z}_j - \boldsymbol{z}_{j-1}$, where

$$z_j = g_T(t_j) \left(\begin{array}{c} \frac{t_j + a_{i-1} - \tau_{i-1}}{\theta_0} \\ (t_j + a_{i-1} - \tau_{i-1})x_i + a_{i-1}^* \end{array} \right), \quad j = 1, ..., L, \qquad [6.11]$$

$$a_{i-1}^* = \frac{1}{\lambda_i} \sum_{l=1}^{i-1} \lambda_l \left(\tau_l - \tau_{l-1} \right) \left(-x_i + x_l \right), \quad i = 2, .., k, \qquad [6.12]$$

$z_{-1} = z_{L+1} = 0$ and i is the stress level at which the units are tested after the j-th inspection time.

The next theorem states the asymptotic distribution of the restricted MDPDE for nondestructive one-shot devices under the step-stress ALT model.

THEOREM 6.1.– *Let* $\boldsymbol{\theta}_0$ *be the true value of the parameter* $\boldsymbol{\theta}$ *and assume that* $g(\boldsymbol{\theta}_0) = 0$ *with* $g(\cdot)$ *defined in [6.8]. The asymptotic distribution of the restricted MDPDE for the step-stress ALT model with nondestructive one-shot devices under exponential lifetimes,* $\widetilde{\boldsymbol{\theta}}^\beta$, *obtained under the constraint* $g(\boldsymbol{\theta}) = 0$, *is given by*

$$\sqrt{N} \left(\widetilde{\boldsymbol{\theta}}^\beta - \boldsymbol{\theta}_0 \right) \xrightarrow[N \to \infty]{L} \mathcal{N} \left(\boldsymbol{0}, \Sigma_\beta(\boldsymbol{\theta}_0) \right)$$

where

$$\Sigma_\beta(\boldsymbol{\theta}_0) = \boldsymbol{P}_\beta(\boldsymbol{\theta}_0) \boldsymbol{K}_\beta(\boldsymbol{\theta}_0) \boldsymbol{P}_\beta(\boldsymbol{\theta}_0),$$

$$\boldsymbol{P}_\beta(\boldsymbol{\theta}_0) = \boldsymbol{J}_\beta(\boldsymbol{\theta}_0)^{-1} - \boldsymbol{Q}_\beta(\boldsymbol{\theta}_0) \boldsymbol{m}^T \boldsymbol{J}_\beta(\boldsymbol{\theta}_0)^{-1}, \qquad [6.13]$$

$$\boldsymbol{Q}_\beta(\boldsymbol{\theta}_0) = \boldsymbol{J}_\beta(\boldsymbol{\theta}_0)^{-1} \boldsymbol{m} (\boldsymbol{m}^T \boldsymbol{J}_\beta(\boldsymbol{\theta}_0)^{-1} \boldsymbol{m})^{-1},$$

with

$$\boldsymbol{J}_\beta(\boldsymbol{\theta}_0) = \boldsymbol{W}^T D_{\pi(\theta_0)}^{\beta-1} \boldsymbol{W},$$

$$\boldsymbol{K}_\beta(\boldsymbol{\theta}_0) = \boldsymbol{W}^T \left(D_{\pi(\theta_0)}^{2\beta-1} - \boldsymbol{\pi}(\boldsymbol{\theta}_0)^\beta \boldsymbol{\pi}(\boldsymbol{\theta}_0)^{\beta T} \right) \boldsymbol{W}, \qquad [6.14]$$

$D_{\pi(\theta_0)}$ *denotes the diagonal matrix with entries* $\pi_j(\boldsymbol{\theta}_0)$, $j = 1, ..., L+1$, *and* $\boldsymbol{\pi}(\boldsymbol{\theta}_0)^\beta$ *denotes the vector with components* $\pi_j(\boldsymbol{\theta}_0)^\beta$.

The proof follows Theorem 2 of Basu et al. (2018) and Result 3 of Balakrishnan et al. (2022a).

6.3. Influence function of the restricted minimum density power divergence estimator

The robustness of an estimator is widely analyzed using the concept of influence function (IF), first introduced by Hampel et al. (1986). Intuitively, the IF describes the effect of an infinitesimal contamination of the model on the estimate. Therefore, IFs associated with locally robust estimators should be bounded. The IF of the MDPDE for the step-stress ALT model with nondestructive one-shot devices was established by Balakrishnan et al. (2022a), and the boundedness of the function was discussed there, concluding that the IF of the MDPDE is always bounded for positive values of the tuning parameter. Here, we derive the IF of the restricted MDPDE, $\widetilde{\boldsymbol{\theta}}^{\beta}$, defined in section 6.2. Note that in this case, the functional associated with the restricted estimator must also satisfy the subspace constraint. The statistical functional and influence function of the estimators under parametric restrictions have been rigorously studied in Ghosh (2015). Here, we study the IF of the restricted MDPDE when the subspace constraint has a linear form. We consider F_θ and G the assumed and real distribution functions with associated mass functions $\boldsymbol{\pi}(\boldsymbol{\theta})$ and g, respectively. We define $\widetilde{\boldsymbol{T}}_\beta$ the functional associated with the restricted MDPDE, $\widetilde{\boldsymbol{\theta}}^{\beta}$, computed as the minimizer of the DPD given in [6.6] between the mass functions $\boldsymbol{\pi}(\boldsymbol{\theta})$ and g subject to the linear constraint $\boldsymbol{m}^T\boldsymbol{\theta} - d = 0$.

For influence function analysis, we could derive the IF expression from the estimating equations of the restricted MDPDE in terms of Lagrange multipliers given in [6.10]. However, Ghosh (2015) proposed an alternative approach where the functional $\widetilde{\boldsymbol{T}}_\beta$ associated with the restricted MDPDE is calculated as a solution of the estimating equations of the (unconstrained) MDPDE over the subspace Θ_0. The existence of such a solution is guaranteed by the implicit function theorem. Hence, the IF of the restricted MDPDE at the contamination point $\boldsymbol{n}$ and the model distribution with the true parameter value $\boldsymbol{\theta}_0$, $F_{\boldsymbol{\theta}_0}$, must simultaneously verify the expression of the IF of the MDPDE stated in Balakrishnan et al. (2022a):

$$\mathrm{IF}\left(\boldsymbol{n}, \widetilde{\boldsymbol{T}}_\beta, F_{\boldsymbol{\theta}_0}\right) = \boldsymbol{J}_\beta^{-1}(\boldsymbol{\theta}_0)\boldsymbol{W}^T\boldsymbol{D}_{\boldsymbol{\pi}(\boldsymbol{\theta}_0)}^{\beta-1}\left(-\boldsymbol{\pi}(\boldsymbol{\theta}_0) + \Delta_{\boldsymbol{n}}\right)$$

and the subspace constraint $\boldsymbol{m}^T\widetilde{\boldsymbol{T}}_\beta - d = 0$. Differentiating on the previous subspace constraint, we have

$$\boldsymbol{m}^T\mathrm{IF}\left(\boldsymbol{n}, \widetilde{\boldsymbol{T}}_\beta, F_{\boldsymbol{\theta}_0}\right) = 0$$

and therefore, combining both equations, we get

$$\begin{pmatrix}\boldsymbol{J}_\beta(\boldsymbol{\theta}_0)\\\boldsymbol{m}^T\end{pmatrix}\mathrm{IF}\left(\boldsymbol{n}, \widetilde{\boldsymbol{T}}_\beta, F_{\boldsymbol{\theta}_0}\right) = \begin{pmatrix}\boldsymbol{W}^T\boldsymbol{D}_{\boldsymbol{\pi}(\boldsymbol{\theta}_0)}^{\beta-1}\left(-\boldsymbol{\pi}(\boldsymbol{\theta}_0) + \Delta_{\boldsymbol{n}}\right)\\0\end{pmatrix}.$$

Now, multiplying both terms by $\left(J_\beta(\theta)^T, m\right)$ and inverting in both sizes of the equation, the expression of the IF of the restricted MDPDE is given by

$$\text{IF}\left(n, \widetilde{T}_\beta, F_{\theta_0}\right) = \left(J_\beta(\theta_0)^T J_\beta(\theta_0) + mm^T\right)^{-1} J_\beta(\theta_0)^T W^T D_{\pi(\theta_0)}^{\beta-1}$$
$$\times \left(-\pi(\theta_0) + \Delta_n\right).$$

[6.15]

Since the matrix $\left(J_\beta(\theta_0)^T J_\beta(\theta_0) + mm^T\right)^{-1} J_\beta(\theta_0)^T$ is typically assumed to be bounded, the robustness of the restricted MDPDE depends only on the boundedness of the IF of the (unrestricted) MDPDE. Therefore, the restricted MDPDE is robust for all types of outliers when using positive values of β, whereas the restricted MLE (corresponding to $\beta = 0$) lacks robustness against stress level or inspection times contamination, i.e. bad leverage points.

6.4. Applications of the restricted MDPDE

An interesting application of the restricted MDPDE is robust testing procedures based on the DPD for testing linear null hypothesis of the form

$$\text{H}_0 : m^T\theta = d.$$

[6.16]

with $m \in \mathbb{R}^2$ and $d \in \mathbb{R}$. In this section, we develop two families of test statistics based on the DPD for testing [6.16] for one-shot devices under the step-stress ALT model, namely Rao-type test statistics and DPD-based test statistics. These two families were studied for general statistical models in Basu et al. (2018, 2021). Let us consider $\widetilde{\theta}^\beta$ the restricted MDPDE with the restricted parameter space defined by the null hypothesis in [6.16],

$$\Theta_0 = \{\theta|\ m^T\theta = d\}$$

and recall $\widehat{\theta}^\beta$ denotes the MDPDE for θ computed in all parameter space.

6.4.1. Rao-type test statistics

Let us consider the score of the DPD loss function for the step-stress ALT model with nondestructive one-shot devices

$$U_{\beta,N}(\theta) = W^T D_{\pi(\theta)}^{\beta-1}(\widehat{p} - \pi(\theta))$$

[6.17]

where matrices W and $D_{\pi(\theta)}$ are defined in section 6.2. That is, the MDPDE verifies the estimating equations given by

$$U_{\beta,N}(\widehat{\theta}^\beta) = 0.$$

DEFINITION 6.1.– *The Rao-type statistics, based on the restricted to the linear null hypothesis [6.16] MDPDE, $\widetilde{\boldsymbol{\theta}}^{\beta}$, for testing [6.16] is given by*

$$
\begin{aligned}
\boldsymbol{R}_{\beta,N}(\widetilde{\boldsymbol{\theta}}^{\beta}) =& N\boldsymbol{U}_{\beta,N}(\widetilde{\boldsymbol{\theta}}^{\beta})^{T}\boldsymbol{Q}_{\beta}(\widetilde{\boldsymbol{\theta}}^{\beta}) \left[\boldsymbol{Q}_{\beta}(\widetilde{\boldsymbol{\theta}}^{\beta})^{T}\boldsymbol{K}_{\beta}(\widetilde{\boldsymbol{\theta}}^{\beta})\boldsymbol{Q}_{\beta}(\widetilde{\boldsymbol{\theta}}^{\beta})\right]^{-1} \\
&\times \boldsymbol{Q}_{\beta}(\widetilde{\boldsymbol{\theta}}^{\beta})^{T}\boldsymbol{U}_{\beta,N}(\widetilde{\boldsymbol{\theta}}^{\beta}),
\end{aligned}
\tag{6.18}
$$

where matrices $\boldsymbol{K}_{\beta}(\boldsymbol{\theta})$, $\boldsymbol{Q}_{\beta}(\boldsymbol{\theta})$ and $\boldsymbol{U}_{\beta,N}(\boldsymbol{\theta})$, are defined in [6.14], [6.13] and [6.17], respectively.

The matrix $\boldsymbol{Q}_{\beta}(\boldsymbol{\theta})$ depends on the null hypothesis through m, and the term d is only used to obtain the restricted MDPDE. Moreover, if $m = (0,1)$ (simple null hypothesis), then the restricted estimate of θ_1 must be necessarily d.

THEOREM 6.2.– *The asymptotic distribution of the score $\boldsymbol{U}_{\beta,N}(\widetilde{\boldsymbol{\theta}}^{\beta})$ for the step-stress ALT model with nondestructive one-shot devices under exponential lifetimes is given by*

$$
\sqrt{N}\boldsymbol{U}_{\beta,N}(\widetilde{\boldsymbol{\theta}}^{\beta}) \xrightarrow[N\to\infty]{L} \mathcal{N}\left(\boldsymbol{0}, \boldsymbol{K}_{\beta}(\boldsymbol{\theta})\right)
$$

where the variance–covariance matrix $\boldsymbol{K}_{\beta}(\boldsymbol{\theta})$ is defined in [6.14].

PROOF.– It is well known that

$$
\sqrt{N}(\widehat{\boldsymbol{p}} - \boldsymbol{\pi}(\boldsymbol{\theta})) \xrightarrow[N\to\infty]{L} \mathcal{N}\left(\boldsymbol{0}, \boldsymbol{D}_{\boldsymbol{\pi}(\boldsymbol{\theta})} - \boldsymbol{\pi}(\boldsymbol{\theta})\boldsymbol{\pi}(\boldsymbol{\theta})^{T}\right).
$$

since $\widehat{\boldsymbol{p}}$ is the MLE of the multinomial model, and $\boldsymbol{D}_{\boldsymbol{\pi}(\boldsymbol{\theta})} - \boldsymbol{\pi}(\boldsymbol{\theta})\boldsymbol{\pi}(\boldsymbol{\theta})^{T}$ is the inverse of the Fisher information matrix of that model. Therefore, the score $\sqrt{N}\boldsymbol{U}_{\beta,N}(\boldsymbol{\theta})$ is asymptotically normal with the mean vector

$$
\mathbb{E}\left[\boldsymbol{U}_{\beta,N}(\boldsymbol{\theta})\right] = \mathbb{E}\left[\boldsymbol{W}^{T}\boldsymbol{D}_{\boldsymbol{\pi}(\boldsymbol{\theta})}^{\beta-1}(\widehat{\boldsymbol{p}} - \boldsymbol{\pi}(\boldsymbol{\theta}))\right] = \boldsymbol{0}
$$

and variance–covariance matrix

$$
\begin{aligned}
\mathrm{Cov}\left[\boldsymbol{U}_{\beta,N}(\boldsymbol{\theta})\right] &= \boldsymbol{W}^{T}\boldsymbol{D}_{\boldsymbol{\pi}(\boldsymbol{\theta})}^{\beta-1}\mathrm{Cov}\left[\widehat{\boldsymbol{p}} - \boldsymbol{\pi}(\boldsymbol{\theta})\right]\boldsymbol{D}_{\boldsymbol{\pi}(\boldsymbol{\theta})}^{\beta-1}\boldsymbol{W} \\
&= \boldsymbol{W}^{T}\left[\boldsymbol{D}_{\boldsymbol{\pi}(\boldsymbol{\theta})}^{2\beta-1} - \boldsymbol{D}_{\boldsymbol{\pi}(\boldsymbol{\theta})}^{\beta-1}\boldsymbol{\pi}(\boldsymbol{\theta})\boldsymbol{\pi}(\boldsymbol{\theta})^{T}\boldsymbol{D}_{\boldsymbol{\pi}(\boldsymbol{\theta})}^{2\beta-1}\right]\boldsymbol{W} \\
&= \boldsymbol{K}_{\beta}(\boldsymbol{\theta}).
\end{aligned}
$$

Now, the following result states the asymptotic distribution of the Rao-type test statistics

THEOREM 6.3.– *The asymptotic distribution of the Rao-type test statistics defined in [6.18] under the linear null hypothesis [6.16] is a chi-square with one degree of freedom.*

PROOF.– The MDPDE restricted to the null hypothesis [6.16], $\widetilde{\boldsymbol{\theta}}^{\beta}$, is defined as the minimum of the DPD loss restricted to the condition $\boldsymbol{m}^T\boldsymbol{\theta} = d$. Then, it satisfies the restricted equations

$$\widetilde{\boldsymbol{U}}_{\beta,N}(\widetilde{\boldsymbol{\theta}}^{\beta}) + \boldsymbol{m}\widetilde{\boldsymbol{\lambda}} = \boldsymbol{0}, \tag{6.19}$$

for some vector $\widetilde{\boldsymbol{\lambda}}$ of Lagrangian multipliers. Then, we can write $\boldsymbol{U}_{\beta,N}(\widetilde{\boldsymbol{\theta}}^{\beta}) = -\boldsymbol{m}\widetilde{\boldsymbol{\lambda}}$ and consequently

$$\boldsymbol{U}_{\beta,N}(\widetilde{\boldsymbol{\theta}}^{\beta})^T\boldsymbol{Q}_{\beta}(\widetilde{\boldsymbol{\theta}}^{\beta}) = -\widetilde{\boldsymbol{\lambda}}\boldsymbol{m}^T\boldsymbol{Q}_{\beta}(\widetilde{\boldsymbol{\theta}}^{\beta}) = -\widetilde{\boldsymbol{\lambda}}$$

where $\boldsymbol{Q}_{\beta}(\widetilde{\boldsymbol{\theta}}^{\beta})$ is defined in [6.13]. Furthermore, the Rao-type test statistics defined in [6.18] can be computed in terms of the vector of Lagrange multipliers as follows:

$$\boldsymbol{R}_{\beta,N}(\boldsymbol{\theta}) = N\widetilde{\boldsymbol{\lambda}}^T\left[\boldsymbol{Q}_{\beta}(\widetilde{\boldsymbol{\theta}}^{\beta})^T\boldsymbol{K}_{\beta}(\widetilde{\boldsymbol{\theta}}^{\beta})\boldsymbol{Q}_{\beta}(\widetilde{\boldsymbol{\theta}}^{\beta})\right]^{-1}\widetilde{\boldsymbol{\lambda}}.$$

Consider the second-order Taylor expansion series of the score function $\boldsymbol{U}_{\beta,N}(\boldsymbol{\theta})$ around the true parameter value $\boldsymbol{\theta}_0$:

$$\boldsymbol{U}_{\beta,N}(\widetilde{\boldsymbol{\theta}}^{\beta}) = \boldsymbol{U}_{\beta,N}(\boldsymbol{\theta}_0) + \left.\frac{\partial\boldsymbol{U}_{\beta,N}(\boldsymbol{\theta})}{\partial\boldsymbol{\theta}}\right|_{\boldsymbol{\theta}=\boldsymbol{\theta}_0}\left(\widetilde{\boldsymbol{\theta}}^{\beta} - \boldsymbol{\theta}_0\right) + o\left(||\widetilde{\boldsymbol{\theta}}^{\beta} - \boldsymbol{\theta}_0||^2\boldsymbol{1}_2\right).$$

Since $\widehat{p}\xrightarrow[N\to\infty]{P}\boldsymbol{\pi}(\boldsymbol{\theta}_0)$, it is not difficult to show that

$$\left.\frac{\partial\boldsymbol{U}_{\beta,N}(\boldsymbol{\theta})}{\partial\boldsymbol{\theta}}\right|_{\boldsymbol{\theta}=\boldsymbol{\theta}_0}\xrightarrow[N\to\infty]{P}-\boldsymbol{J}_{\beta}(\boldsymbol{\theta}_0),$$

where the matrix $\boldsymbol{J}_{\beta}(\boldsymbol{\theta})$ is defined in [6.14]. Therefore, we can approximate the score function at the restricted MDPDE by

$$\boldsymbol{U}_{\beta,N}(\widetilde{\boldsymbol{\theta}}^{\beta}) = \boldsymbol{U}_{\beta,N}(\boldsymbol{\theta}_0) - \boldsymbol{J}_{\beta}(\boldsymbol{\theta}_0)\left(\widetilde{\boldsymbol{\theta}}^{\beta} - \boldsymbol{\theta}_0\right) + o\left(||\widetilde{\boldsymbol{\theta}}^{\beta} - \boldsymbol{\theta}_0||^2\boldsymbol{1}_2\right) + o\left(\boldsymbol{1}_2\right).$$

Based on [6.19], we have that

$$\boldsymbol{U}_{\beta,N}(\boldsymbol{\theta}_0) - \boldsymbol{J}_{\beta}(\boldsymbol{\theta}_0)\left(\widetilde{\boldsymbol{\theta}}^{\beta} - \boldsymbol{\theta}_0\right) + \boldsymbol{m}\widetilde{\boldsymbol{\lambda}} = o\left(\boldsymbol{1}_2\right)$$

so under the null hypothesis, we can write

$$\boldsymbol{m}^T\widetilde{\boldsymbol{\theta}}^{\beta} - d = \boldsymbol{m}^T\left(\widetilde{\boldsymbol{\theta}}^{\beta} - \boldsymbol{\theta}_0\right) = 0.$$

By joining both equations and solving for $\widetilde{\boldsymbol{\theta}}^{\beta} - \boldsymbol{\theta}_0$ and $\widetilde{\boldsymbol{\lambda}}$, we get

$$\begin{pmatrix} \widetilde{\boldsymbol{\theta}}^{\beta} - \boldsymbol{\theta}_0 \\ \widetilde{\boldsymbol{\lambda}} \end{pmatrix} = \begin{pmatrix} -\boldsymbol{J}_{\beta}(\boldsymbol{\theta}_0) & \boldsymbol{m} \\ \boldsymbol{m}^T & 0 \end{pmatrix}^{-1} \begin{pmatrix} -\boldsymbol{U}_{\beta,N}(\boldsymbol{\theta}_0) \\ 0 \end{pmatrix} + \begin{pmatrix} o(\boldsymbol{1}_2) \\ 0 \end{pmatrix}.$$

But from Theorem 6.2,

$$\begin{pmatrix} \sqrt{N}(\widetilde{\boldsymbol{\theta}}^{\beta} - \boldsymbol{\theta}_0) \\ \sqrt{N}\widetilde{\boldsymbol{\lambda}} \end{pmatrix} \xrightarrow[N\to\infty]{L} \mathcal{N}\left(\boldsymbol{0}_3, \boldsymbol{V}_{\beta}(\boldsymbol{\theta}_0)\right)$$

with

$$\boldsymbol{V}_{\beta}(\boldsymbol{\theta}_0) = \begin{pmatrix} \boldsymbol{P}_{\beta}(\boldsymbol{\theta}_0) & \boldsymbol{Q}_{\beta}(\boldsymbol{\theta}_0) \\ \boldsymbol{Q}_{\beta}(\boldsymbol{\theta}_0)^T & \left(\boldsymbol{m}^T\boldsymbol{J}_{\beta}(\boldsymbol{\theta}_0)^{-1}\boldsymbol{m}\right)^{-1} \end{pmatrix} \begin{pmatrix} \boldsymbol{K}_{\beta}(\boldsymbol{\theta}_0) & 0 \\ \boldsymbol{0}^T & 0 \end{pmatrix}$$

$$\begin{pmatrix} \boldsymbol{P}_{\beta}(\boldsymbol{\theta}_0) & \boldsymbol{Q}_{\beta}(\boldsymbol{\theta}_0) \\ \boldsymbol{Q}_{\beta}(\boldsymbol{\theta}_0)^T & \left(\boldsymbol{m}^T\boldsymbol{J}_{\beta}(\boldsymbol{\theta}_0)^{-1}\boldsymbol{m}\right)^{-1} \end{pmatrix}.$$

Thus, the asymptotic distribution of the vector of Lagrangian multipliers is given by

$$\sqrt{N}\widetilde{\boldsymbol{\lambda}} \xrightarrow[N\to\infty]{L} \mathcal{N}\left(0, \boldsymbol{Q}_{\beta}(\boldsymbol{\theta}_0)^T \boldsymbol{K}_{\beta}(\boldsymbol{\theta}_0)\boldsymbol{Q}_{\beta}(\boldsymbol{\theta}_0)\right).$$

Using the previous convergence and the consistency of the restricted MDPDE, it follows that the asymptotic distribution of the Rao-type test statistics, $\boldsymbol{R}_{\beta,N}(\widetilde{\boldsymbol{\theta}}^{\beta})$, is a chi-square distribution with one degree of freedom.

6.4.2. *DPD-based statistics*

We develop a class of test statistics based on the DPD between the model evaluated under the null hypothesis and under the whole parameter space, respectively. Let $\pi(\widehat{\boldsymbol{\theta}}^{\beta})$ and $\pi(\widetilde{\boldsymbol{\theta}}^{\beta})$ denote the probability vector of the multinomial model estimated in the whole parameter space and the restricted parameter space, respectively. The DPD for $\tau > 0$ between these two mass functions is given by

$$d_{\tau}(\widehat{\boldsymbol{\theta}}^{\beta}, \widetilde{\boldsymbol{\theta}}^{\beta}) = \sum_{i=1}^{L+1} \left(\pi_j(\widehat{\boldsymbol{\theta}}^{\beta})^{1+\tau} + \left(1 + \frac{1}{\tau}\right) \pi_j(\widehat{\boldsymbol{\theta}}^{\beta})\pi_j(\widetilde{\boldsymbol{\theta}}^{\beta})^{\tau} + \frac{1}{\tau}\pi_j(\widetilde{\boldsymbol{\theta}}^{\beta})^{\tau+1} \right).$$

[6.20]

Note that here we should deal with two different tuning parameters controlling the trade-off between robustness and efficiency in the estimation (β) and in the DPD between the estimated mass functions (τ). Many authors choose $\tau = \beta$ for the sake of simplicity. If the true parameter $\boldsymbol{\theta}_0$ verifies the null hypothesis, then the distance in [6.20] must be near zero. Then, the reject region for the test with null hypothesis [6.16] is given by

$$RC = \{(n_1, ..., n_{L+1}) s.t. \ d_\tau(\widehat{\boldsymbol{\theta}}^\beta, \widetilde{\boldsymbol{\theta}}^\beta) > k\}$$

with k being a constant computed such that the test has size α. The exact distribution of the test statistic $d_\tau(\widehat{\boldsymbol{\theta}}^\beta, \widetilde{\boldsymbol{\theta}}^\beta)$ is not easy to get, but using similar arguments as in Jaenada et al. (2022) is not difficult to establish that

$$T_\tau(\widehat{\boldsymbol{\theta}}^\beta, \widetilde{\boldsymbol{\theta}}^\beta) = 2nd_\tau(\widehat{\boldsymbol{\theta}}^\beta, \widetilde{\boldsymbol{\theta}}^\beta)$$

is asymptotically distributed, under the null hypothesis, as a linear combination of chi-squared random variables with one degree of freedom. Furthermore, asymptotic results under some particular kind of alternative hypotheses, such as contiguous alternative hypotheses, may also be of interest.

6.5. Simulation study

We empirically analyze the performance of the restricted MDPDEs for one-shot device data under the step-stress model with nondestructive one-shot devices under exponential lifetime distributions, $\widetilde{\boldsymbol{\theta}}^\beta$. Furthermore, we evaluate their robustness properties under different scenarios of contamination.

For the multinomial model, we should consider "outlying cells" rather than "outlying devices". Then, we introduce contamination by increasing (or decreasing) the probability of failure in [6.4] for (at least) one interval (i.e. one cell). The probability of failure is switched in such contaminated cells as

$$\tilde{\pi}_j(\boldsymbol{\theta}) = G_{\boldsymbol{\theta}}(IT_j) - G_{\tilde{\boldsymbol{\theta}}}(IT_{j-1}) \tag{6.21}$$

for some $j = 2, ..., L$, where $\tilde{\boldsymbol{\theta}} = (\tilde{\theta}_0, \tilde{\theta}_1)$ is a contaminated parameter with $\tilde{\theta}_0 \le \theta_0$ and $\tilde{\theta}_1 \le \theta_1$. The resulting probability vector must be normalized after introducing contamination.

Let us consider a two-step stress ALT experiment with $L = 11$ inspection times and a total of $N = 180$ nondestructive one-shot devices. The devices are tested at two stress levels, $x_1 = 35$ and $x_2 = 45$. The first stress level is maintained from the beginning of the experiment until $\tau_1 = 25$, and the experiment ends at $\tau_2 = 70$. During the experiment, device inspection is performed at a grid of inspection times, containing the times of stress change, $IT = (10, 15, 20, 25, 30, 35, 40, 45, 50, 60, 70)$. At each inspection time, all surviving units under test are examined. We set the true value of the parameter $\theta_0 = (0.003, 0.03)$, and then generate data from the corresponding multinomial model described in section 6.2. Additionally, we contaminate the described model by increasing the probability of failure in the third interval following [6.21], with $\widetilde{\theta} = (\varepsilon\theta_0, \theta_1)$ for the first scenario of contamination and $\widetilde{\theta} = (\theta_0, \varepsilon\theta_1)$ for the second scenario of contamination. Note that in both scenarios, the mean lifetime is decreased for the outlying cell. Furthermore, we consider the linearly restricted parameter space of the form

$$\Theta_0 = \{\theta \in \Theta|\ \theta_1 = d\}$$

with $d \in \mathbb{R}$. We evaluate the performance of the restricted estimators when the true parameter verifies the subspace constraints as well as when θ_0 does not belong to the restricted subspace Θ_0. For the first scenario ($\theta_0 \in \Theta_0$), we set $d = 0.03$ and for the second one ($\theta_0 \notin \Theta_0$) we set $d = 0.027$. Note that, in the second case, the true parameter is close to the restricted space.

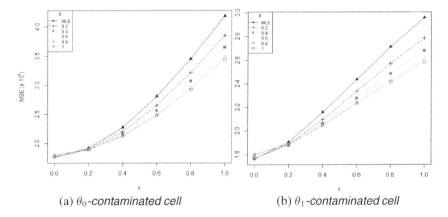

(a) θ_0-*contaminated cell*   (b) θ_1-*contaminated cell*

Figure 6.1. *MSE of the restricted MDPDE when the true parameter belongs to the restricted space over $R = 10,000$ repetitions. For a color version of this figure, see www.iste.co.uk/dimotikalis/data3.zip*

Figure 6.1 shows the mean squared error (MSE) of the restricted MDPDE when the true parameter value satisfies the subspace restrictions over $R = 10,000$ repetitions, for the two scenarios of contamination and different values of β. Larger values of the tuning parameter produce more robust estimates, although less efficient. From these empirical results, moderately large values of the tuning parameter β over 0.4 could produce the best trade-off between efficiency and robustness. Similarly, Figure 6.2 shows the MSE of the restricted MDPDE for similar scenarios when the true parameter value does not belong to the restricted parameter space. Similar conclusions are drawn, but the MSE on the estimation increases considerably in this context.

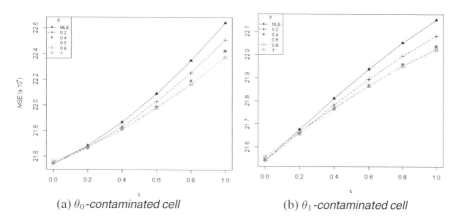

(a) θ_0-contaminated cell   (b) θ_1-contaminated cell

Figure 6.2. *MSE of the restricted MDPDE when the true parameter does not belong to the restricted space over $R = 10,000$ repetitions. For a color version of this figure, see www.iste.co.uk/dimotikalis/data3.zip*

6.6. Conclusions

In this chapter, we have developed the restricted minimum MDPDE for nondestructive one-shot device data tested under step-stress ALTs. We have derived its asymptotic distribution and analyzed its robustness properties through its IF. Furthermore, we have defined two families of robust testing procedures based on the restricted DPD estimators, Rao-type test statistics and DPD-based statistics, and we have established the asymptotic distribution for the first one. Finally, all properties stated theoretically have been illustrated empirically through simulation, showing certain advantage in terms of robustness of DPD-based inference methods.

The robustness of the two proposed families of test statistics would be interesting to study theoretically through their IF analysis, and furthermore, empirical performance comparison of these two families, together with well-known Wald-type test statistics based on the DPD for one-shot devices tested under step-stress ALT model, will be interesting to examine in future research.

6.7. References

Balakrishnan, N., Castilla, E., Jaenada M., Pardo, L. (2022a). Robust inference for non-destructive one-shot device testing under step-stress model with exponential lifetimes. *Quality and Reliability Engineering International*, 39(4), 1192–1222.

Balakrishnan, N., Castilla, E., Jaenada M., Pardo, L. (2022b). Non-destructive one-shot device testing under step-stress model with Weibull lifetime distributions. doi: 10.48550/arxiv.2208.02674.

Balakrishnan, N., Castilla, E., Jaenada M., Pardo, L. (2022c). Robust Rao-type tests for non-destructive one-shot device testing under step-stress model with exponential lifetimes. In *Proceedings of the 10th International Conference on Soft Methods in Probability and Statistics (SMPS2022)*.

Basu, A., Harris, I.R., Hjort, N.L., Jones, M.C. (1998). Robust and efficient estimation by minimising a density power divergence. *Biometrika*, 85(3), 549–559.

Basu, A., Mandal, A., Martin, N., Pardo, L. (2018). Testing composite hypothesis based on the density power divergence. *Sankhya B: The Indian Journal of Statistics*, 80(2), 222–262.

Basu, A., Ghosh, A., Martin, N., Pardo, L. (2021). A robust generalization of the Rao test. *Journal of Business & Economic Statistics*. doi: 10.1080/07350015.2021.1876711.

Ghosh, A. (2015). Inuence function analysis of the restricted minimum divergence estimators: A general form. *Electronic Journal of Statistics*, 9, 1017–1040.

Hampel, F.R., Ronchetti, E., Rousseauw, P.J., Stahel, W. (1986). *Robust Statistics: The Approach Based on Inuence Functions*. John Wiley & Sons, New York.

Jaenada, M., Miranda, P., Pardo, L. (2022). Robust test statistics based on restricted minimum Rényi's pseudodistance estimators. *Entropy*, 24(5), 616.

PART 3

Finance

7

Properties of American Options Under a Semi-Markov Modulated Black-Scholes Model

In this research, we consider the valuation of the American option when the asset price dynamics follow a geometric Brownian motion driven by a varying economic situation. We assume that the economic situation transits based on a semi-Markov chain, where the option will be evaluated at each epoch of economic situation transition. The decision-maker can decide whether to early exercise or hold the option, based on the asset price, economic situation and holding time. The decision-making problem is formulated using a semi-Markov decision process. Based on simulation results, some properties on the optimal exercise regions and the monotonicity of option prices are discussed. In addition, the conditions of the transition probability matrix for maintaining the monotonicity of the option price are examined.

7.1. Introduction

A financial option is a derivative traded in a market which gives its holder a right, but not the obligation, to buy or sell an underlying asset at a predetermined strike price. If the holder has the right to buy, it is called the call option, and if the holder has the right to sell, it is a put option. Options have a maturity that enables the exercising of rights. Typically, they are divided into European options that can be exercised only on their maturity, and American options that can be exercised at any time before their maturity.

Option prices mainly fluctuate depending on asset prices, and volatilities of asset prices differ depending on the economic situation. By using the semi-Markov decision

Chapter written by Kouki TAKADA, Marko DIMITROV, Lu JIN and Ying NI.
For a color version of all the figures in this chapter, see www.iste.co.uk/dimotikalis/data3.zip.

process, economic situations can be taken into account when pricing American options. It is possible, by using this, to continuously express changes in economic situations in the same way as in the actual market. Also, to consider the impact of economic situations on asset prices, an extended geometric Brownian motion with stochastic volatility driven by a semi-Markov decision process is used; this models changes in asset prices.

There are several models suitable for option pricing. Kim and Byun (2004) defined a simple binomial model with constant volatility. Guo and Zhang (2004) studied an optimal stopping time problem for pricing of an American put option in a regime switching model, and described the value function in a closed form. Carriere (1996) focused on valuing American options using simulations of stochastic processes and showed how to value the optimal stopping time for any Markovian process in finite discrete-time. Kijima and Yoshida (1993) used the Black–Scholes model to price options when asset price changes followed the binomial model.

From here, previous studies using the geometric Brownian motion to change asset prices are introduced. Broadie and Detemple (1999) considered the properties of the optimal exercise region of the option, assuming that asset prices follow the geometric Brownian motion. Yin et al. (2006) set the price of American put options under the regime switching model and numerically examined the stochastic optimization algorithm. Klimsiak et al. (2015) used the backward stochastic differential equation to formulate the option price and analytically proved the properties of the option price. Hanyan (2017) used the fractional Black–Scholes model to derive an approximation formula of the American option price as a closed form. Gapeev et al. (2021) presented a closed-form solution to some discounted optimal stopping problems using the geometric Brownian motion with state-dependent payoffs.

Geometric Brownian motion is often used as an asset price model for the Black–Scholes model. However, using the Black–Scholes model cannot consider a fat tail for the asset return distribution or create a volatility smile (Shi et al. 2016). Therefore, Nasir (2020) proposed a Markov decision process for option pricing as a model that incorporates uncertainties and features that affect option pricing. Also, Nasir (2020) highlighted that the literature on this proposal shows that the option trading problem can be formulated as an optimal stopping problem using a Markov decision process (Bertsekas 2000). In addition, Bertsekas and Tsitsiklis (1995) showed that the optimal policy could be determined using a dynamic decision-making method of a Markov decision process.

The following is a list of previous studies on pricing options that use a Markov decision process. Sato and Sawaki (2012) assumed that the economic situation could be directly observed and that transitions follow a Markov chain; they priced options using a discrete-time Markov decision process and examined the properties of the optimal exercise region. After that, Sato and Sawaki (2018) made the economic situations unobservable; priced options used a partially observable Markov decision process and considered the optimal strategy. Jin et al. (2019) followed the framework in Sato and Sawaki (2018), and considered valuation and optimal strategies by using a partially observable Markov decision process. Dimitrov et al. (2021) represented the transitions of asset prices using a binomial model that uses risk-neutral distribution, and numerically considered the properties of the threshold of the optimal exercise region by using the partially observable Markov decision process of three states. In these studies, time intervals between changes in the economic situation are assumed to be discrete and equal. Option prices should be considered in which transitions may randomly change, along with random changes in a real economy. D'Amico et al. (2009) priced the options using a semi-Markov process, where the time intervals between changes in the economic situation are continuous, when the economic situation was steady, and when the changes in the option prices for each remaining period were numerically examined.

In this study, we price an American option when transitions in economic situations are represented by semi-Markov chains, where the time interval in each economic situation before a transition follows a general distribution. Also, asset price changes follow an extended geometric Brownian motion with stochastic volatility driven by a semi-Markov decision process. In addition, we numerically examine changes in option prices, the optimal exercise region, and conditions of the transition probability matrix.

The remainder of this chapter is as follows. In section 7.2, American options are formulated using a semi-Markov decision process. Section 7.3 numerically examines the properties of changes in American options and changes in the optimal exercise region. Also, the conditions of the transition probability matrix for satisfying the monotonicity of the option price transition are considered. In section 7.4, our work is summarized, and future research is discussed.

7.2. American option pricing

Consider an American option with a strike price K, an asset price s and a maturity T in a changing economic situation.

Let Z_0 be the initial economic situation at the start of option trading. For $t \geq 0$, let Z_t denote the economic situation at time t, and let S_t be the asset price at time t. The dynamic in the asset price is within time interval m given by

$$S_{t+m} = S_t X_{t+m}^{Z_{t+m}},$$

where the price relative to X_t depends on the economic situation Z_t.

Next, assume that the economic situation Z_t takes a value from a finite state space $\mathbb{Z} = \{1, 2, 3\}$. The economic situations are in ascending order, with 1 being the worst economic situation and 3 being the best. Assume that the transition of economic situation Z follows a known transition law given by $\mathbf{P} = [p_{ij}]_{i,j \in \mathbb{Z}}$ where p_{ij} is the probability that the economic situation transits from level i to level j. Let

$$F_{ij}(m) = P(l \leq m | Z_t = i, Z_{t+m} = j),$$

represent the distribution function that an economic situation's transition will take place within an amount of time m, given that the process has just entered i and will enter j next.

Let $r > 0$ be the continuously compounded risk-free interest rate, and let δ be the continuously compounded dividend yield. Assume that changes in asset prices are distributed as an extended geometric Brownian motion with stochastic volatility driven by a semi-Markov decision process. Using this, the fluctuation rate of the asset price $x_j(m)$ follows a log-normal distribution $g_{jm}(x)$ as follows:

$$x_j(m) = e^{\left(r - \delta - \frac{1}{2}\sigma_j^2\right)m + \sigma_j z_m}$$

$$g_{jm}(x) = \frac{1}{\sqrt{2\pi\sigma_j^2 m x}} \exp\left\{ -\frac{(\ln x - (r - \delta - \frac{1}{2}\sigma_j^2)m)^2}{2\sigma_j^2 m} \right\}$$

Here, z_m is a normal R.V that follows a normal distribution with mean zero and variance m. In this chapter, the risk-neutral dynamic $X_t^{Z_t}$ is expressed as the fluctuation rate $x_j(m)$.

The economic situations are ordered based on volatility σ_j. The larger the σ_j value, the worse the economy; and the smaller the σ_j value, the better the economy.

During each transition between economic situations, the investors decide whether to exercise or hold their options, based on the current information. The payoff function for put (call) option is given by $v^e(s) = \max\{K - s, 0\}(v^e(s) = \max\{s - K, 0\})$ with domain $s \in [0, \infty)$.

Consider the American option when an information vector of the current asset price, economic situation and time is (s, i, t). The option price $v(s, i, t)$ is determined as

$$v(s, i, t) = \max \begin{cases} v^e(s) = \max\{K - s, 0\} \quad \text{or} \quad \max\{s - K, 0\} \\ v^h(s, i, t) \end{cases}$$

where

$$v^h(s, i, t) = \sum_{j=1}^{3} p_{ij} \int_0^{T-t} \int_0^{\infty} e^{-rm} v(sx_j(m), j, t + m) g_{jm}(x) dx f_{ij}(m) dm.$$

Here, $f_{ij}(m)$ is the probability density function of the distribution function $F_{ij}(m)$.

Recall that $v^e(s)$ is the payoff function which gives the exercise value of the option. On the other hand, $v^h(s, i, t)$ is the hold value of the option. Since the hold value at maturity is zero, $v(s, i, T) = \max\{v^e(s), v^h(s, i, T)\} = v^e(s)$.

7.3. Exercising strategies

Section 7.3 provides some numerical examples under the proposed model in section 7.2. We consider changes in the option price and optimal exercise region when the parameters are changed, and the conditions of the transition probability matrix for maintaining the monotonicity of the option price.

7.3.1. *Setting parameters*

The properties of option prices are examined, based on simulated results. The parameters are set as shown in Table 7.1, which is partially based on the work of Dimitrov et al. (2021).

Item	Notation	Parameter
Time interval of a step	τ	$1/252$
Maturity time	T	$15/252$
Volatility vector	σ	$(0.7, 0.4, 0.2)$
Strike price	K	100
Interest rate	r	0.02
Dividend yield	δ	0.1
Transition probability matrix	$\boldsymbol{P}$	$[p_{ij}]_{i,j=1,2,3}$

Table 7.1. *Each parameter used in this study*

In the simulation, equidistant time intervals $\tau = \frac{1}{252}$ were prepared, and the expected value of option price can be calculated as follows:

$$v^h(s, i, t) = \sum_{j=1}^{3} p_{ij} \sum_{m=1}^{\frac{T-t}{\tau}} \sum_{x} e^{-rm\tau} v(sx_j(m\tau), j, t + m\tau) g_{j,m\tau}(x) 0.01 f_{ij}(m\tau)\tau$$

In the numerical calculation, a dataset $X = \{0, 0.01, 0.02, ..., 2.00\}$ in increments of 0.01 for the fluctuation rate of the asset price and $S = \{0, 0.02, 0.04, ..., 200\}$ in increments of 0.02 for the asset price, were prepared. As before, we used the option price of the American put option from $s = 70$ to $s = 100$, and the asset price of the American call option from $s = 100$ to $s = 130$.

We assume that the distribution function $F_{ij}(m)$ is a CDF of a gamma distribution with the shape parameter $\alpha = 2$ and scale parameter $\theta = 160$. The probability density function $f_{ij}(m)$ is given as follows:

$$f_{ij}(m) = \frac{1}{\Gamma(\alpha)\theta^\alpha} m^{\alpha-1} e^{-\frac{m}{\theta}}$$

Consider the matrix P given by

$$P = \begin{bmatrix} 0.70 & 0.20 & 0.10 \\ 0.10 & 0.40 & 0.50 \\ 0.05 & 0.25 & 0.70 \end{bmatrix} .$$

Numerical calculations were performed using the above datasets and parameters in Table 7.1. The calculated and output graph is presented in the following section.

7.3.2. *Relationship between the option price and "economic situation, asset price and maturity"*

Figure 7.1 shows the relationship between the holding value of the option, economic situation, asset price and maturity in the American put option and American call option when holding is selected currently.

From Figure 7.1, it can be seen that the holding value of the option decreases as the asset price increases in the American put option, and the holding value of the option increases as the asset price increases in the American call option. This occurs because the value of the asset price approaches the strike price for the American put option as the asset price increases, and the future payoff decreases, so the holding value of the option is considered to be smaller. Also, the asset price value deviates from the strike price for the American call option as the asset price increases, and the future payoff increases, so the holding value of the option is considered to be greater.

Regarding maturity, the holding value of the option increases as the maturity increases in the American put option and American call option. If the maturity is long, asset prices are more likely to fluctuate, and there is a greater chance of exercising at a better price in the future, so the holding value of the option will increase. Conversely, if the maturity is short, asset prices are less likely to fluctuate, and there is a smaller chance of exercising at a better price in the future, so the holding value of the option will decrease. Also, regarding the "maturity" axis of the graph, the value written in the graph multiplied by $\tau = \frac{1}{252}$ is the actual maturity.

In addition, since it is difficult to see the relationship between the holding value of the option and economic conditions from Figure 7.1, a two-dimensional graph of the holding value of the option and economic conditions is shown in Figure 7.2.

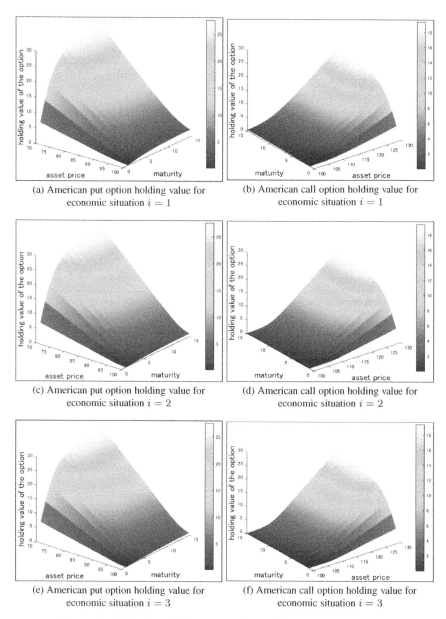

(a) American put option holding value for economic situation $i = 1$

(b) American call option holding value for economic situation $i = 1$

(c) American put option holding value for economic situation $i = 2$

(d) American call option holding value for economic situation $i = 2$

(e) American put option holding value for economic situation $i = 3$

(f) American call option holding value for economic situation $i = 3$

Figure 7.1. *Relationship between the holding value of the option and "economic situation, asset price and maturity"*

As shown in Figure 7.2, the holding value of the option decreases as the economic situation improves for the American put and call options. This happens because the volatility of the asset price will increase if the economic situation is bad, and there is a greater chance of exercising at a better price in the future, so the holding value of the option will increase. Conversely, the volatility of the asset price will decrease if the economic situation is good, and there is less chance of exercising at a better price in the future, so the holding value of the option will increase.

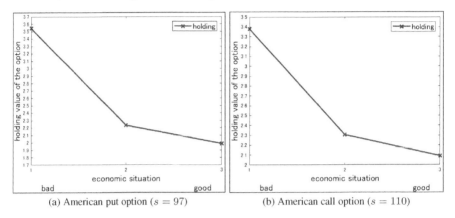

(a) American put option ($s = 97$)   (b) American call option ($s = 110$)

Figure 7.2. *Relationship between the holding value of the option and economic situation*

(a) American put option

	Economic situation i		
	1	2	3
Holding	3.5392	2.2333	1.9776

(b) American call option

	Economic situation i		
	1	2	3
Holding	3.3776	2.3045	2.0904

Table 7.2. *Details of option prices used in Figure 7.2*

7.3.3. *Relationship between option price and transition probability matrix*

Figure 7.3 shows a graph of the holding value of the option, when the transition probability matrix changes in the American put option when $s = 97$ and the American call option when $s = 110$.

The three types of transition probability matrices used in Figure 7.3 are shown as follows:

$$P_s = \begin{bmatrix} 0.85\ 0.10\ 0.05 \\ 0.10\ 0.75\ 0.15 \\ 0.05\ 0.15\ 0.80 \end{bmatrix}, \quad P_n = \begin{bmatrix} 0.70\ 0.20\ 0.10 \\ 0.10\ 0.40\ 0.50 \\ 0.05\ 0.25\ 0.70 \end{bmatrix}, P_u = \begin{bmatrix} 0.40\ 0.30\ 0.30 \\ 0.25\ 0.35\ 0.40 \\ 0.20\ 0.30\ 0.50 \end{bmatrix}$$

Here, P_s represents a stable economy in which the economic situation is difficult to change, and P_u represents an unstable economy in which the economic situation is easy to change.

Figure 7.3 shows a graph created using these transition probability matrices.

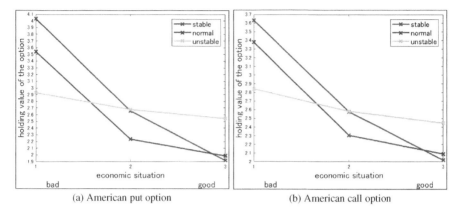

(a) American put option   (b) American call option

Figure 7.3. *Relationship between the holding value of the option and transition probability matrix*

(a) American put option

P	Economic situation i		
	1	2	3
Stable	4.0319	2.6548	1.9178
Normal	3.5392	2.2333	1.9864
Unstable	2.9269	2.6750	2.5420

(b) American call option

P	Economic situation i		
	1	2	3
Stable	3.6301	2.5751	2.0176
Normal	3.3776	2.3045	2.0904
Unstable	2.88388	2.5808	2.4448

Table 7.3. *Details of option prices used in Figure 7.3*

From Figure 7.3, it can be seen that the holding value of the option of both the American put option and American call option is significantly higher in a stable economy than in a normal economy when the economic situation is $i = 1, 2$. A stable economy is less likely to transition into other economic situations than a normal economy, and the volatility of the asset price of $i = 1, 2$ is larger than that of $i = 3$. Therefore, when the economic situation is $i = 1, 2$, there will be an even greater chance of exercising at a better price in the future, so the holding value of the option will increase.

It can also be seen that in an unstable economy, the holding value of the option hardly changes, even though the economic situation changes. This is because it is difficult to predict the future of an unstable economy, so the holding value of the option will be the same, regardless of the current economic situation.

All of the above transition probability matrices have a property of TP_2. Previous studies have shown that the transition probability matrix having TP_2 leads to the monotonicity of the holding value of the option transitions. Therefore, in the following, we investigate the property of the holding value of the option using the transition probability matrix with a property of SI, which has looser restrictions than TP_2, and the transition probability matrix that does not have a property of both TP_2 and SI.

Also, the partial ordering, TP_2 and SI, are defined as follows:

– Totally Positive of Order 2 (TP_2) (Karlin 1968)

Let $P = [p_{ij}]$ be an $n \times m$ matrix for which

$$\begin{vmatrix} p_{ij} & p_{ij'} \\ p_{i'j} & p_{i'j'} \end{vmatrix} \geq 0$$

for any $1 \leq i < i' \leq n$ and $1 \leq j < j' \leq m$, then the matrix P has a property of TP_2.

– Stochastic Increasing (SI) (Marshall et al. 1979)

Let $P = [p_{ij}]$ be an $n \times m$ matrix for which

$$\sum_{j=k}^{m} x_{ij} \leq \sum_{j=k}^{m} y_{i'j}$$

for any $1 \leq i < i' \leq n$ and $1 \leq k \leq m$, then the matrix P has a property of SI.

The transition probability matrix used in Figure 7.4 is shown as follows:

$$P_{\text{SI}} = \begin{bmatrix} 0.50 & 0.20 & 0.30 \\ 0.30 & 0.30 & 0.40 \\ 0.20 & 0.30 & 0.50 \end{bmatrix}, \qquad P_{\text{None}} = \begin{bmatrix} 0.20 & 0.40 & 0.40 \\ 0.40 & 0.20 & 0.40 \\ 0.40 & 0.40 & 0.20 \end{bmatrix}$$

Here, P_{SI} does not have a property of TP_2, but has only the property of SI and P_{None} does not have a property of either TP_2 or SI.

Figure 7.4 shows a graph created using these transition probability matrices.

From Figure 7.4, it can be seen that the monotonicity of the holding value of the option is maintained when the transition probability matrix has a property of SI, and the monotonicity of the holding value of the option is not maintained when the transition probability matrix does not have a property of SI. This result implies that the TP_2 property may be sufficient but not necessary, and the SI property may be sufficient for the establishment of monotonicity of the holding value of the option.

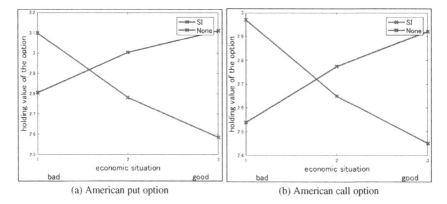

(a) American put option   (b) American call option

Figure 7.4. *Changes in the holding value of the option due to partial ordering*

(a) American put option

P	1	2	3
SI	3.0983	2.7813	2.5845
None	2.8041	3.0020	3.1102

Economic situation i

(b) American call option

P	1	2	3
SI	2.9696	2.6488	2.4506
None	2.5381	2.7732	2.9204

Economic situation i

Table 7.4. *Details of option prices used in Figure 7.4*

7.3.4. *Consideration of the optimal exercise region*

Figure 7.5 shows the asset price, which is the threshold for exercising and holding when the maturity is changed; this is for each economic situation in the American put option.

From Figure 7.5, it can be seen that as the economic situation improves, the value of the asset price (the threshold for exercising and holding) increases; and as the economic situation improves, the region of holding becomes smaller and the region of exercising increases. This occurs because the worse the economic situation, the greater the chance of exercising at a better price in the future, so the holding region increases. Conversely, the better the economic situation, the lower the possibility of exercising at a better price in the future, so the holding region decreases.

Comparing Figure 7.6(a)–(c), the longer the maturity, the larger the holding region and the smaller the exercising region. The holding region grows larger because the longer the maturity, the greater the chance of exercising at a better price in the future. However, the shorter the maturity, the smaller the chance of exercising at a better price in the future, so the holding region will decrease.

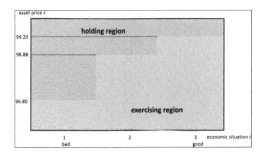

(a) Optimal exercise region with maturity $T = \frac{8}{252}$

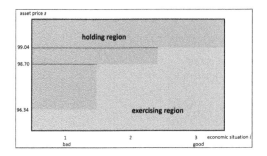

(b) Optimal exercise region with maturity $T = \frac{10}{252}$

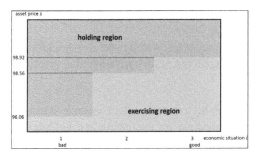

(c) Optimal exercise region with maturity $T = \frac{12}{252}$

Figure 7.5. *Optimal exercise region for the American put option*

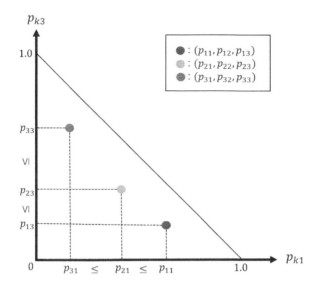

Figure 7.6. *A two-dimensional plane diagram of the transition probability matrix P having the property of SI*

7.3.5. *Condition of transition probability matrix for option price transition to be monotonous*

A transition probability matrix that has the property of SI is shown on a two-dimensional plane. Since the transition probability matrix P used in our study is a 3×3 matrix, it can be expressed as follows:

$$P = \begin{bmatrix} p_{11} & p_{12} & p_{13} \\ p_{21} & p_{22} & p_{23} \\ p_{31} & p_{32} & p_{33} \end{bmatrix}$$

From the definition of SI in section 7.3.3, the condition that the transition probability matrix has the property of SI is $p_{31} \leq p_{21} \leq p_{11}$ and $p_{13} \leq p_{23} \leq p_{33}$. Therefore, a two-dimensional plane diagram in which the transition probability matrix of this study has the property of SI can be expressed as follows.

The red, green and blue dots in Figure 7.6 represent $p_1 = (p_{11}, p_{12}, p_{13})$, $p_2 = (p_{21}, p_{22}, p_{23})$ and $p_3 = (p_{31}, p_{32}, p_{33})$, respectively. Since the summation of elements in each vector is equal to 1, it can be expressed in a two-dimensional plane by extracting only the first and third element of each vector. As mentioned above, since the condition for SI is $p_{31} \leq p_{21} \leq p_{11}$ and $p_{13} \leq p_{23} \leq p_{33}$, as shown in Figure 7.6, when the point of p_2 is on the upper left of the point of p_1 and the point of p_3 is on the upper left of the point of p_2, the transition probability matrix has a property of SI.

Some diagrams of a two-dimensional plane, when the transition probability matrix has a property of SI, are shown. The following four transition probability matrices have a property of SI up to the second row:

$$P_{example1} = \begin{bmatrix} 0.40 & 0.30 & 0.30 \\ 0.30 & 0.40 & 0.30 \\ p_{31} & 1 - p_{31} - p_{33} & p_{33} \end{bmatrix} \quad P_{example2} = \begin{bmatrix} 0.40 & 0.30 & 0.30 \\ 0.20 & 0.30 & 0.50 \\ p_{31} & 1 - p_{31} - p_{33} & p_{33} \end{bmatrix}$$

$$P_{example3} = \begin{bmatrix} 0.70 & 0.10 & 0.20 \\ 0.30 & 0.45 & 0.25 \\ p_{31} & 1 - p_{31} - p_{33} & p_{33} \end{bmatrix} \quad P_{example4} = \begin{bmatrix} 0.30 & 0.60 & 0.10 \\ 0.25 & 0.40 & 0.35 \\ p_{31} & 1 - p_{31} - p_{33} & p_{33} \end{bmatrix}$$

Figures of the two-dimensional plane created using these transition probability matrices are shown below.

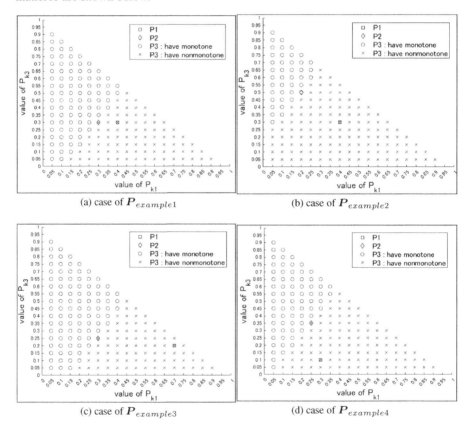

(a) case of $P_{example1}$

(b) case of $P_{example2}$

(c) case of $P_{example3}$

(d) case of $P_{example4}$

Figure 7.7. *Two-dimensional planes that determine whether the transition probability matrix has a property of SI*

These two-dimensional planes will be described using Figure 7.7(a) as an example. The elements used in this figure are p_1, p_2 and p_3 described in the previous section. In the figure, p_1 is represented by a square, and p_2 is represented by a diamond. Here, p_1 and p_2 are fixed, but p_3 is fluctuating. The values of p_{31} and p_{33} are varied under the condition of $p_{31}, p_{32}, p_{33} > 0$, and $p_{31} + p_{32} + p_{33} = 1$, and the circle is plotted when the monotonicity of the holding value of the option is satisfied, and the cross is plotted when the monotonicity of the holding value of the option is not satisfied.

In Figure 7.7, when the transition probability matrix has a property of SI, the monotonicity of the holding value of the option transition is satisfied. In addition, even though the transition probability matrix does not have a property of SI, there is a part where the monotonicity of the holding value of the option transition is satisfied. This result implies that the property of SI may be sufficient but not necessary for the establishment of monotonicity of the holding value of the option.

Also, areas where the monotonicity of the holding value of the option transitions is satisfied, and areas where it is not, are clearly divided into two areas. Looking at Figure 7.8(a)–(d), it can be seen that there is no significant difference in the inclination of the boundary between the two areas.

7.4. Conclusion

We used a semi-Markov decision process to price American options, when asset price dynamics followed the extended geometric Brownian motion with stochastic volatility driven by a semi-Markov decision process. We found monotonic option prices in the economic situation, asset price and maturity. Furthermore, we examined the conditions of the transition probability matrix for satisfying the monotonicity of changes in the option price.

In this study, we examined the properties of option prices using numerical calculations. Therefore, the analytical proof will be performed to more reliably clarify the properties of option prices. Also, it does not take into account situations such as the Lehman shock, where economic situations and asset prices suddenly, significantly change. So, we will propose a model with shock.

7.5. References

Bertsekas, D.P. (2000). *Dynamic Programming and Optimal Control: 1*, 4th edition. Athena Scientific, Belmont, MA.

Bertsekas, D.P. and Tsitsiklis, J.N. (1995). Neuro-dynamic programming: An overview. *Proceedings of 1995 34th IEEE Conference on Decision & Control*, New Orleans, LA.

Broadie, M. and Detemple, J. (1999). American options on dividend-paying assets. *Fields Institute Communications*, 22, 22–97.

Carriere, J.F. (1996). Valuation of the early-exercise price for options using simulations and nonparametric regression. *Mathematics and Economics*, 19(1996), 19–30.

D'Amico, G., Janssen, J., Manca, R. (2009). European and American options: The Semi-Markov case. *Physica A*, 388, 3181–3194.

Dimitrov, M., Jin, L., Ni, Y. (2021). Properties of American options under a Markovian regime switching model. *Communications in Statistics: Case Studies, Data Analysis and Applications*, 1–7.

Gapeev, P.V., Kort, P.M., Lavrutich, M.N. (2021). Discounted optimal stopping problems for maxima of geometric Brownian motions with switching payoffs. *Advances in Applied Probability*, 53(1), 189–219.

Guo, X. and Zhang, Q. (2004). Closed-form solutions for perpetual American put options with regime switching. *SIAM Journal on Applied Mathematics*, 64(6), 2034–2049.

Hanyan, L. (2017). An approximate formula for pricing American option in the fractional Black-Scholes model. *Proceedings of 2017 9th International Conference on Measuring Technology and Mechatronics Automation*, 260–262.

Jin, L., Dimitrov, M., Ni, Y. (2019). Valuation and optimal strategies for American options under a Markovian regime-switching model. In *Stochastic Processes and Algebraic Structures, Volume 1. Stochastic Processes, Statistical Methods, and Engineering Mathematics 1*, Malyarenko, A., Ni, Y., Rancić, M. (eds). Springer International Publishing, Cham, Forthcoming.

Karlin, S. (1968). *Total Positivity*. Stanford University Press, Palo Alto, CA.

Kijima, M. and Yoshida, T. (1993). A simple option pricing model with Markovian volatilities. *Journal of the Operations Research Society of Japan*, 36(3).

Kim, I.J. and Byun, S.J. (2004). Optimal exercise boundary in a binomial option pricing model. *Journal of Financial Engineering*, 3(2), 137–158.

Klimsiak, T., Rozkosz, A., Ziemkiewicz, B. (2015). Valuing American options by simulation: A BSDEs approach. *Mathematics and Computers in Simulation*, 123.

Marshall, A.W., Olkin, I., Arnold, B.C. (1979). *Inequalities: Theory of Majorization and Its Applications*. Academic Press, Orlando, FL.

Nasir, A., Khursheed, A., Ali, K., Mustafa, F. (2020). A Markov decision process model for optimal trade of options using statistical data. *Computational Economics*, 58, 327–346.

Sato, K. and Sawaki, K. (2012). The valuation of callable financial options with regime switches: A discrete-time model (financial modeling and analysis) *RIMS Kokyuroku*, 1818, 22–46.

Sato, K. and Sawaki, K. (2018). The dynamics valuation of callable contingent claims with a partially observable regime switch. doi: 10.2139/ssrn.3284489.

Shi, X., Zhang, L., Kim, Y.S.A. (2016). A Markov chain approximation for American option pricing in the tempered stable GARCH models. *Frontiers in Applied Mathematics and Statistics*, 1(13), 1–12.

Yin, G., Wang, J.W., Zhang, Q., Liu, Y.J. (October 2006). Stochastic optimization algorithms for pricing American put options under regime-switching models. *Journal of Optimization Theory and Applications*, 131(1), 37–52.

8

Numerical Studies of Implied Volatility Expansions Under the Gatheral Model

The Gatheral double stochastic volatility model is a three-factor model with mean-reverting stochastic volatility that reverts to a stochastic long-run mean. Our previous paper investigated the performance of the first- and second-order implied volatility expansions under this model. Moreover, a simple partial calibration method has been proposed. This chapter reviews and extends previous results to the third-order implied volatility expansions under the same model. Using the Monte Carlo simulation as the benchmark method, extensive numerical studies are conducted to investigate the accuracy and properties of the third-order expansion.

8.1. Introduction

Since the advent of the Black–Scholes model (1973), option pricing has been under the spotlight and received significant attention. The model was the first nontrivial model that was completely solved in the sense that it gives mathematical rigor to option pricing. It calculates the theoretical price of European-style options that is unique regardless of the underlying asset's expected returns. Although the Black–Scholes model has been incredibly successful in the financial world, with their finding winning a Nobel prize in 1997, it was not without its drawbacks. The main issue of the model is the assumption that the underlying asset follows a geometric Brownian motion with constant volatility. This was strongly conflicting with empirical findings.

For example, Macbeth and Merville (1979) noted that implied volatilities are not constant and often exhibit a volatility smile or smirk pattern. Implied volatility is the volatility value of the underlying asset, which, when input into the option

Chapter written by Mohammed ALBUHAYRI, Marko DIMITROV, Ying NI and Anatoliy MALYARENKO.

pricing model, returns the market option price. The challenge of the constant volatility hypothesis prompted research along dimensions relaxing the restrictive assumptions, and many well-known models have been obtained to capture empirical features of financial prices. For instance, Cox and Ross (1976) proposed the constant elasticity of the variance diffusion process, which can be regarded as the generalized version of the Black–Scholes model. The main characteristic of the CEV model is that it allows volatility to change with the stock price.

Assuming that the underlying asset follows a Black–Scholes-type stochastic process but with a stochastic variance that follows the Cox et al. process, Heston (1993) came up with a revolutionary approach to the pricing option, known as stochastic volatility modeling. The proposed single factor model with mean reversion property assumes that the volatility of an asset follows a random process rather than a constant or deterministic process. Although the Heston model was not the first stochastic model to be introduced in options pricing, it has become one of the most popular models because the option price is available in closed form, and the model's versatility gives a realistic representation of implied volatilities extracted from options prices.

Despite the popularity of single-factor stochastic volatility models such as the Heston model, solid empirical evidence emerged to suggest that a multi-factor volatility framework led by at least two volatilities of mean reversion type is needed. For instance, Christoffersen et al. (2009) find that using a two-factor framework improves the ability to capture the slope and level of volatility smile, which largely move independently of each other.

In the earlier works of Albuhayri et al. (2019, 2021), three-factor stochastic volatilities with double mean reverting type, first proposed by Gatheral (2008), were considered. Such a model has no analytical solutions for European option price nor implied volatility. Thus, a result by Pagliarani and Pascucci (2017) is used to obtain option price and implied volatility under the Gatheral model. In their paper, Pagliarani and Pascucci derived the exact Taylor formula for the implied volatility as a function of both strike and maturity within the parabolic region close to expiry. Their method was applied to some popular models in mathematical finance, for example, Heston, CEV and SABR. Hence, applying the previous method, asymptotic implied volatility expansions up to third order under the Gatheral model have been obtained. It should be noted that using this general Taylor formula to a specific three-factor model is a complicated and time-consuming task.

A thorough numerical analysis is needed to check the performance of the asymptomatic expansions formulas as approximation formulas for the implied volatility obtained in Albuhayri et al. (2019, 2021). This chapter is organized as follows. In section 8.1, we recall the asymptotic expansions formulas under the Gatheral model up to the third order. Then, sections 8.2 and 8.3 show numerical studies on these expansions using Monte Carlo as the benchmark and calculated the relative errors for the implied volatilities. Finally, section 8.4 gives a conclusion and information on future works.

8.2. Previous results

Let $d \geq 2$ be a positive integer, $T_0 > 0$ be a time horizon, $T \in (0, T_0]$ and $\{ \mathbf{Z}_t : 0 \leq t \leq T \}$ be a continuous $\mathbb{R}^d$-valued adapted Markov stochastic process on a probability space $(\Omega, \mathfrak{F}, \mathsf{P})$ with a filtration $\{ \mathfrak{F}_t : 0 \leq t \leq T \}$. Assume that the first coordinate S_t of the process $\mathbf{Z}_t$ represents the risk-neutral price of a financial asset, and the $d - 1$ remaining coordinates $\mathbf{Y}_t$ represent stochastic factors in a market with zero interest rate and no dividends.

On the one hand, the time t no-arbitrage price of a European call option with strike price $K > 0$ and maturity T is $C_{t,T,K} = v(t, S_t, \mathbf{Y}_t, T, K)$, where

$$v(t, s, \mathbf{y}, T, K) = \mathsf{E}[\max\{0, S_T - K\} \mid \mathfrak{F}_t, S_t = s, \mathbf{Y}_t = \mathbf{y}],$$

for $(t, s, \mathbf{y}) \in [0, T] \times (0, \infty) \times \mathbb{R}^{d-1}$. We change to *logarithmic variables* and define the option price by:

$$u(t, x, \mathbf{y}, T, k) = v(t, \mathrm{e}^x, \mathbf{y}, T, \mathrm{e}^k),$$

where x is the time t log-price of the underlying asset, k is the log-strike of the option and $(t, x, \mathbf{y}) \in [0, T] \times \mathbb{R} \times \mathbb{R}^{d-1}$.

On the other hand, the Black–Scholes price in logarithmic variables is

$$u^{\mathrm{BS}}(\sigma, \tau, x, k) = \mathrm{e}^x \mathcal{N}(d_+) - \mathrm{e}^k \mathcal{N}(d_-), \quad \text{where} \quad d_{\pm} = \frac{1}{\sigma \sqrt{\tau}} \left(x - k \pm \frac{\sigma^2 \tau}{2} \right),$$

and $\tau = T - t \in [0, T]$, $x, k \in \mathbb{R}$, $\mathcal{N}$ is the cumulative distribution function of the standard normal random variable.

DEFINITION 8.1.– *The implied volatility* $\sigma = \sigma(t, x, \mathbf{y}, T, k)$ *is the unique positive solution of the nonlinear equation*

$$u^{\mathrm{BS}}(\sigma, \tau, x, k) = u(t, x, \mathbf{y}, T, k).$$

Following Dupire (1997), we *postulate* that under a martingale measure the underlying asset price $S(t), t \in [0, T]$ satisfies the following equation:

$$dS(t) = \eta(t, S(t))S(t)\, dW^*(t), \qquad S(0) = s.$$

where s is a deterministic positive number and the coefficient $\eta(t, S(t))$ is called the *local volatility function*.

A more recent and general extension is given in Pagliarani and Pascucci (2017). Assuming that under a martingale probability measure, the market model is described by an $\mathbb{R}^d$-valued stochastic process $(S(t), Y_2(t), \ldots, Y_d(t))^\top$ that satisfies the following system of stochastic differential equations:

$$dS(t) = \eta_1(t, S(t), \mathbf{Y}(t))S(t)\, dW_1^*(t), \qquad\qquad S(0) = s,$$

$$dY_i(t) = \mu_i(t, S(t), \mathbf{Y}(t))\, dt + \eta_i(t, S(t), \mathbf{Y}(t))\, dW_i^*(t), \quad \mathbf{Y}(0) = \mathbf{y},$$

where $2 \leq i \leq d$ and $\mathbf{Y}(t)$ is a vector with components $Y_i(t)$, $\mathbf{y} \in \mathbb{R}^{d-1}$ is a deterministic vector, and the time t correlation matrix of the $\mathbb{R}^d$-valued stochastic process with components $W_i^*(t)$ has entries

$$\rho_{ij}(t, S(t), \mathbf{Y}(t)) \in [-1, 1].$$

In the following, we refer to this model as a *local stochastic volatility model*.

The model under consideration is the Gatheral model from this family of local stochastic volatility models. The Gatheral model is a double-mean-reverting market model proposed by Gatheral (2008). In a subsequent publication, Bayer et al. (2013), the model is given by

$$dS(t) = \sqrt{v(t)}S(t)\, dW_1^*(t),$$

$$dv(t) = \kappa_1(v'(t) - v(t))\, dt + \xi_1 v^{\alpha_1}(t)\, dW_2^*(t), \qquad\qquad [8.1]$$

$$dv'(t) = \kappa_2(\theta - v'(t))\, dt + \xi_2 v'^{\alpha_2}(t)\, dW_3^*(t),$$

and the time t correlation matrix of the $\mathbb{R}^3$-valued stochastic process with components $W_i^*(t)$ has entries

$$\rho_{ij}(t, S(t), \mathbf{Y}(t)) = ij \in [-1, 1].$$

The issue with such models is the general lack of closed form characteristic function, which makes pricing much more challenging. Therefore, in Albuhayri et al. (2019, 2021), the following asymptotic expansions under the model in equation [8.1] were proven.

THEOREM 8.1.– *The asymptotic expansion of order* 1 *of the implied volatility under Gatheral model has the form*

$$\sigma(t, x_0, \nu_0; T, k) = \sqrt{\nu_0} + \frac{1}{4}\rho_{12}\xi_1 \nu_0^{\alpha_1 - 1}(k - x_0) + o\left(\sqrt{T - t} + |k - x_0|\right).$$

THEOREM 8.2.– *The asymptotic expansion of order* 2 *of the implied volatility under Gatheral model has the form*

$$\sigma(t, x_0, \nu_0, \nu_0'; T, k) = \sqrt{\nu_0} + \frac{1}{4}\rho_{12}\xi_1 v^{\alpha_1 - 1}(t)(k - x_0)$$

$$- \frac{3}{16}\rho_{12}^2\xi_1^2 v^{2\alpha_1 - 5/2}(t)(k - x_0)^2$$

$$+ \left[\frac{\kappa_1(v'(t) - v(t))}{4\sqrt{v(t)}} + \frac{1}{8}\rho_{12}\xi_1 v^{\alpha_1}(t) \right.$$

$$\left. + \frac{3}{32}\rho_{12}^2\xi_1^2 v^{2\alpha_1 - 3/2}(t) \right] (T - t)$$

$$+ o(T - t + (k - x_0)^2).$$

THEOREM 8.3.– *The asymptotic expansion of order* 3 *of the implied volatility under Gatheral model has the form*

$$\sigma(t, x_0, \nu_0, \nu_0'; T, k) = \sqrt{\nu_0} + \frac{1}{4}\rho_{12}\xi_1 v^{\alpha_1 - 1}(t)(k - x_0)$$

$$- \frac{3}{16}\rho_{12}^2\xi_1^2 v^{2\alpha_1 - 5/2}(t)(k - x_0)^2$$

$$+ \left[\frac{\kappa_1(v'(t) - v(t))}{4\sqrt{v(t)}} + \frac{1}{8}\rho_{12}\xi_1 v^{\alpha_1}(t) \right.$$

$$\left. + \frac{3}{32}\rho_{12}^2\xi_1^2 v^{2\alpha_1 - 3/2}(t) \right] (T - t)$$

$$+ \frac{1}{128}[16\kappa_1(v'(t) - v(t))\rho_{12}\xi_1\nu^{\alpha_1 - 3} + 8\rho_{12}^2\xi_1^2\nu_0^{2\alpha_1 - 5/2}$$

$$- 32\rho_{12}^3\xi_1^3\nu_0^{3\alpha_1 - 4}](k - x_0)^3$$

$$+ \frac{1}{128}[24\kappa_1(v'(t) - v(t))\rho_{12}\xi_1\nu^{\alpha_1 - 2} + 12\rho_{12}^2\xi_1^2\nu_0^{2\alpha_1 - 3/2}$$

$$+ 35\rho_{12}^3\xi_1^3\nu_0^{3\alpha_1 - 3}](T - t)(k - x_0)$$

$$+ o((T - t)^{3/2} + |k - x_0|^3).$$

Here, $x_0 = \ln S_0$, k is the logarithmic strike price of a European call option and the quantity $k - x_0$ will hereafter be called the log-moneyness. Discarding the $o(\cdot)$ terms, we can use these expansions as approximation formulas for the model's implied volatility.

8.3. Accuracy of the asymptotic expansions

Since the model in equation [8.1] is not affine unless the correlation coefficients ρ_{13} and ρ_{13} are zero and $\alpha_1 = \alpha_2 = 0.5$, then the standard Fourier-based option pricing method cannot be applied for the general case. This means the expansions can only be benchmarked using the Monte Carlo simulation. Therefore, numerical studies have been conducted to check the performance of these asymptotic expansions of the implied volatility. We use the Monte Carlo simulation to generate benchmark values for the implied volatilities. All errors are calculated by treating the benchmark values by the Monte Carlo simulation as the reference values.

The parameters used for the simulation are given in Table 8.1. Here, the initial asset price is denoted by S_0, the number of time steps by M, the number of paths by I, and the rest are the Gatheral model parameters.

Parameter	Value	Parameter	Value	Parameter	Value	Parameter	Value
r	0.3	κ_1	1	ρ_{12}	-0.4	α_1	1
S_0	100	κ_2	1	ρ_{13}	0	α_2	1
M	500	v_0	0.04	ρ_{23}	0	ξ_1	0.1
I	500,000	v_0'	0.05	θ	0.04	ξ_2	0.2

Table 8.1. *Fixed parameters used for the numerical study*

The parameter choices come from Bayer et al. (2013). Here, $\rho_{13} = \rho_{23} = 0$ is the most realistic situation. Indeed, the correlation between the underlying asset and the long-run mean and the correlation between the volatility and its long-run mean should be close to zero. Correlation ρ_{12} is set to be negative as the underlying price and the volatility are usually negatively correlated.

As we are pricing a plain vanilla European option, the traditional Euler–Maruyama discretization scheme in combination with the moment matching method for the set of generated standard normal pseudo-random numbers, volatility, underlying asset's price series and a control variate were used (see Hilpisch (2015)).

We consider 100 options with maturities ranging from 30 days to 2 years and with log-moneyness between -0.2 and 0.2 as well as for shorter range of log-moneyness between -0.1 and 0.1.

Figure 8.1 gives examples of the asymptotic expansions of orders 1, 2 and 3 of the implied volatility and the benchmark values for four different times to maturities, 30 days, 60 days, 1 year and 2 years, respectively. The number of time steps is $M = 500$. From this example, it could be seen that the asymptotic expansions of orders 2 and 3 give better approximations compared to first-order expansion as expected. In addition, asymptotic expansions of orders 2 and 3 are almost identical, we hoped that order 3 is better.

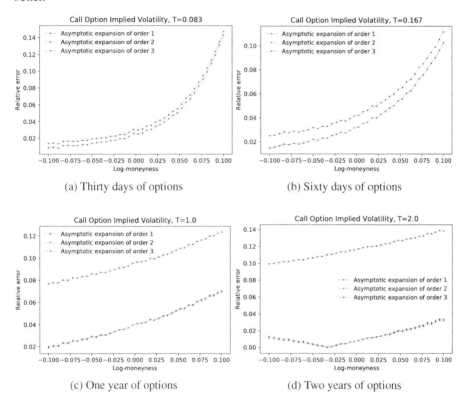

(a) Thirty days of options   (b) Sixty days of options

(c) One year of options   (d) Two years of options

Figure 8.1. *The asymptotic expansions of orders 1, 2 and 3 of the implied volatility and the benchmark value for a call option with log-moneyness ranging between* -0.1 *and* 0.1*. For a color version of this figure, see www.iste.co.uk/dimotikalis/ data3.zip*

Once again, the accuracy of the expansions is checked, and this time for the same range of maturities from 30 days to 2 years, but with a longer range of log-moneyness between -0.2 and 0.2.

The asymptotic expansions seem to perform well for different log-moneyness and maturities. Moreover, the obtained results for the two different ranges of log-moneyness considered are similar. The proportion of options that can be approximated within a relative error of 5% using the first-order expansion is around 67% in Figure 8.1a, and that accuracy decreases for 60 days of maturities to 60% in

Figure 8.1b, and then accuracy deteriorates for the first-order expansion against the benchmark in Figure 8.1c and 8.1d, which is to be expected.

In contrast, the accuracy becomes higher for the second- and third-order expansions in Figure. 8.1 with almost 70% of options within relative error of 5% in Figure 8.1a, 8.1b and 8.1c and a 100% of options within error of 5% for 2 years of options.

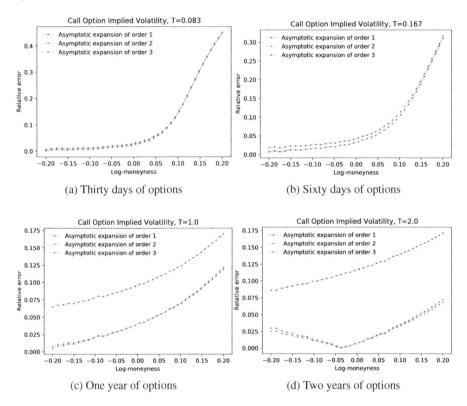

(a) Thirty days of options   (b) Sixty days of options

(c) One year of options   (d) Two years of options

Figure 8.2. *The asymptotic expansions of orders 1, 2 and 3 of the implied volatility and the benchmark value for a call option with log-moneyness ranging between* -0.2 *and* 0.2. *For a color version of this figure, see www.iste.co.uk/dimotikalis/ data3.zip*

On the contrary, the performance of the expansions in Figure 8.2 is similar of accuracy with an overall accuracy of more than 66% of options within a relative error of 5% for the second- and third-order expansions and less accuracy for the first-order expansion for the same range of log-moneyness, as expected. It is worth mentioning that the expansions seem to perform well against the Monte Carlo benchmark, especially for a short range of log-moneyness. However, they still perform well for a higher order of expansions for a longer range of log-moneyness.

8.4. Numerical analysis

Following the previous experiments on the performance of the asymptotic expansions under the Gatheral model. The same set of data is used with time to maturities ranging from 30 days to 2 years and strike prices varying from 80 to 120 to calculate the options prices as well as implied volatility for the fixed set of data using the asymptotic expansions of orders 1, 2 and 3 under our model and compare them with the reference price of the Monte Carlo. A part of the experiment is presented in Table 8.2.

Monte Carlo ImpVol	ImpVol order1	impVol order2	ImpVol order3
0.20399	0.201875	0.202845	0.203074
0.204258	0.201751	0.202728	0.202918
0.203948	0.201629	0.202612	0.202769
0.203589	0.201508	0.202497	0.202625
0.203734	0.201389	0.202383	0.202486
0.203833	0.201271	0.20227	0.202352

Table 8.2. *Implied volatilities calculated by Monte Carlo simulation (MC) compared to implied volatilities given by asymptotic expansions of orders 1, 2 and 3 under the Gatheral model*

Relative error of order 1	Relative error of order 2	Relative error of order 3
0.0098	0.0049	0.0049
0.0147	0.0098	0.0049
0.0098	0.0049	0.0049
0.0098	0.0049	0.0049
0.0147	0.0098	0.0098
0.0147	0.0098	0.0098

Table 8.3. *Illustrations of relative (Rel) errors given for previous data of the asymptotic expansions of orders 1, 2 and 3 against the Monte Carlo benchmark in Table 8.2*

In Table 8.3, the relative errors are defined according to this following formula:

$$\text{error}(IV) = \frac{|IV_{mc} - IV_{ex}|}{IV_{mc}}.$$

where IV_{mc} and IV_{ex} are implied volatilities by the Monte Carlo and model implied volatilities by expansions, respectively. It can be said that the figures indicate that the accuracy of the asymptotic expansion or order 2 is better than the asymptotic expansion of order 1. In addition, the accuracy becomes much better for the third-order expansion compared to the first order and with a slight improvement in the accuracy compare to the second order. Moreover, both results in Tables 8.2 and 8.3 prove that our asymptotic expansion approximations give plausible results.

8.5. Conclusion and future work

As is shown in the numerical analysis, the accuracy of the asymptotic expansions has been checked using the Monte Carlo benchmark as it is the only means for this purpose. The numerical studies have been performed on fixed datasets described by Bayer et al. (2013). The accuracy in the asymptotic expansion of order 1 was plausible as long as the short time to maturities (30 days and 60 days) is concerned; however, as we test the expansion with longer maturities, the accuracy becomes less. Moreover, we can confirm that the asymptotic expansions of orders 2 and 3 yield good approximations not only for a longer range of maturities up to two years but also for different ranges of the log-moneyness. The relative errors were also calculated to confirm the validity of our expansions.

We recommend that more extensive studies should be done by considering a wider choice of stocks and options so that the accuracy of our expansions is confirmed. Further numerical studies can be carried out to study how much of an improvement we can make by using the third-order expansion. Having analytical formulas will motivate us to do a full calibration of the model.

8.6. Acknowledgments

This work was funded by the Saudi Arabia Cultural Bureau in Germany (SACUOF) in cooperation with the scholarship program of the Saudi Arabian Ministry of Education (MOE). Moreover, this work would not have been accomplished without the support of the International Science Programme (ISP) at Uppsala University which handles the coordination of collaboration between Al-Baha University, Saudi Arabia and Mälardalen University, Sweden.

8.7. References

Albuhayri, M., Engström, C., Malyarenko, A., Ni, Y., Silvestrov, S. (2019). An improved asymptotics of implied volatility in the Gatheral model. In *Stochastic Processes, Statistical Methods, and Engineering Mathematics*, Malyarenko, A., Ni, Y., Rančić, M., Silvestrov, S. (eds). Springer, Cham, 3–13.

Albuhayri, M., Malyarenko, A., Silvestrov, S., Ni, Y., Engström, C., Tewolde, F., Zhang, J. (2021). Asymptotics of implied volatility in the gatheral double stochastic volatility model. In *Applied Modeling Techniques and Data Analysis 2*, Dimotikalis, Y., Karagrigoriou, A., Parpoula, C., Skiadas, C.H. (eds). ISTE Ltd, London, and John Wiley & Sons, New York.

Bayer, C., Gatheral, J., Karlsmark, M. (2013). Fast Ninomiya–Victoir calibration of the double-mean-reverting model. *Quant. Finance*, 13(11), 1813–1829.

Berestycki, H., Busca, J., Florent, I. (2002). Asymptotics and calibration of local volatility models. *Quant. Finance* 2(1), 61–69.

Christoffersen, P., Heston, S., Jacobs, K. (2009). The shape and term structure of the index option smirk: Why multifactor stochastic volatility models work so well. *Management Sci.*, 55(12), 1914–1932.

Cox, J.C. and Ross, S.A. (1976). The valuation of options for alternative stochastic processes. *J. Financ. Economics*, 3(1–2), 145–166.

Dupire, B. (1997). Pricing and hedging with smiles. In *Mathematics of Derivative Securities (Cambridge, 1995)*, Dempster, M.A.H. and Pliska, S.R. (eds). Cambridge University Press, Cambridge.

Fouque, J.P., Papanicolaou, G., Sircar, R., K. Sølna. (2011). *Multiscale Stochastic Volatility for Equity, Interest Rate, and Credit Derivatives*. Cambridge University Press, Cambridge.

Gatheral, J. (2008). Consistent modeling of SPX and VIX options. *The Fifth World Congress of the Bachelier Finance Society*, London.

Heston, S.L. (1993). A closed-form solution for options with stochastic volatility with applications to bond and currency options. *Rev. Financ. Studies*, 6(2), 327–343.

Hilpisch, Y. (2015). *Derivatives Analytics with Python. Data Analysis, Models, Simulation, Calibration and Hedging*. John Wiley & Sons, New York.

Macbeth, J.D. and Merville, L.J. (1979). An empirical examination of the Black-Scholes call option pricing model. *J. Finance*, 34(5), 1173–1186.

Pagliarani, S. and Pascucci, A. (2017). The exact Taylor formula of the implied volatility. *Finance Stoch.*, 2(3), 661–718.

9

Constructing Trinominal Models Based on Cubature Method on Wiener Space: Applications to Pricing Financial Derivatives

This contribution deals with an extension to our developed novel cubature methods of degrees 5 on Wiener space. In our previous studies, we studied cubature formulae that are exact for all multiple Stratonovich integrals up to dimension equal to the degree. In fact, cubature method reduces solving a stochastic differential equation to solving a finite set of ordinary differential equations. Now, we apply the above methods to construct trinomial models and to price different financial derivatives. We will compare our numerical solutions with the Black's and Black–Scholes models' analytical solutions. The constructed model has practical usage in pricing American options and American-style derivatives.

9.1. Introduction and outline of this chapter

In mathematical finance, it is common to describe the random changes in risky asset prices by stochastic differential equations (SDEs). SDEs can be rewritten in their integral forms. However, it is not possible to calculate all stochastic integrals in closed form. Therefore, proper numerical methods should be used to estimate the value of such stochastic integrals.

One of the most popular numerical methods to estimate stochastic integrals is the Monte Carlo method (estimate). In particular, according to Nohrouzian et al. (2022), cubature methods and consequently cubature formulae construct a

Chapter written by Hossein NOHROUZIAN, Anatoliy MALYARENKO and Ying NI.
For a color version of all the figures in this chapter, see www.iste.co.uk/dimotikalis/data3.zip.

probability measure with finite support on a finite-dimensional real linear space, which approximates the standard Gaussian measure. A generalization of this idea, when a finite-dimensional space is replaced with the Wiener space, can be used for constructing modern Monte Carlo estimates (see Bayer and Teichmann (2008) for the exact sense of modern Monte Carlo estimate). The idea of cubature method on Wiener space, among others, was developed in Lyons and Victoir (2002). The extension of this idea was developed and studied in Malyarenko et al. (2017), Nohrouzian (2019), Malyarenko and Nohrouzian (2021) and Nohrouzian et al. (2022).

The objective here is to use the cubature method and a cubature formula of degree 5 on Wiener space to estimate the expected values of functionals defined on the solutions of SDEs. This means that we use an extension to our developed novel cubature methods of degrees 5 to estimate the (discounted) expected values of European call and put payoff functions, which are defined on the solutions of Black–Scholes and Black's SDEs. This extension includes a construction of a recombining trinomial tree model. The underlying asset prices in Black–Scholes and Black's models are log-normally distributed, and the price dynamics follow geometric Brownian motion. Moreover, both models have closed-form solutions to find the price of European call and put options. Availability of closed-form solutions of these models provides an opportunity to investigate whether or not the sequence of our trinomial models converges to a geometric Brownian motion. Also, we can compare our numerical results with analytical ones and consequently estimate the corresponding errors of our method. We would like to emphasize that the constructed trinomial tree has practical usage and applications in pricing path-dependent and American-style options.

The outline of this chapter is as follows. In section 9.2, we look at the cubature method on Wiener space and at the applications of cubature formula in Black–Scholes and Black's models. Then, in section 9.3, we construct a trinomial model based on cubature formula on Black–Scholes model. After that, in section 9.4, we study the convergence of the sequences of constructed trinomial model to a geometric Brownian motion. In section 9.5, we will study the conditions that make the probability measure in our trinomial model a martingale measure, i.e. risk-neutral probability measure. Later, in section 9.6, we will extend our results for more cases and give concrete examples of studying the behavior of the constructed trinomial model in Black–Scholes and Black's models. Finally, we conclude this chapter with a discussion section.

9.2. Cubature formula in Black–Scholes and Black's models

In this section, we briefly review how the cubature method on Wiener space can be used in the Black–Scholes and Black's models.

9.2.1. *Black–Scholes model via cubature formula*

Given a filtered probability space $(\Omega, \mathfrak{F}, \mathsf{P}, (\mathfrak{F})_{t \geq 0})$, let $S(t)$ be time-t price of a (non-dividend-paying) risky asset, r and σ be drift (risk-free interest rate) and diffusion (volatility of asset price) coefficients, and $\{W(t)\}_{t \geq 0}$ be the standard one-dimensional Wiener process. The dynamics of risky asset prices in the Black–Scholes model (Black and Scholes 1973; Merton 1973), under equivalent martingale probability measure $\mathsf{Q} \sim \mathsf{P}$, satisfies the following SDE (originally proposed by Samuelson (1965)):

$$\mathrm{d}S(t) = rS(t)\mathrm{d}t + \sigma S(t)\mathrm{d}W(t), \qquad 0 \leq t \leq T. \tag{9.1}$$

The solution to the SDE [9.1] is an Itô process. After applying the Stratonovich correction, the above equation can be written in its Stratonovich form (see Øksendal (2013))

$$\mathrm{d}S(t) = (r - \frac{1}{2}\sigma^2)S(t)\mathrm{d}t + \sigma S(t) \circ \mathrm{d}W(t). \tag{9.2}$$

Note that the cubature formula is valid in time interval of length 1. Applying the results of cubature method on Wiener space in equation [9.2] yields to Nohrouzian (2019) and Nohrouzian et al. (2022)

$$\mathrm{d}S_k(t) = (r - \frac{1}{2}\sigma^2)S_k(t)\mathrm{d}t + \sigma S_k(t)\mathrm{d}\omega_k(t)t, \qquad 0 \leq t \leq 1,$$

where ω_k, $(1 \leq k \leq l)$ is the kth possible trajectory, and l, $(l \in \mathbb{Z}^+)$ stands for the number of trajectories in the cubature formula of degree M.

Rearranging the last equation and calculating the integral of both hand sides gives

$$\hat{S}_k(t_j) = \hat{S}_k(t_{j-1}) \exp\left\{(r - \frac{1}{2}\sigma^2)[t_j - t_{j-1}] + \sigma[\omega_k(t_j) - \omega_k(t_{j-1})]\right\},$$
$$\tag{9.3}$$

with $j = 1, \ldots, l$ and $0 \leq t_j \leq 1$. In a cubature formula of degree $M = 5$, the number of trajectories is $l = 3$ and one of the possible solutions becomes

$$\omega_k(t_j) = 3\theta_{k,j}(t_j - t_{j-1}) + \omega_k(t_{j-1}), \quad j = 1, 2, 3, \quad \omega_k(0) = 0, \tag{9.4}$$

where $0 = t_0 < t_1 < t_2 < t_3 = 1$, i.e. the trajectories start from time 0 and stop at time 1, $j = 1, 2, 3$, $t_j - t_{j-1} = 1/3$ and with weight λ_k and coefficients θ_k summarized in Table 9.1.

Using equation [9.4], we calculate $\omega_3(t_3) = -\omega_1(t_3) = \sqrt{3}$ and $\omega_2(t_3) = 0$. For simplicity, denote $\omega_k(t_3)$ by ω_k. Now, let us ignore the intermediate partitions in $0 = t_0 < t_1 < t_2 < t_3 = 1$. This reduces equation [9.3] to

$$\hat{S}_k(1) = \hat{S}_k(0) \exp\left\{(r - \frac{1}{2}\sigma^2) + \sigma\omega_k\right\}. \tag{9.5}$$

k	λ_k	$\theta_{k,1} = \theta_{k,3}$	$\theta_{k,2}$	$\theta_{k,3} = \theta_{k,1}$
1	1/6	$(-2\sqrt{3} \mp \sqrt{6})/6$	$(-\sqrt{3} \pm \sqrt{6})/3$	$(-2\sqrt{3} \mp \sqrt{6})/6$
2	2/3	$\pm\sqrt{6}/6$	$\mp\sqrt{6}/3$	$\pm\sqrt{6}/6$
3	1/6	$(2\sqrt{3} \pm \sqrt{6})/6$	$(\sqrt{3} \mp \sqrt{6})/3$	$(2\sqrt{3} \pm \sqrt{6})/6$

Table 9.1. *Information for cubature formulae of degree 5*

Equation [9.5] works for the time interval of length 1, i.e. $t \in [0, 1]$. Now, consider the time to maturity of an option as a time interval of length 1; we also need to calculate (estimate) the corresponding interest rate r and volatility σ. For example, for a three-month option, we need three-month interest rate and volatility, and for a six-month option, we need six-month interest rate and volatility.

However, we would like to consider the yearly interest rate, yearly volatility and yearly time to maturity in a more flexible way. Therefore, we modify the drift and diffusion terms in equation [9.5]. This modification yields to:

$$\hat{S}_k(T) = \hat{S}_k(0) \exp \left\{ (r - \frac{1}{2}\sigma^2)T + \sigma\sqrt{T}\omega_k \right\}. \tag{9.6}$$

Now, it is easy to calculate $\hat{S}_k(T)$ for $k = 1, 2, 3$. Then, the price of an option will be equal to its discounted expected payoff. For example, the price of an European call option (π_c) and the price of an European put option (π_p) with strike price K will be given by

$$\pi_c = e^{-rT} \sum_{k=1}^{3} \lambda_k \max \left(\hat{S}_k(T) - K, 0 \right),$$

$$\pi_p = e^{-rT} \sum_{k=1}^{3} \lambda_k \max \left(K - \hat{S}_k(T), 0 \right).$$

Equation [9.6] works better for a very small time to maturity. Later, in this chapter, we will try to improve the performance of our model by extending it into a trinomial tree model.

9.2.2. *Black's model via cubature formula*

In the Black's model (Black 1976), the dynamics of risky forward rate prices $F(t)$ satisfies

$$dF(t) = \sigma F(t)dW(t), \quad 0 \le t \le T.$$

The Stratonovich form of the above SDE becomes

$$dF(t) = -\frac{1}{2}\sigma^2 F(t)dt + \sigma F(t) \circ dW(t).$$

Following the same procedure as in section 9.2.1, we get

$$\hat{F}_k(T) = \hat{F}_k(0)\exp\left\{-\frac{1}{2}\sigma^2 T + \sigma\sqrt{T}\omega_k\right\}. \qquad [9.7]$$

9.3. Constructing a trinomial tree via cubature formula

In this section, we develop, modify and revise the idea of constructing a trinomial model via cubature formula on Wiener space presented in Nohrouzian (2019). The idea of constructing an n-step trinomial tree is to divide the time interval $[0, T]$ by n steps. In each step, the price can go up by an amount of u_0 with probability p_u, go in middle by an amount of m_0 with probability p_m and go down by an amount d_0 with probability p_d; also, $0 \le p_u, p_m, p_d \le 1$, $p_u + p_m + p_d = 1$ and $u_0 > m_0 > d_0$. In other words, we create more trajectories (paths) for the underlying process in discrete time in order to get more accurate possible prices. If a trinomial model is recombining, then the number of nodes in the constructed recombining trinomial tree is $2n + 1$. Using trinomial expansion, we can find all $(n+1)(n+2)/2$ trinomial coefficients which represent the number of possible paths to reach each node. Note that the sum of all trinomial coefficients is equal to the number of all possible paths in the constructed trinomial tree, i.e. to 3^n. Moreover, we can simply calculate the corresponding probabilities and prices at each step of the tree, and for each node. Figure 9.1 illustrates the idea, where the dashed arrows represent a recombining binomial tree (see, for example, CRR binomial model in Cox et al. (1979)). Note that, for example, in node $(3, 4)$, $S_0 u_0 m_0^2 = S_0 u_0^2 d_0$ and in node $(3, 3)$ $S_0 m_0^3 = S_0 u_0 m_0 d_0$.

The constructed tree can (among other possible applications) be used for pricing European, American-style and path-dependent derivative options.

9.3.1. *A trinomial tree approximation for the Black–Scholes model*

Let $h = T/n$, substituting $\omega_3 = -\omega_1 = \sqrt{3}$ and $\omega_2 = 0$ in equation [9.6] (from now on, we type S instead of $\hat{S}$), we introduce up, middle and down factors by

$$\begin{cases} u = \ln(u_0) = \ln\dfrac{S_3(h)}{S(0)} = (r - \dfrac{1}{2}\sigma^2)h + \sigma\sqrt{3h}, \\[2mm] m = \ln(m_0) = \ln\dfrac{S_2(h)}{S(0)} = (r - \dfrac{1}{2}\sigma^2)h, \\[2mm] d = \ln(d_0) = \ln\dfrac{S_1(h)}{S(0)} = (r - \dfrac{1}{2}\sigma^2)h - \sigma\sqrt{3h}. \end{cases} \qquad [9.8]$$

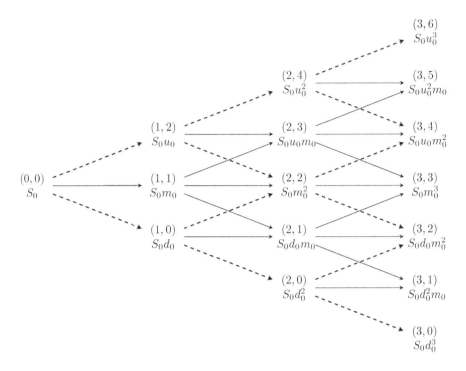

Figure 9.1. *A three-step trinomial tree*

Note that the factors u, m and d depend on n through h. To simplify the notation, we omit this dependence.

PROPOSITION 9.1.– *The above trinomial construction produces a recombining trinomial tree.*

PROOF.– We simply calculate

$$u_0 d_0 = \exp\left\{2(r - \frac{1}{2}\sigma^2)h\right\} = m_0 m_0 = m_0^2.$$

Since u_0, m_0 and d_0 are positive, $m_0 = \sqrt{u_0 d_0}$. Equivalently, $m = (u + d)/2$.

As an example, assume that the stock price $S_0 = \$100$, time to maturity $T = 0.5$ of a year, strike price $K = \$120$, yearly interest rate $r = 2.5\%$, yearly volatility $\sigma = 25\%$ and the number of steps in our trinomial tree $n = 252$.

Now, given the above parameters, a script is written in MATLAB®, where we use the Black–Scholes formulae to calculate analytical prices and apply the constructed trinomial tree model to estimate numerical prices of European call and put options. The option prices are summarized in Table 9.2. Moreover, the behavior of trinomial tree prices (for call option) is shown in Figure 9.2. The absolute value of difference between Black–Scholes and trinomial prices for call option is 0.0020704969, and for put is 0.00207049733.

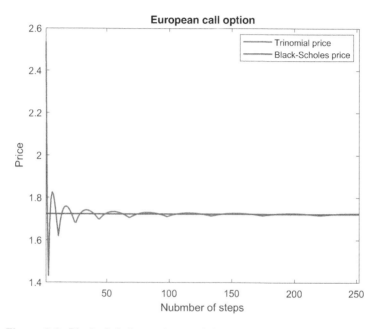

Figure 9.2. *Black–Scholes and trinomial prices for European call option*

$\pi_c(\$)$ Black–Scholes	$\pi_c(\$)$ Trinomial	$\pi_p(\$)$ Black–Scholes	$\pi_p(\$)$ Trinomial
1.722901670	1.724972167	20.23223773	20.234308227

Table 9.2. *Black–Scholes model example*

9.4. Convergence to geometric Brownian motion

As Figure 9.2 suggests, our (numerical) trinomial price may converge to the (analytical) Black–Scholes price. Now, we will consider a more general case and show that the sequence of our trinomial model (weakly) converges to a geometric Brownian motion. We first prove the convergence in distribution, and then prove the sequence of measures is tight. We will start by reviewing the necessary definitions and a theorem given in Billingsley (1999).

Let (S, d) be a metric space. For the purposes of this chapter, it is enough to consider the case of $S = C[0, T]$ with the distance

$$d(a, b) = \max_{t \in [0,T]} |a(t) - b(t)|.$$

Let $\mathfrak{S}$ be the σ-field of Borel sets in S. For a probability space $(\Omega, \mathfrak{F}, \mathsf{P})$, consider a measurable map $X: \Omega \to S$. By this definition, for a point $w \in \Omega$, the image $X(w)$ is a continuous function on $[0, T]$. That is, $X(t, w) = X(w)(t)$ is a stochastic process with continuous sample paths.

DEFINITION 9.1.– *The distribution of X is the probability measure P on the σ-field $\mathfrak{S}$ given by*

$$P(A) = \mathsf{P}(X^{-1}(A)), \qquad A \in \mathfrak{S}.$$

REMARK 9.1.– *In other words, we describe the one-to-one correspondence between the family of stochastic processes X with continuous trajectories and the family of probability measures P on $C[0, T]$.*

DEFINITION 9.2.– *A sequence $\{X_n: n \geq 1\}$ of stochastic processes* converges in distribution *to a stochastic process X if the sequence $\{P_n: n \geq 1\}$ of their distributions weakly converges to the distribution P of the stochastic process X, i.e. for any continuous function $v: S \to \mathbb{R}$, we have*

$$\lim_{n \to \infty} \int_S v(f) \, \mathrm{d}P_n(f) = \int_S v(f) \, \mathrm{d}P(f).$$

Let k be a positive integer, and let $t_1, \ldots, t_k$ be arbitrary distinct points in $[0, T]$; then we have the following definitions.

DEFINITION 9.3.– *The* natural projection *is the map $\pi_{t_1, \ldots, t_k}: S \to \mathbb{R}^k$ given by*

$$\pi_{t_1, \ldots, t_k}(f) = (f(t_1), \ldots, f(t_k))^{\top}.$$

DEFINITION 9.4.– *The* finite-dimensional distributions *of a stochastic process X are the measures $P\pi_{t_1, \ldots, t_k}^{-1}$ on the Borel σ-field $\mathfrak{R}^k$ of the space $\mathbb{R}^k$ given by*

$$P\pi_{t_1, \ldots, t_k}^{-1}(A) = P(\pi_{t_1, \ldots, t_k}^{-1}(A)), \qquad A \in \mathfrak{R}^k.$$

DEFINITION 9.5.– *A family Π of probability measures on $\mathfrak{S}$ is called* relatively compact *if every sequence of elements of Π contains a weakly converging subsequence.*

THEOREM 9.1.– *If the sequence $\{P_n: n \geq 1\}$ of the distributions of stochastic processes $\{X_n: n \geq 1\}$ is relatively compact and the finite-dimensional distributions* *of X_n converge weakly to those of a stochastic process X, then $\{X_n \colon n \geq 1\}$ converges in distribution to X.*

Thus, proof of convergence in distribution of the sequence of trinomial trees to the geometric Brownian motion is naturally divided into two parts, which will be given in the following two sections.

9.4.1. *Convergence of finite-dimensional distribution*

The convergence of our model will be studied in the following three steps.

9.4.1.1. *Step 1 (Preliminaries)*

Consider equation [9.8] and let $0 = t_0 < t_1 < \cdots < t_n$, where $t_n = T$. Then, the price at each step of the tree can be found using

$$S(t_i) = \begin{cases} S(t_{i-1})e^u & \text{with probability} \quad p_u, \\ S(t_{i-1})e^m & \text{with probability} \quad p_m, \quad i = 1, \ldots, n \\ S(t_{i-1})e^d & \text{with probability} \quad p_d. \end{cases} \qquad [9.9]$$

Denote the amount of times that the price goes up, up to time t_n, i.e. step n, by $n_u(t_n)$, down by $n_d(t_n)$ and middle by $n_m(t_n) = n - n_u(t_n) - n_d(t_n)$, then the set of possible prices can be expressed by

$$S(t_n) \in \{S_0 \exp\left(un_u(t_n) + dn_d(t_n) + m[n - n_u(t_n) - n_d(t_n)]\right)\}.$$

If we substitute $m = (u + d)/2$, the above set reduces to

$$S(t_n) \in \{S_0 \exp\left([n_u(t_n) - n_d(t_n)](u - d)/2 + n(u + d)/2\right)\}.$$

Put $\Omega = C[0, T]$, the space of paths, and $\mathfrak{S}$ as the σ-field of Borel sets. Let $p = (p_u, p_m, p_d)$ such that $0 \leq p_u, p_m, p_d \leq 1$ and $p_u + p_m + p_d = 1$ be given. Now, we define the probability measure P_n on $\mathfrak{S}$ supported by a finite subset of sample space $C[0, T]$ with 3^n elements.

9.4.1.2. *Step 2 (Description of the measure P_n)*

Consider the set of 3^n "words" $w = w_1 \ldots w_n$ consisting of n letters, where each letter is either u, m or d. Let

– $\{\xi_k \colon k \geq 1\}$ be the sequence of independent and identically distributed (IDD) random variables with $\mathsf{P}\{\xi_1 = \ln(w_1)\} = p_{w_1}$;

– $\Xi_0 = 0$ and $\Xi_k = \xi_1 + \cdots + \xi_k, k \geq 1$;

– $f_w \in C[0,T]$ be the function that takes the following values:

1) $f_w(0) = \ln(S_0)$,

2) $f_w\left(\dfrac{(k+1)T}{n}\right) = f_w\left(\dfrac{kT}{n}\right) + \xi_{k+1}$, $0 \leq k \leq n-1$,

the value in an arbitrary "intermediate" point, say t, is given by linear interpolation, i.e.

3) $f_w(t) = \ln(S_0) + \Xi_{\lfloor nt/T \rfloor} + (nt/T - \lfloor nt/T \rfloor)\xi_{\lfloor nt/T \rfloor+1}$, $0 \leq t \leq T$;

– $n_u(w)$ represent the number of letters u;

– $n_m(w)$ represent the number of letters m;

– $n_d(w)$ represent the number of letters d.

Now, we define the probability measure P_n on the Borel σ-field supported by the subset of sample space $C[0,T]$ with 3^n atoms $f_w(t)$ by

$$\mathsf{P}_n(f_w(t)) = p_u^{n_u(w)} p_m^{n_m(w)} p_d^{n_d(w)}.$$

Finally, let P be the measure that corresponds to the geometric Brownian motion

$$S(t) = S_0 \exp\left\{(r - \frac{1}{2}\sigma^2)t + \sigma W(t)\right\},   0 \leq t \leq T,$$

i.e. $\mathsf{P}(A) = \mathsf{P}\{S(t) \in A\}$, $A \in \mathfrak{G}$.

9.4.1.3. *Step 3 (Proof of convergence)*

Define the sequence of random variables $\{X_i\}_{i=1}^n$ on the probability space $(\Omega, \mathfrak{F}, \mathsf{P}_n, (\mathfrak{F}_t)_{t\geq 0})$ and on $w = (\xi_1, \ldots, \xi_n) \in \Omega$ as $X(w) = \xi_i$. Following the theories and discussions in Pascucci (2011), Pascucci and Runggaldier (2009) and Silvestrov (2014), we define

$$X_i(w) = \begin{cases} 1 & \text{if } \xi_i = u, \\ 0 & \text{if } \xi_i = m, \\ -1 & \text{if } \xi_i = d. \end{cases}$$

Note that the sequence $\{X_i\}_{i=1}^n$ is a sequence of independent and identically distributed (IID) random variables.

Let $S^n(t)$ be the stochastic process that corresponds to the measure P_n. By the constructions in "*Step 2.*", the values of the process $S^n(t_i)$ (for simplicity, denote it by $S(t_i)$) in our trinomial tree can be expressed by rewriting equation [9.9] as the following trinomial stock price

$$S(t_i) = S(t_{i-1}) \exp \left\{ \frac{(u+d)}{2} + \frac{(u-d)}{2} X_i \right\}, \qquad i = 1, \ldots, n. \qquad [9.10]$$

Note that $E[X_i] = p_u(1) + p_m(0) + p_d(-1) = p_u - p_d$ and $E[X_i^2] = p_u(1)^2 + p_m(0)^2 + p_d(-1)^2 = p_u + p_d$. Using the equation above, we obtain the following mean:

$$E\left[\ln \frac{S(t_i)}{S(t_{i-1})}\right] = E\left[\frac{(u+d)}{2} + \frac{(u-d)}{2} X_i\right] = \frac{(u+d)}{2} + \frac{(u-d)}{2} E[X_i],$$

$$= \frac{1}{2}[u + d + (u - d)(p_u - p_d)], \qquad [9.11]$$

and variance:

$$\text{Var}\left[\ln \frac{S(t_i)}{S(t_{i-1})}\right] = E\left[\left(\ln \frac{S(t_i)}{S(t_{i-1})}\right)^2\right] - \left(E\left[\ln \frac{S(t_i)}{S(t_{i-1})}\right]\right)^2,$$

where for the first term on the right-hand side of the above equation, we have

$$E\left[.^2\right] = \frac{1}{4} E\left[(u+d)^2 + 2(u+d)(u-d)X_i + (u-d)^2 X_i^2\right]$$

$$= \frac{1}{4}\left((u+d)^2 + 2(u+d)(u-d)E[X_i] + (u-d)^2 E\left[X_i^2\right]\right)$$

$$= \frac{1}{4}\left((u+d)^2 + 2(u+d)(u-d)(p_u - p_d) + (u-d)^2(p_u + p_d)\right),$$

and for the second term

$$(E\left[.\right])^2 = \frac{1}{4}[(u+d)^2 + 2(u+d)(u-d)(p_u - p_d) + (u-d)^2(p_u - p_d)^2.$$

Subtracting the second term from the first one gives

$$E\left[.^2\right] - (E\left[.\right])^2 = \frac{1}{4}\left[(u-d)^2(p_u + p_d) - (u-d)^2(p_u - p_d)^2\right]$$

$$= \frac{1}{4}[(p_u + p_d) - (p_u - p_d)^2](u - d)^2.$$

Thus,

$$\text{Var}\left[\ln \frac{S(t_i)}{S(t_{i-1})}\right] = \frac{1}{4}[p_u + p_d - (p_u - p_d)^2](u - d)^2. \qquad [9.12]$$

Substituting the values $\lambda_1 = p_u = p_d = \lambda_3 = 1/6$, u and d, confirms the construction of our trinomial tree. That is,

$$\mathrm{E}\left[\ln \frac{S(t_i)}{S(t_{i-1})}\right] = \frac{1}{2}[u + d + (p_u - p_d)(u - d)]$$

$$= \frac{1}{2}(\mu h + \mu h + 0 \cdot (u - d)) = \mu h,$$

where $\mu = (r - \frac{1}{2}\sigma^2)$. Moreover,

$$\mathrm{Var}\left[\ln \frac{S(t_i)}{S(t_{i-1})}\right] = \frac{1}{4}[p_u + p_d - (p_u - p_d)^2](u - d)^2$$

$$= \frac{1}{4}\left[\frac{2}{6}\right](2\sigma\sqrt{3h})^2 = \sigma^2 h.$$

In the next step, we would like to prove that the sequence of finite-dimensional distributions of our trinomial trees converges to those of the geometric Brownian motion. In a one-dimensional case, we prove $S(t_n)$ in our trinomial model converges in distribution to $S(T)$ in geometric Brownian motion as $n \to \infty$. First, we iterate equation [9.10]. This yields to

$$S(t_n) = S_0 \exp\left\{n\frac{(u + d)}{2} + \frac{(u - d)}{2}\sum_{i=1}^{n} X_i\right\}. \tag{9.13}$$

Note that for $i = 1, \ldots, n$, the random variables $\ln \dfrac{S(t_i)}{S(t_{i-1})}$ are IID random variables. Now, we use equation [9.10] and define Z_n as the standardized random variable of the sum, $\sum_{i=1}^{n} \ln \dfrac{S(t_i)}{S(t_{i-1})}\left(= \ln \dfrac{S(t_n)}{S_0}\right)$. That is,

$$Z_n := \frac{\sum_{i=1}^{n} \ln \dfrac{S(t_i)}{S(t_{i-1})} - n\mathrm{E}\left[\ln \dfrac{S(t_i)}{S(t_{i-1})}\right]}{\left(n\mathrm{Var}\left[\ln \dfrac{S(t_i)}{S(t_{i-1})}\right]\right)^{1/2}}.$$

Using the obtained mean and variance values in equations [9.11] and [9.12]

$$Z_n = \frac{\sum_{i=1}^{n} \ln \dfrac{S(t_i)}{S(t_{i-1})} - \dfrac{n}{2}[u + d + (p_u - p_d)(u - d)]}{\sqrt{\dfrac{n}{4}[p_u + p_d - (p_u - p_d)^2](u - d)^2}}$$

$$= \frac{\dfrac{(u - d)}{2}\sum_{i=1}^{n} X_i + n\dfrac{u + d}{2} - n\dfrac{u + d}{2} + n\dfrac{(p_u - p_d)(u - d)]}{2}}{\sqrt{n}\sqrt{\dfrac{1}{4}[p_u + p_d - (p_u - p_d)^2](u - d)^2}},$$

multiplying the numerator and the denominator by $2/(u - d)$,

$$Z_n = \frac{\sum_{i=1}^{n} X_i - n(p_u - p_d)}{\sqrt{n}\sqrt{p_u + p_d - (p_u - p_d)^2}} = \frac{X_1 + \ldots + X_n - n(p_u - p_d)}{\sqrt{n}\sqrt{p_u + p_d - (p_u - p_d)^2}},$$

where for all X_i and $i = 1, \ldots, n$

$$E[X_i] = p_u(1) + p_m(0) + p_d(-1) = p_u - p_d = \mu_X,$$

$$\mathrm{Var}[X_i] = E[X_i^2] - (E[X_i])^2 = p_u(1)^2 + p_m(0)^2 + p_d(-1)^2 - (p_u - p_d)^2$$

$$= p_u + p_d - (p_u - p_d)^2 = \sigma_X^2.$$

Thus,

$$Z_n = \frac{X_1 + \ldots + X_n - n\mu_X}{\sigma_X \sqrt{n}},$$

and using the central limit theorem (see Kijima 2013), we have

$$\lim_{n \to \infty} P\{Z_n \leq z\} = \mathcal{N}(z), \qquad z \in \mathbb{R},$$

where $\mathcal{N}(z)$ is the standard normal distribution function.

Using a little algebra, we calculate the following terms in equation [9.13]:

$$n\left(\frac{u + d}{2}\right) = (r - \frac{1}{2}\sigma^2)nh = (r - \frac{1}{2}\sigma^2)T,$$

$$\frac{u - d}{2}\sum_{i=1}^{n} X_i = \frac{u - d}{2}\left[n(p_u - p_d) + Z_n\sqrt{n}\sqrt{p_u + p_d - (p_u - p_d)^2}\right]$$

$$= (\sigma\sqrt{3h})(Z_n\sqrt{n}\sqrt{1/3})] = \sigma\sqrt{nh}Z_n = \sigma\sqrt{T}Z_n, \qquad [9.14]$$

where $p_u = p_d = 1/6$, $T = t_n = nh$ and u, d are given in equation [9.8]. Substituting the above values into equation [9.13] (for an arbitrary T), we get

$$S(T) = S_0 \exp\left\{(r - \frac{1}{2}\sigma^2)T + \sigma\sqrt{T}Z_n\right\}.$$

As a result, we have shown that the one-dimensional distributions of our trinomial tree model converge (in distribution) to those of the geometric Brownian motion as $n \to \infty$. The generalization to k-dimensional distributions is straightforward and uses the fact that the stochastic processes X_n and X have independent increments (for details, see Billingsley (1999)). It remains to prove that the corresponding sequence of measures is relatively compact.

9.4.2. *Relative compactness*

To prove the relative compactness of the sequence of measures, we first denote the stock price, up, middle and down factors as functions of n. That is, S^n, u_n, m_n and d_n. Second, we use the *modulus of continuity*'s definition given in equation 7.1 and theorem 7.5 in Billingsley (1999).

DEFINITION 9.6 (MODULUS OF CONTINUITY).– *The* modulus of continuity *for (an arbitrary) function $S^n(\cdot)$ on $[0, T]$ is defined by*

$$g(S^n, \delta) = \sup_{|z - z_0| \leq \delta} |S^n(z) - S^n(z_0)|.$$

THEOREM 9.2 (TIGHTNESS AND COMPACTNESS IN C).– *Let $S, S^1, S^2, \ldots$ be random functions. If for all $t_1, \ldots, t_k$*

$$(\mathcal{C}_1) \qquad (S^n_{t_1}, \ldots, S^n_{t_k}) \Rightarrow_n (S_{t_1}, \ldots, S_{t_k}),$$

holds and if for each positive ϵ

$$(\mathcal{C}_2) \qquad \lim_{\delta \downarrow 0} \lim_{n \to \infty} \sup P\left\{g(S^n, \delta) \geq \epsilon\right\} = 0,$$

holds, then $S^n \Rightarrow_n S$.

On the one hand, we have already shown that the sequence of our trinomial models converges (in distribution) to the geometric Brownian motion. Therefore, condition $(\mathcal{C}_1)$ holds. On the other hand, using Definition 9.6 and since $|S^n(z) - S^n(z_0)|$ are piecewise linear, we have

$$g(S^n, \delta) = \sup_{|z - z_0| \leq \delta} |S^n(z) - S^n(z_0)| = \max\{e^{u_n}, e^{m_n}, e^{d_n}\}\delta.$$

Let $C_n = \{e^{u_n}, e^{m_n}, e^{d_n}\}$, then $\lim_{n \to \infty} \max\{C_n\} = 1$. Thus, for condition $(\mathcal{C}_2)$ in Theorem 9.2, we have

$$\lim_{\delta \downarrow 0} \lim_{n \to \infty} \sup P\left\{g(S^n, \delta) \geq \epsilon\right\}$$

$$= \lim_{\delta \downarrow 0} \lim_{n \to \infty} \sup P\left\{\max(\{C_n\})\delta \geq \epsilon\right\}$$

$$= \lim_{\delta \downarrow 0} P\left\{\delta \geq \epsilon\right\} = 0.$$

9.5. Martingale probability measure

In this section, we will investigate whether there is a *martingale (risk-neutral) probability measure* Q equivalent to the physical probability measure P such that the discounted price process $S(t_n)$ becomes a martingale.

On the one hand, using the fundamental asset pricing theorem, *no arbitrage opportunity* is possible if and only if there exists a risk-neutral probability measure (see Kijima (2013)). This means that the average return on an asset should be equal to risk-free return, i.e.

$(\mathcal{NA})$ $\mathsf{E}^{\mathbb{Q}}[S(t_i)|S(t_{i-1})] = e^{r(t_i - t_{i-1})}S(t_{i-1}) = e^{rh}S(t_{i-1}).$

On the other hand, by definition, the martingale conditions for an arbitrary discrete time stochastic process $\{X(t)\}_{t\geq 0}$ are:

$(\mathcal{M}_1)$ $\mathsf{E}^{\mathbb{Q}}[|X(t_n)|] < \infty,$
$(\mathcal{M}_2)$ $\mathsf{E}^{\mathbb{Q}}[X(t_i)|X(t_{i-1})] = X(t_{i-1}).$

In order to see under which conditions the *discounted* asset price process $S(t)$ in a risk-neutral world is a martingale, we first define the stochastic process $\{Y(t)\}_{t\in[0,T]}$ by $Y(t_n) = \prod_{i=1}^{n} y_i$ on $w = (\xi_1, \ldots, \xi_n) \in \Omega$ as $y(w) = \xi_i$, where

$$y_i(w) = \begin{cases} u_0 & \text{if} \quad \xi_i = u, \\ m_0 & \text{if} \quad \xi_i = m, \\ d_0 & \text{if} \quad \xi_i = d. \end{cases}$$

Now, we can write the stock price $S(t_n)$ as

$S(t_n) = S_0 Y(t_n).$

First, for condition $(\mathcal{M}_2)$, we have

$$\mathsf{E}^{\mathbb{Q}}[S(t_i)|S(t_{i-1})] = \mathsf{E}^{\mathbb{Q}}[S(t_{i-1})Y(t_i)|S(t_{i-1})] = S(t_{i-1})\mathsf{E}^{\mathbb{Q}}[y_i]$$
$$= S(t_{i-1})(p_u u_0 + p_m m_0 + p_d d_0).$$

Equating the above equation with the no arbitrage condition $(\mathcal{NA})$ yields to

$$e^{rh} = p_u u_0 + p_m m_0 + p_d d_0 = p_u e^u + p_m e^{\frac{u+d}{2}} + p_d e^d. \qquad [9.15]$$

Second, for condition $(\mathcal{M}_1)$ and since $S(t_n), S_0 > 0$, we have

$$\mathsf{E}^{\mathbb{Q}}[|S(t_n)|] = \mathsf{E}^{\mathbb{Q}}[S(t_n)] = \mathsf{E}^{\mathbb{Q}}[S_0 Y(t_n)] = S_0 \prod_{i=1}^{n} \mathsf{E}^{\mathbb{Q}}[y_i]$$

$$= S_0(p_u u_0 + p_m m_0 + p_d d_0)^n = S_0(e^{rh})^n = S_0 e^{rt_n}.$$

Consequently, the expected value of *discounted* risky asset price becomes

$$\mathsf{E}^{\mathbb{Q}}[|e^{-rt_n}S(t_n)|] = e^{-rt_n} S_0 e^{rt_n} = S_0 < \infty.$$

Thus, the discounted stock price is a martingale if equation [9.15] holds. Moreover, note that if $h \to 0$, then both hand sides of equation [9.15] tend to 1. This condition will be investigated in an example given in the following section.

9.6. Extension of the results and examples

The proof of convergence suggests that there could be many solutions to a recombining trinomial tree.

We extend equation [9.8] by introducing a finite positive parameter $c > 1$, i.e.

$$
\begin{cases}
u = (r - \frac{1}{2}\sigma^2)h + \sigma\sqrt{ch}, \\
m = (r - \frac{1}{2}\sigma^2)h, \\
d = (r - \frac{1}{2}\sigma^2)h - \sigma\sqrt{ch}.
\end{cases}
$$

Also, we put $p = p_u = p_d = 1/(2c)$ and $p_m = 1 - 2p = 1 - 1/c$. Note that, with the above general formulations, our proof of convergence remains to be valid. Indeed, equation [9.14] holds for different values of c. In our trinomial tree, $c = 3$, $p_u = p_d = 1/6 = 1/(2c)$ and $p_m = 1 - 2p = 1 - 1/c$. We would like to examine the convergence of Black–Scholes (BS) price and extension of our trinomial (Tri.) model price, where $c = \{1, 3/2, 2, 3, 4, 5, 10, 20, 30\}$.

Let the current stock price $S_0 = \$100$, time to maturity $T = 1$ year, yearly interest rate $r = 3.5\%$ and yearly volatility $\sigma = 30\%$ be given. We set (number of steps in the tree) $n = 252$ (business days in one year). Now, we calculate the price of European call (π_c) and put (π_p) options with the described parameters for strike prices $K = \{\$80, \$100, \$120\}$. We calculate the absolute error (Abs. error) by the absolute value of the difference between the analytical Black–Scholes (BS) price and the trinomial price (Tri.). Using MATLAB®, the results are given in Tables 9.3–9.5.

Moreover, we investigate whether the martingale condition holds for this example. This means that the following absolute value of difference (let us call it the martingale condition) as $n \to \infty$ or equivalently $h \to 0$ should tend to zero:

$$
\text{Martingale condition} = |(p_u u_0 + p_m m_0 + p_d d_0) - e^{rh}| \xrightarrow[h \to 0]{} 0.
$$

The martingale conditions for different values of c are shown in Table 9.6.

REMARK 9.2.– *We note that, when $c = 1$, our trinomial model reduces to a binomial model where $p_u = p_d = 1/2$ (see the dashed lines in Figure 9.1). In the limit case, i.e. when $h \to 0$, our reduced trinomial model matches the Jarrow–Rudd binomial model proposed in Jarrow and Rudd (1983) (see also Jarrow and Turnbull (2000)).*

c	p_u	$\pi_c(\$)$ BS	$\pi_c(\$)$ Tri.	Abs. error π_c	$\pi_p(\$)$ BS	$\pi_p(\$)$ Tri.	Abs. error π_p
1	1/2	25.578	25.583	0.0050237	2.8262	2.8315	0.0052915
3/2	1/3	25.578	25.579	0.0008575	2.8262	2.8272	0.0010584
2	1/4	25.578	25.574	0.0034202	2.8262	2.8229	0.0032862
3	1/6	25.578	25.581	0.0035653	2.8262	2.8297	0.0035653
4	1/8	25.578	25.581	0.0031566	2.8262	2.8292	0.0030227
5	1/10	25.578	25.568	0.0102440	2.8262	2.8157	0.0105120
10	1/20	25.578	25.585	0.0071857	2.8262	2.8324	0.0062482
20	1/40	25.578	25.591	0.0134450	2.8262	2.8374	0.0111680
30	1/60	25.578	25.511	0.0662680	2.8262	2.7563	0.0698850

Table 9.3. $K = \$80$

c	p_u	$\pi_c(\$)$ BS	$\pi_c(\$)$ Tri.	Abs. error π_c	$\pi_p(\$)$ BS	$\pi_p(\$)$ Tri.	Abs. error π_p
1	1/2	13.517	13.523	0.0058724	10.078	10.084	0.00614020
3/2	1/3	13.517	13.522	0.0051641	10.078	10.083	0.00536490
2	1/4	13.517	13.522	0.0047397	10.078	10.083	0.00487370
3	1/6	13.517	13.520	0.0031506	10.078	10.081	0.00315060
4	1/8	13.517	13.518	0.0009543	10.078	10.079	0.00082035
5	1/10	13.517	13.516	0.0016326	10.078	10.076	0.00190050
10	1/20	13.517	13.500	0.0177320	10.078	10.059	0.01867000
20	1/40	13.517	13.460	0.0570400	10.078	10.018	0.05931700
30	1/60	13.517	13.416	0.1008700	10.078	9.9733	0.10449000

Table 9.4. $K = \$100$

c	p_u	$\pi_c(\$)$ BS	$\pi_c(\$)$ Tri.	Abs. error π_c	$\pi_p(\$)$ BS	$\pi_p(\$)$ Tri.	Abs. error π_p
1	1/2	6.4401	6.4333	0.006796	22.313	22.306	0.00652820
3/2	1/3	6.4401	6.4424	0.002330	22.313	22.315	0.00253110
2	1/4	6.4401	6.4401	0.000055	22.313	22.313	0.00018848
3	1/6	6.4401	6.4363	0.003782	22.313	22.309	0.00378220
4	1/8	6.4401	6.4317	0.008373	22.313	22.304	0.00850690
5	1/10	6.4401	6.4481	0.008076	22.313	22.321	0.00780800
10	1/20	6.4401	6.4366	0.003491	22.313	22.308	0.00442890
20	1/40	6.4401	6.4442	0.004160	22.313	22.315	0.00188270
30	1/60	6.4401	6.3995	0.040562	22.313	22.269	0.04417800

Table 9.5. $K = \$120$

c	p_u	Martingale condition
1	1/2	1.0630×10^{-8}
3/2	1/3	7.9724×10^{-9}
2	1/4	5.3151×10^{-9}
3	1/6	3.7947×10^{-13}
4	1/8	5.3145×10^{-9}
5	1/10	1.0629×10^{-8}
10	1/20	3.7206×10^{-8}
20	1/40	9.0369×10^{-8}
30	1/60	1.4355×10^{-7}

Table 9.6. *Martingale condition*

$\pi_c(\$)$ Black	$\pi_c(\$)$ Trinomial	$\pi_p(\$)$ Black	$\pi_p(\$)$ Trinomial
1.496683230	1.497311844	21.248239239	21.248867854

Table 9.7. *Black's model example*

9.6.1. *A trinomial tree approximation for Black's model*

So far, we have considered the Black–Scholes model. Constructing a trinomial model and a recombining tree in the Black's model is similar. Proofs of convergence to the geometric Brownian motion and martingale conditions can be achieved, similarly to previously done in the preceding sections. We only have different up, middle and down factors. That is, using equation [9.7]

$$
\begin{cases}
u = \ln(u_0) = \ln \dfrac{F_3(h)}{F(0)} = -\dfrac{1}{2}\sigma^2 h + \sigma\sqrt{3h}, \\
m = \ln(m_0) = \ln \dfrac{F_2(h)}{F(0)} = -\dfrac{1}{2}\sigma^2 h, \\
d = \ln(d_0) = \ln \dfrac{F_1(h)}{F(0)} = -\dfrac{1}{2}\sigma^2 h - \sigma\sqrt{3h}.
\end{cases}
$$

Now, we try an example inspired by Hull (2017). Assume that the current future price of a commodity $F_0 = \$100$, time to maturity $T = 0.5$ of a year, strike price $K = \$120$, yearly interest rate $r = 2.5\%$, yearly volatility $\sigma = 25\%$ and the number of steps in our trinomial tree $n = 252$. Programming in MATLAB®, we find the prices of European call futures and put futures options given in Table 9.7. Moreover, the behavior of trinomial trees (for put futures option) as the number of steps increases, is shown in Figure 9.3.

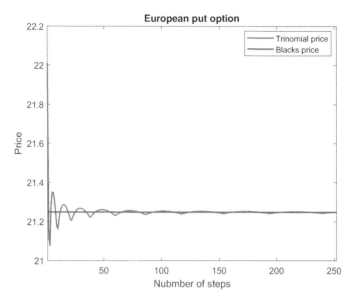

Figure 9.3. *Black's and trinomial prices for European put futures option*

The absolute value of difference between Black's and trinomial prices for call futures option is 0.0006286140 and for put is 0.0006286144.

9.6.2. *Pricing American options using the trinomial tree*

In this section, we will investigate the performance of our model in pricing American call and put options, and compare it with the classical CRR model. Let the current stock price $S_0 = \$100$, time to maturity $T = 0.5$ year, yearly interest rate $r = 2.5\%$ and yearly volatility $\sigma = 25\%$ be given. We increase the number of steps in the tree up to $n = 126$ (business days in half a year). We would like to calculate the price of American call and put options with the described parameters for strike prices $K = \{\$90, \$100, \$110\}$. The stock is non-dividend paying; thus, the optimal time to exercise such an American call option is at maturity, and therefore, its price should coincide with a European call option. This fact help us to calculate the Black–Scholes (BS) price of European call option and calculate absolute errors of our trinomial model and CRR model for a call option.

Using MATLAB®, we implement *backward recursion* to perform these calculations. The results are given in Figures 9.4–9.7.

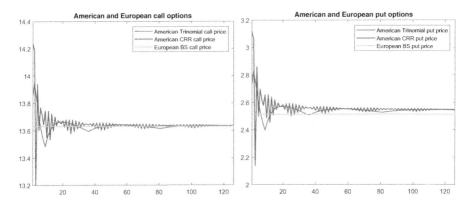

Figure 9.4. *Trinomial and CRR prices for American call and put options,* $K = 90$

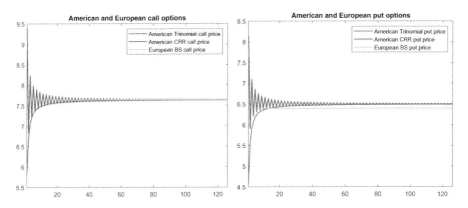

Figure 9.5. *Trinomial and CRR prices for American call and put options,* $K = 100$

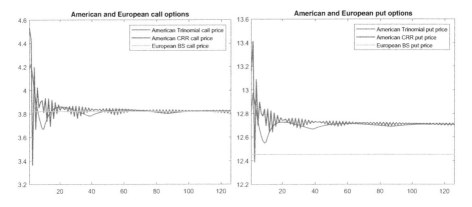

Figure 9.6. *Trinomial and CRR prices for American call and put options,* $K = 110$

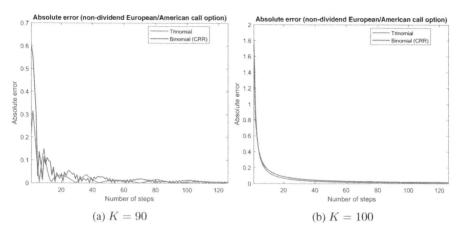

(a) $K = 90$ (b) $K = 100$

Figure 9.7. *Absolute errors of trinomial and CRR prices versus Black–Scholes price for non-dividend paying European/American call options, $K = \{90, 100\}$*

9.7. Discussion

In this chapter, we briefly reviewed the cubature method on Wiener space, where we specifically applied the cubature method and cubature formula on the Black–Scholes and Black's models. We saw that using cubature formula of degree 5, solving Black–Scholes and Black's SDEs reduces to solving three ordinary differential equations. This approach is inaccurate for long time intervals, and therefore, we constructed a trinomial tree model for very small time intervals using the result of cubature formula. Then, we find the numerical prices of European call and put options using our developed cubature formula and compare our results with analytical prices of Black–Scholes model. Moreover, we proved that the sequences of constructed trinomial tree converge to the geometric Brownian motion. We then studied the martingale conditions and extended the results. The extension of results (among other possible applications) included pricing American options.

9.8. References

Bayer, C. and Teichmann, J. (2008). Cubature on Wiener space in infinite dimension. *Proceedings of The Royal Society of London, Series A: Mathematical, Physical and Engineering Sciences*, 464(2097), 2493–2516.

Billingsley, P. (1999). *Convergence of Probability Measures*, 2nd edition. John Wiley & Sons, New York.

Black, F. (1976). The pricing of commodity contracts. *J. Financial Economics*, 3(1–2), 167–179.

Black, F. and Scholes, M. (1973). The pricing of options and corporate liabilities. *J. Political Economy*, 81(3), 637–654.

Cox, J., Ross, S., Rubinstein, M. (1979). Option pricing: A simplified approach. *J. Financial Economics*, 7(3), 229–263.

Glasserman, P. (2004). *Monte Carlo Methods in Financial Engineering*. Springer, New York.

Hull, J. (2017). *Options, Futures, and Other Derivatives*, 10th edition. Pearson, London.

Jarrow, R. and Rudd, A. (1983). *Option Pricing*. Dow Jones-Irwin, Homewood, IL.

Jarrow, R. and Turnbull, S.M. (2000). *Derivative Securities*. South-Western College Pub, Cincinnati, OH.

Kijima, M. (2013). *Stochastic Processes with Applications to Finance*, 2nd edition. CRC Press, Boca Raton, FL.

Lyons, T. and Victoir, N. (2002). Cubature on Wiener space. *Proceedings of The Royal Society of London, Series A: Mathematical, Physical and Engineering Sciences*, 460(2041), 169–198.

Malyarenko, A. and Nohrouzian, H. (2021). Evolution of forward curves in the Heath–Jarrow–Morton framework by cubature method on Wiener space. *Communications in Statistics: Case Studies, Data Analysis and Applications*, 7(4), 717–735.

Malyarenko, A., Nohrouzian, H., Silvestrov, S. (2017). An algebraic method for pricing financial instruments on post-crisis market. In *Algebraic Structures and Applications. SPAS 2017*, Silvestrov, S., Malyarenko, A., Rančić, M. (eds). Springer, Cham, 839–856.

Merton, R. (1973). Theory of rational option pricing. *The Bell Journal of Economics and Management Science*, 4(1), 141–183.

Nohrouzian, H. and Malyarenko, A. (2019). Testing cubature formulae on Wiener space vs explicit pricing formulae. In *Stochastic Processes, Statistical Methods and Engineering Mathematics. SPAS 2019*, Anatoliy, M., Ying, N., Milica, R., Sergei, S (eds). Springer, Cham, 223–248.

Nohrouzian, H., Ni, Y., Malyarenko, A. (2021). An arbitrage-free large market model for forward spread curves. In *Applied Modeling Techniques and Data Analysis 2*, Dimotikalis, Y., Karagrigoriou, A., Parpoula, C., Skiadas, C.H. (eds). ISTE Ltd, London, and John Wiley & Sons, New York, 75–90.

Nohrouzian, H., Malyarenko, A., Ni, Y. (2022). *Pricing Financial Derivatives in the Hull–White Model Using Cubature Methods on Wiener Space*. John Wiley & Sons, New York.

Øksendal, B. (2013). *Stochastic Differential Equations: An Introduction with Applications*. Springer, Berlin.

Pascucci, A. (2011). *PDE and Martingale Methods in Option Pricing*. Springer, Milan.

Pascucci, A. and Runggaldier, W. (2009). *Financial Mathematics: Theory and Problems for Multi-period Models*. Springer, Milan.

Samuelson, P. (1965). Rational theory of warrant pricing. *Industrial Management Review*, 6(2), 13–31.

Silvestrov, D. (2014). *American-Type Options: Stochastic Approximation Methods*, volume 1. De Gruyter, Berlin.

10

A Bayesian Approach to Measuring Risk on Portfolios with Many Assets

Hedge fund companies typically deal with huge liquid multi-asset portfolios, and modeling the risk of these investments can be challenging. Furthermore, their susceptibility to global market crashes makes modeling their risk even more important. Fitting multivariate models to such portfolios can be challenging given their size, while modeling them univariately runs the risk of ignoring dependencies between the different assets. In this study, a three-stage method for measuring risk on a hedge fund portfolio with many assets is proposed. The first step is that of performing dimension reduction using dynamic principal component analysis which yields orthogonal components that can then be modeled separately avoiding the need to consider multivariate models. This is followed by volatility modeling and forecasting of the individual principal components using a Bayesian generalized autoregressive conditional heteroscedastic (GARCH) model with t-distributed innovations. This allows us to construct a posterior predictive distribution for the whole portfolio. Finally, from this posterior predictive distribution, direct estimation of the risk of the portfolio is obtained using value at risk and expected shortfall. To determine the optimal balance between dimension reduction and accurate forecasts, this method is applied on 4, 11 and 36 dynamic principal components cut-off points determined by the elbow method and the total variation accounted for. Cross-validation over 135 trading days of the different modeling approaches is performed using log pseudo-maximum likelihood as measure of predictive ability. In this case study, it is found that the model with 11 dynamic principal components yields the most accurate forecasts, while the model with four principal components yields the least favorable ones.

10.1. Introduction

Over the past few decades, regulations surrounding financial markets have gone through substantial changes to match the pace of technological advancements as well as globalization. Nowadays, a country's stock market can no longer be

Chapter written by Samuel BONELLO, David SUDA and Monique BORG INGUANEZ.

considered to function independently since a crash in one country has the potential to cause a significant domino effect all around the world. The US subprime mortgage crash in 2008 and China's "Black Monday" crash in 2015 are just two of the many examples of such global market chain reactions that for the financial industry have been eye openers to the importance of employing an effective model to measure risk. One of the most commonly used tools for measuring the potential losses incurred by financial services as a result of market risk is the Value at Risk (VaR). However, VaR is often criticized for its lack of subadditivity and for the fact that it fails to say anything about the tail behavior of the distribution of losses. To overcome these shortfalls, Artzner et al. (1999) introduced the concept of coherent measures. The simplest and most popular coherent measure is the expected shortfall (ES), sometimes referred to as conditional VaR. Hedge fund companies typically deal with huge liquid multi-asset portfolios and modeling the risk of these investments can be challenging. Furthermore, their susceptibility to global market crashes makes modeling their risk even more important. Fitting multivariate models to such portfolios can be challenging given their size, while modeling them univariately runs the risk of ignoring dependencies between the different assets. Many authors have extended GARCH models to multivariate GARCH (MGARCH) models (see Tsay 2010). When applied to multi-asset portfolios, given the large number of parameters, the likelihood function becomes flat and its optimization becomes increasingly difficult (Orskaug 2009). These difficulties can be overcome using a Bayesian approach. An extensive overview of several Bayesian MGARCH models is provided by Virbickaite et al. (2015). Galeano and Ausín (2010) note that most of the proposed multivariate models aim at describing the correlation of several return series, with features such as leverage getting very little attention.

Since the univariate GARCH model has been extensively adapted to account for many different phenomena, many analysts prefer to operate in the univariate space. For this reason, Alexander (2003) introduced the orthogonal GARCH (O-GARCH) model. The O-GARCH model makes use of principal component analysis (PCA) to reduce the dimensions of the dataset, and then the univariate GARCH model is implemented on each principal component (PC) individually. This method contains a clear drawback: when performing PCA on a time series, although the covariance matrix of the PCs will be diagonal, it has been shown that the PCs still display lagged cross-correlations, and thus treating them as independent is inaccurate (Hörmann et al. 2015). This problem can be circumvented by applying dynamic principal component analysis (DPCA) instead of PCA. Contrary to classical PCA, which operates in the time domain, DPCA operates in the frequency domain and obtains the PCs using spectral analysis. As a result, once the PCs are transformed back into the time domain using the inverse discrete Fourier transform, they are uncorrelated across all lags. It is important to acknowledge that, like many other techniques, performing DPCA has some disadvantages; the main one being its complexity. Classical PCA, and more specifically the time domain, tends to be much more comprehensible than DPCA and the frequency domain, especially for those that may not have a mathematical background. It is likely that the reason why DPCA is not as popular as its classical counterpart. In this study, a method for measuring risk on a hedge fund portfolio with many assets consisting of three main steps is proposed: (1) perform dimension reduction using DPCA which yields orthogonal components that can then be modeled separately avoiding the need to consider multivariate models; (2) model and forecast volatility of the individual principal components using a Bayesian GARCH model with t-distributed innovations; and (3) reconstruct a posterior predictive distribution for the whole portfolio. From this posterior predictive distribution in the third step, direct estimation of the risk of the portfolio can be obtained using value at risk (VaR) and expected shortfall (ES). Finally, a method that mimics the ideas of the popular method of cross-validation is applied to compare the predictive ability of fitted models. Apart from the results presented in this chapter, supplementary results and material can be found in Bonello et al. (2022).

10.2. Dynamic principal component analysis

DPCA is applied in the frequency domain rather than the time domain and hence considers the spectral representation of a time series. The spectral representation of a stationary process X_t decomposes the process into a sum of sinusoidal components with uncorrelated random coefficients (see, for example, Brockwell and Davis 1991). In this chapter, it is assumed that the reader is familiar with the basic concepts of the frequency domain. Let $\mathbf{X}_t = \left(X_{1,t}, X_{2,t}, \dots, X_{p,t}\right)'$ denote a p-variate asset vector at time t belonging to a stationary multivariate time series with mean vector $\mathbf{0}$ and covariance matrix function $\mathbf{P_{XX}}(\cdot)$. The function $f_{mn}(\omega) = \sum_{h=-\infty}^{\infty} \rho_{mn}(h) e^{-i2\pi\omega h}$, $-\frac{1}{2} \leq \omega \leq \frac{1}{2}$ is called the cross-spectrum or cross-spectral density of the time series $X_{m,t}$ and $X_{n,t}$ where $m, n \in \{1, 2, \dots, p\}$ and $m \neq n$, and $\rho_{mn}(h)$ refers to the covariance between the series $X_{m,t}$ and $X_{n,t}$ at lag h. The $p \times p$ matrix

$$\mathbf{F_{XX}}(\omega) = \sum_{h=-\infty}^{\infty} \mathbf{P_{XX}}(h) e^{-i2\pi\omega h} = \begin{bmatrix} f_{11}(\omega) & f_{12}(\omega) & \cdots & f_{1n}(\omega) & \cdots & f_{1p}(\omega) \\ f_{21}(\omega) & f_{22}(\omega) & & f_{2n}(\omega) & \cdots & f_{2p}(\omega) \\ \vdots & \vdots & \ddots & \vdots & \ddots & \vdots \\ f_{m1}(\omega) & f_{m2}(\omega) & \cdots & f_{mn}(\omega) & \cdots & f_{mp}(\omega) \\ \vdots & \vdots & \ddots & \vdots & \ddots & \vdots \\ f_{p1}(\omega) & f_{p2}(\omega) & \cdots & f_{pn}(\omega) & \cdots & f_{pp}(\omega) \end{bmatrix}$$

is the spectral density matrix of $\mathbf{X}_t$ at frequency ω. For a fixed frequency ω, it is desired to find a complex-valued univariate process $Y_t(\omega)$ such that the univariate spectral density $f_Y(\omega)$ is maximized. In other words, the aim of DPCA is to find a complex vector $\mathbf{c}(\omega)$ of unit length such that:

$$\max_{\mathbf{c}(\omega) \neq 0} \mathbf{c}(\omega)' \mathbf{F}_{XX}(\omega) \mathbf{c}(\omega) \tag{10.1}$$

where $f_Y(\omega) = \mathbf{c}(\omega)' \mathbf{F}_{XX}(\omega) \mathbf{c}(\omega)$. Brillinger (1975) can be viewed as the pioneer of DPCA. The method that he proposed makes use of discrete Fourier transform (DFT) to jump from the time domain to the frequency domain and the inverse DFT to transform a time series that is represented in the frequency domain into the time domain. Further detail can be found in Brillinger (1981). The following is a brief overview. Let $\left\{ \left(\lambda_1(\omega), \mathbf{e}_1(\omega) \right), \ldots, \left(\lambda_p(\omega), \mathbf{e}_p(\omega) \right) \right\}$ denote the eigenvalue–eigenvector pairs $\mathbf{F}_{XX}(\omega)$. Then, the solution to equation [10.1] is choosing $\mathbf{c}(\omega) = \mathbf{e}_1(\omega)$, in which case $Y_t(\omega) = \mathbf{e}_1(\omega)' \mathbf{X}_t$ maximises the spectral density $f_Y(\omega) = \lambda_1(\omega)$. The first PC series is then defined as $Y_{1,t} = \sum_{h=-\infty}^{\infty} \mathbf{e}_{1,h}' \mathbf{X}_{t-h}$, where $\mathbf{e}_1(\omega) = \sum_{h=-\infty}^{\infty} \mathbf{e}_{1,h}' e^{-i2\pi h\omega}$. This process can be repeated for k series such that $k \leq p$, where the kth dynamic PC series is formulated as follows:

$$Y_{k,t} = \sum_{h=-\infty}^{\infty} \mathbf{e}_{k,h}' \mathbf{X}_{t-h} \tag{10.2}$$

and the coherency between $Y_{i,t}$ and $Y_{q,t}$ for $i \neq q$ is zero. In this way, $\mathbf{Y}_t = (Y_{1,t}, \ldots, Y_{q,t})'$ has spectral density $\mathbf{F}_{YY}(\omega) = diag\left(\lambda_1(\omega), \ldots, \lambda_q(\omega) \right)$.

So far, DPCA has been reviewed in the context of a population. Next, a brief overview of the method for performing DPCA when dealing with observed data is provided. Given observations $\mathbf{x}_t = \left(x_{1,t}, \ldots, x_{p,t} \right)'$, equation [10.3] determines the empirical lagged covariances between $x_{m,t}$ and $x_{n,t}$. More precisely, it determines $\hat{\rho}_{mn}(h)$ for h lags. For a sample of size v, set $\hat{\mu}_m = \frac{1}{v}\sum_{t=1}^{v} x_{m,t}$ and $\hat{\mu}_n = \frac{1}{v}\sum_{t=1}^{v} x_{n,t}$ such that

$$\hat{\rho}_{mn}(h) = \frac{1}{v}\sum_{t=1}^{v-h} \left(x_{m,t+h} - \hat{\mu}_m \right)\left(x_{n,t} - \hat{\mu}_n \right)' \tag{10.3}$$

The spectral density f is often estimated by a function of the form

$$\hat{f}_{mn}(\omega) = \frac{1}{2\pi}\sum_{|h|<q} K\left(\frac{h}{q}\right) \hat{\rho}_{mn}(h) e^{-i2\pi h\omega} \tag{10.4}$$

where $\hat{\rho}(\cdot)$ is the sample autocovariance function and $K(x)$ is a kernel smoother with window size q. By default, in the *freqdom* package in R, which will be used for DPCA (Hörmann and Kidzinski 2022), $K(x)$ is the Bartlett kernel. This is calculated for all $m, n \in \{1, 2, \ldots, p\}$ and $m \neq n$, to estimate the $p \times p$ cross-spectral matrix, $\hat{\mathbf{F}}_{XX}(\omega)$. Equation [10.4] is repeated for all $\omega_j = \frac{j}{n}$, $j = 1, \ldots, n$. Next, using singular value decomposition (SVD), we can retrieve the dynamic eigenvectors and eigenvalues of $\hat{\mathbf{F}}_{\mathbf{xx}}(\omega)$ for each ω_j. Denote the estimated dynamic eigenvectors as $\boldsymbol{\phi}_1(\omega), \dots, \boldsymbol{\phi}_p(\omega)$. To obtain the linear filter, Hörmann et al. (2015) used the Fourier inverse as follows:

$$\boldsymbol{\phi}_{l,h} = \frac{1}{2\pi} \int_{-\pi}^{\pi} \boldsymbol{\phi}_l(\omega) e^{ih\omega} d\omega \qquad [10.5]$$

for $|h| < q$ and $1 \leq l \leq p$. To reduce the dimensions, take $k < p$ PCs and calculate [10.5] for $1 \leq l \leq k$. In this way, k vector-valued filters $\{\boldsymbol{\phi}_{l,h}\}$ of dimension $p \times 1$ are estimated for each h, where $-q \leq h \leq q$. Compute the estimated scores for each PC, $\hat{Y}_{1,t}, \dots, \hat{Y}_{p,t}$, using [10.2] with $\hat{Y}_{k,t} = \sum_{h=-q}^{q} \boldsymbol{\phi}_{l,h}' \mathbf{x}_{t-h}$, $k = 1, \dots p$. Finally, using these estimated scores, the reconstruction of $\mathbf{X}_t$ is performed using the dynamic Karhunen–Loève expansion

$$\hat{\mathbf{X}}_t = \sum_{l=1}^{k} \sum_{h=-q}^{q} Y_{l,t+h}\, \boldsymbol{\phi}_{l,h} \qquad [10.6]$$

Ultimately, the aim is to model the estimated $\hat{Y}_{k,t}$'s using the Bayesian GARCH(1,1) model.

10.3. The Bayesian GARCH(1,1) model

Nowadays, modeling and forecasting the volatility of the returns of a financial asset is crucial, given that numerous asset-pricing models use volatility estimates to measure risk, and it is also known that financial time series are typically conditionally heteroscedastic in nature. In this section, the usefulness of the GARCH model in modeling portfolio risk shall be discussed. A detailed discussion is provided on how to infer the parameters of a GARCH(1,1) model with t-distributed innovations using Bayesian methods. Since the GARCH(1,1) model shall be used on the dynamic PCs, in the notation Y_t shall be used to denote the observed series. The classical t-distributed GARCH(1,1) model (Bollerslev 1987) has the following formulation:

$$Y_t = Z_t \sigma_t; \; Z_t \overset{iid}{\sim} S(0,1,v) \; \sigma_t^2 = \alpha_0 + \alpha_1 Y_{t-1}^2 + \beta_1 \sigma_{t-1}^2 \qquad [10.7]$$

where $S(0,1,v)$ refers to a scaled Student's t-distribution with mean zero, unit variance and v degrees of freedom. It is important to note that the standard Student's t-distribution is not what is being used here, as that would have a variance of $\frac{v}{v-2}$ which would skew the conditional variance. Ardia (2008) explains that the model described in [10.7] has been shown to be problematic when considering Bayesian inference since it is difficult to find proposal densities for the parameters when applying the Metropolis Hastings (MH) algorithm. To address this issue, Ardia and Hoogerheide (2010) propose the following reparameterization:

$$Y_t = Z_t \left(\frac{v-2}{v} \omega_t \sigma_t^2\right)^{\frac{1}{2}}; Z_t \overset{iid}{\sim} N(0,1), \omega_t \overset{iid}{\sim} IG\left(\frac{v}{2},\frac{v}{2}\right)$$
$$\sigma_t^2 = \alpha_0 + \alpha_1 Y_{t-1}^2 + \beta \sigma_{t-1}^2 \qquad\qquad [10.8]$$

where $\alpha_0 > 0, \alpha_1, \beta \geq 0$ and $v > 2$; $N(0,1)$ denotes the standard normal distribution and $IG\left(\frac{v}{2},\frac{v}{2}\right)$ denotes the inverted gamma distribution with shape and scale parameter equal to $\frac{v}{2}$. A derivation of the equivalence of [10.7] and [10.8] can be found in Bonello et al. (2022).

To begin to make inferences, define the observed values as $\mathbf{y} := (y_1, \ldots, y_T)'$, and the vectors of parameters to be estimated $\boldsymbol{\omega} := (\omega_1, \ldots, \omega_T)'$ and $\boldsymbol{\alpha} := (\alpha_0, \alpha_1)'$. The parameters are then grouped such that $\boldsymbol{\theta} := (\boldsymbol{\alpha}', \beta, v)'$. Ultimately, it is desired to estimate $\boldsymbol{\theta}$ and $\boldsymbol{\omega}$. In other words, we wish to find the posterior density $P(\boldsymbol{\theta}, \boldsymbol{\omega} \mid \mathbf{y})$:

$$P(\boldsymbol{\theta}, \boldsymbol{\omega} \mid \boldsymbol{y}) = \frac{\mathcal{L}(\boldsymbol{\theta},\boldsymbol{\omega} \mid y).P(\boldsymbol{\theta},\boldsymbol{\omega})}{\int \mathcal{L}(\boldsymbol{\theta},\boldsymbol{\omega} \mid y).P(\boldsymbol{\theta},\boldsymbol{\omega}) \, d\boldsymbol{\theta} \, d\boldsymbol{\omega}} \qquad\qquad [10.9]$$

where the denominator is a marginal likelihood. The priors used are the following: $P(\boldsymbol{\alpha}) \propto \tilde{\phi}_{N_2}(\boldsymbol{\alpha} \mid \boldsymbol{\mu_\alpha}, \Sigma_\alpha), \boldsymbol{\alpha} \in R_+^2$; $P(\beta) \propto \tilde{\phi}_{N_1}(\beta \mid \mu_\beta, \Sigma_\beta), \beta \in R_+$; $P(\boldsymbol{\omega} \mid v) = \left(\frac{v}{2}\right)^{\frac{Tv}{2}} \left[\Gamma\left(\frac{v}{2}\right)\right]^{-T} (\prod_{t=1}^T \omega_t)^{-\frac{v}{2}-1} e^{-\frac{1}{2}\sum_{t=1}^T \frac{v}{\omega_t}}$; $P(v) = \lambda e^{-\lambda(v-\delta)}; v > \delta$ (see Ardia and Hoogerheide 2010). Here, $\tilde{\phi}_{N_d}$ is the d-dimensional truncated normal density on R_+^d, $\boldsymbol{\mu_\alpha}$, μ_β, Σ_α and Σ_β are hyperparameters, and $P(v)$ is a translated exponential distribution with parameters $\lambda > 0$ and $\delta \geq 2$. Finally, the joint prior $P(\boldsymbol{\theta}, \boldsymbol{\omega}) = P(\boldsymbol{\alpha}).P(\beta).P(\boldsymbol{\omega} \mid v).P(v)$ is obtained. The posterior in [10.9] is estimated empirically using an MCMC simulator with the MH algorithm. Note that the MCMC sampler for this model was created by Ardia (2008) and consists of an algorithm in which the GARCH parameters are not updated in one single block. Rather, the GARCH parameters are updated in two separate blocks: one block for $\boldsymbol{\alpha}$ and another block for β. Further details on the MCMC procedure can be found in Ardia (2008).

In the next section, the extraction of orthogonal dynamic PC components and the use of Bayesian Student's-t GARCH model are discussed. Each of these dynamic PC components is modeled univariately and independently.

10.4. Modeling a portfolio with many assets

The dataset used in this study consists of 106 assets that are traded in various European exchanges. The original dataset is based on a typical portfolio provided to the authors by a risk management professional in an unnamed financial services company, with the intent of designing a procedure for quick and accurate measurements of risk on portfolios with many assets. The daily adjusted closing prices of each asset were observed for five years, from September 10, 2015 to September 10, 2020. All data has been downloaded using Yahoo Finance. The prices are represented by $(\mathbf{P}_t)$. One of the issues encountered was that since these assets operate in different exchanges, the assets experienced inconsistent trading days, which led to the observations of different time series being asynchronous in time. To overcome this problem, the trading days of all exchanges were compared and only those which were common to all were considered. Another issue encountered was that the assets included in the portfolio are being traded in multiple different currencies (EUR, GBX, SEK, NOK, CHF and DKK). It was opted to standardize the currencies of all assets by converting the value of all assets to EUR using the relevant exchange rates at the time. DPCA was applied to $(\mathbf{X}_t)$, the log returns of these assets.

Figure 10.1 shows a scree plot, which provides a summary of the proportion of variation explained by each component in the data. A rule of thumb is to analyze the scree plot and determine the point from which the variance explained seems to level off, known as the "elbow". The components to the left of this point should then be retained. For the given dataset, this seems to happen at around the fourth PC. However, when taking four PCs, these are only accounting for 54.66% of the total variation in the original dataset. Thus, apart from the results obtained when using four PCs, results for when retaining 11 and 36 PCs shall also be obtained, which explain a minimum of 70% and 90% of the total variation in the original dataset, respectively (71.46% and 90.27%, to be precise) shall be obtained for comparison purposes. It would have been ideal to analyze models every k in terms of predictive ability but alas this would have resulted in a very computationally expensive exercise.

Given k, the resulting output will be k independent univariate time series represented by $\widehat{\mathbf{Y}}_t = \left(\widehat{Y}_{1,t}, \widehat{Y}_{2,t}, ..., \widehat{Y}_{k,t}\right)'$, where $\widehat{Y}_{i,t}$ refers to the score of the ith dynamic PC at time t for $i = 1, ..., k$. As a comparison, we must note that the first PC explains 38.21% of the total variation in $\mathbf{X}_t$, while the 36th PC explains only 0.40% of the total variation in $\mathbf{X}_t$. After performing DPCA, we can use the dynamic Karhunen–Loève expansion illustrated in equation [10.6] to recover an estimation of $\mathbf{X}_t$ from $\widehat{\mathbf{Y}}_t$. We can then transform the estimated log returns, $\widehat{\mathbf{X}}_t$, into the estimated prices, $\widehat{\mathbf{P}}_t$.

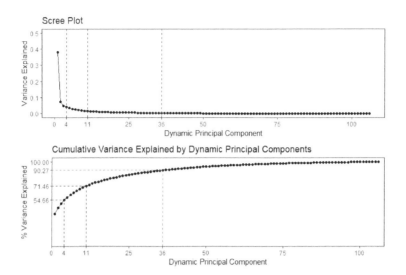

Figure 10.1. *Scree plot (top) and the cumulative variance (bottom) to display the variance captured by each dynamic PC. For a color version of this figure, see www.iste.co.uk/dimotikalis/data3.zip*

When using DPCA on time series data, the dynamic PC obtained after reducing the dimensions are uncorrelated over time. As a result, each dynamic PC can be treated as a univariate time series, allowing us to model the volatility independently. The Bayesian GARCH model is now implemented on all of the first 36 dynamic PCs, and the results are presented for $k = 1,4,11$ and 36. Two chains of length 30,000 with a burn-in period of 25,000 are run, using the average of the two chains to estimate the empirical probability density function of the parameters. The credibility intervals presented are the highest posterior density (HPD) intervals. For diffuse priors on α and β, we take $\mu_\alpha = (0,0)'$, $\mu_\beta = 0$, $\Sigma_\alpha = diag\{1,000, 1,000\}$ and $\Sigma_\beta = 1,000$. On the contrary, for $P(v)$, we take $\lambda = 0.01$ and $\delta = 2$. The parameter α_0 is an intercept term that ensures that the volatility is never equal to zero.

In Table 10.1, we can discern that for larger k, the mean of α_0 shifts closer to 0. This is expected, as for larger k, $Y_{i,t}$ accounts for less and less of the total variation in the data. The role of α_1, on the contrary, is to approximate the degree to which the conditional volatility reacts to market shocks. According to Alexander (2008) (see section III.4.5.6), when α_1 is around 0.1 or larger, then the volatility is said to be sensitive to market events. In Table 10.1, it can be seen that at least until the 11th PC, the mean for α_1 has an HPD interval that is greater than 0.1, indicating that the earlier PCs are rather sensitive to market events. However, it can be seen that for $k = 36$, the density of α_1 shifts closer to zero, indicating that for larger k, dynamic

PCs lose their sensitivity. In fact, from the 31st PC onwards, (see Bonello et al. (2022)), the HPD interval for α_1 lies completely below 0.1. Similar to the previous discussion, since the later PCs explain less of the total variation in the data, the variation due to market events becomes miniscule. In fact, for dimension reduction purposes, we hope that such important variation is fully explained by a small number of the earlier PCs. β represents the degree to which the volatility of the last period affects the next period's volatility. As shown in Table 10.1, the HPD intervals for $k = 4$ and $k = 11$ are similar, with relatively high numbers. Interestingly, the HPD intervals for β have similar ranges up until the 21st PC. The parameter ν is responsible for the heavy tails of the distribution and is a crucial component in accounting for the leptokurtosis that is present in financial data. In the model, the role of the degrees of freedom parameter ν is to magnify the effect of the conditional variance. In Table 10.1, it can be seen that for larger k, the HPD intervals become elongated and the corresponding empirical probability density function indicates more dispersion. For further inspection, trace plots and EPDF plots for these parameters can be found in Bonello et al. (2022). From the higher-order PCs, it was found that the chains for β do not converge, and so the resulting EPDF plot is not accurate. The chains also indicate instability for higher-order PCs when it comes to ν.

	4th PC	11th PC	36th PC
Mean (α_0)	15.87×10^{-5}	6.73×10^{-5}	6.67×10^{-5}
Standard deviation (α_0)	4.11×10^{-5}	2.22×10^{-5}	1.80×10^{-5}
95% HPD LB (α_0)	8.46×10^{-5}	2.98×10^{-5}	3.07×10^{-5}
95% HPD UB (α_0)	23.68×10^{-5}	11.06×10^{-5}	9.60×10^{-5}
Mean (α_1)	0.1605	0.1286	0.0327
Standard deviation (α_1)	0.0279	0.0287	0.0254
95% HPD LB (α_1)	0.1132	0.0777	1.07×10^{-5}
95% HPD UB (α_1)	0.2210	0.1878	0.0819
Mean (β)	0.7578	0.7654	0.2671
Standard deviation (β)	0.0382	0.0541	0.1834
95% HPD LB (β)	0.6834	0.6598	0.0002
95% HPD UB (β)	0.8271	0.8579	0.6174
Mean (ν)	10.9650	24.2921	23.1302
Standard deviation (ν)	2.8084	23.4420	17.8266
95% HPD LB (ν)	6.5518	6.6321	6.8372
95% HPD U.P. (ν)	16.7609	76.1065	61.0999

Table 10.1. *Mean, standard deviation and HPD interval for the 5,000 realizations generated from the posterior distribution of $\alpha_0, \alpha_1, \beta$ and ν for the PCs $\hat{Y}_{4,t}, \hat{Y}_{11,t}$, and $\hat{Y}_{36,t}$. Complete results for all PCs can be found in Bonello et al. (2022)*

Now that an MCMC sample for each parameter has been generated, it is possible to move on to constructing forecasts for the given portfolio. Firstly, however, the theoretical framework for these forecasts is initially provided in section 10.5.

10.5. Forecasting and risk estimation

In this section, the procedure for obtaining forecasts for each PC is introduced, which are then transformed into forecasts for log returns of each asset. Finally, these are converted to asset prices, and ultimately, the value of the portfolio. We can then apply the "direct" approach on these forecasts to estimate VaR and ES. Consider G estimated MCMC realizations. Then, for each $\alpha_0^{(g)}$, $\alpha_1^{(g)}$, $\beta^{(g)}$, and $v^{(g)}$, we can obtain the following forecasts for the dynamic PCs:

$$\hat{Y}_{i,T+m}^{(g)} = Z_{i,T+m}^{(g)} \left(\frac{\hat{v}_{(i)}^{(g)}-2}{\hat{v}_{(i)}^{(g)}} \omega_{i,T+m}^{(g)} \hat{\sigma}_{i,T+m}^2 {}^{(g)} \right)^{\frac{1}{2}}, \ Z_{i,T+m}^{(g)} \overset{iid}{\sim} N(0,1), \ \omega_{i,T+m}^{(g)} \overset{iid}{\sim} IG \left(\frac{\hat{v}_{(i)}^{(g)}}{2}, \frac{\hat{v}_{(i)}^{(g)}}{2} \right)$$

and $\hat{\sigma}_{i,T+m}^2 {}^{(g)} = \hat{\alpha}_{0(i)}^{(g)} + \hat{\alpha}_{1(i)}^{(g)} \hat{Y}_{i,T+m-1}^{(g)} {}^2 + \hat{\beta}_{(i)}^{(g)} \hat{\sigma}_{i,T+m-1}^2 {}^{(g)}$ for $g = 1, 2, \dots, G$ and $m = 1, 2, \dots, M$, where $\hat{Y}_{i,T}^{(g)} \equiv \hat{Y}_{i,T}$. Furthermore, from $\hat{Y}_{i,T+m}^{(g)}$, the forecasts $\hat{X}_{i,T+m}^{(g)}, m = 1, \dots, M$ of the log returns of the original assets are retrieved for a specified number of dynamic PCs using the Karhunen–Loève expansion in (6). Consequently, from these, the forecasts of the prices $\hat{P}_{i,T+m}^{(g)}, m = 1, \dots, M$ are easily recovered. Finally, we can obtain forecasts for the value of the portfolio by assigning the relevant weightings, $\tau_1, \dots, \tau_p$, to each asset

$$\hat{V}_{T+m}^{(g)} = \tau_1 \hat{P}_{1,T+m}^{(g)} + \tau_2 \hat{P}_{2,T+m}^{(g)} + \dots + \tau_p \hat{P}_{p,T+m}^{(g)}$$

for $m = 1, \dots, M$. The simulated sample of size G of the given portfolio's value at time $T + m$ is combined into a vector, i.e. $\hat{\mathbf{V}}_{T+m} := \left(\hat{V}_{T+m}^{(1)}, \hat{V}_{T+m}^{(2)}, \dots, \hat{V}_{T+m}^{(G)} \right)'$ for $m = 1, \dots, M$, with which we can calculate the m-step ahead Bayesian estimation of VaR and ES. The direct approach in Hoogerheide and van Dijk (2010) is used. This approach involves obtaining the forecasted loss at time $T + m$. In order to do this, we may simply calculate $\hat{L}_{T+m}^{(g)} = \hat{V}_{T+m}^{(g)} - V_T$ for all $g = 1, \dots G$. Thus, at the confidence level $\alpha \in (0,1)$, the m-step ahead estimate for the VaR of the given portfolio will be obtained through the sample α-quantile q_α obtained from $\hat{\mathbf{L}}_{T+m} = \left(\hat{L}_{T+m}^{(1)}, \hat{L}_{T+m}^{(2)}, \dots, \hat{L}_{T+m}^{(G)} \right)'$: $\widehat{VaR}_\alpha(\mathbf{L}_{T+m}) = -q_\alpha(\hat{\mathbf{L}}_{T+m})$. The m-step ahead estimate for the ES of the given portfolio can be obtained as follows: $\widehat{ES}_\alpha(\mathbf{L}_{T+m}) =$

$$-\frac{1}{\alpha} \left\{ \frac{\sum_{g=1}^G \hat{L}_{T+m}^{(g)} \mathbb{1}_{\left\{ \hat{L}_{T+m}^{(g)} \leq \hat{q}_\alpha(\mathbf{L}_{T+m}) \right\}}}{\sum_{g=1}^G \mathbb{1}_{\left\{ \hat{L}_{T+m}^{(g)} \leq \hat{q}_\alpha(\mathbf{L}_{T+m}) \right\}}} \right\}.$$

The implementation of the forecast of the value of the portfolio for $k = 4, k = 11$ and $k = 36$ shall now be seen. Consequently, the value at risk and expected shortfall for different time horizons are estimated. Due to space limitations, the forecasts of $\hat{\sigma}^{2}_{i,T+m}{}^{(g)}$ and $\hat{P}^{(g)}_{i,T+m}$ are neither displayed here nor are displayed in Bonello et al. (2022), but they can be requested from the authors if needed. The typical portfolio weightings that were provided to the authors by a hedge fund company also included the number of units to invest into each asset, and these can also be accessed in the same link. These weightings are a combination of buy and short positions. A short position means that we are borrowing the asset from a financial institution such that a fall in the price of the asset that we have shorted will increase the value of the given portfolio. In total, on September 10, 2015, -€111,992,327 have been invested in this portfolio. To gain some insight into the portfolio, the reader is referred to Figure 10.2, which shows how the value of the portfolio has changed over the five year period. Note that there was a huge spike in value at the beginning of 2016, which is a direct result of the fluctuations of one particular asset that has a very large weighting in the given portfolio, namely SPMR.MI in which a short position of $-750,003$ units is held, but otherwise it is relatively stable.

Figure 10.2. *The value of the given portfolio over the past five years*

$\hat{V}_{1186+1}$	$k = 4$	$k = 11$	$k = 36$
Mean	−30,598,530	−30,598,530	−30,598,530
Standard deviation	87,127.01	142,472.90	226,486.40
95% HPD LB	−30,766,041	−30,670,470	−30,744,850
95% HPD UB	−30,425,646	−30,112,297	−29,866,495
$\hat{V}_{1186+5}$	$k = 4$	$k = 11$	$k = 36$
Mean	−30,826,255	−30,459,983	−30,320,170
Standard deviation	321,099	473,519	609,058
95% HPD LB	−31,491,554	−31,356,762	−31,498,444
95% HPD UB	−30,222,764	−29,515,981	−29,141,408

Table 10.2. *Mean, standard deviation and HPD interval for the 5,000 realizations of the 1- and 5-step ahead value of the given portfolio when taking $k = 4, k = 11$ and $k = 36$ dynamic PCs*

Table 10.2 shows the descriptive statistics for the distributions of $\widehat{\mathbf{V}}_{1186+1}$ and $\widehat{\mathbf{V}}_{1186+5}$, respectively. EPDF plots for $\widehat{V}_{1186+m}$ for $m = 1, ... , 5$ when taking $k = 4, k = 11$ and $k = 36$ are provided in Bonello et al. (2022). Furthermore, as we take more PCs, more variation in the dataset becomes accounted for. As a result, the standard deviation of the forecasted portfolio value increases with the number of PCs, capturing the true variation of the portfolio. Finally, in Table 10.3, measures of risk at different time horizons are estimated. To do this, the losses/gains experienced for each MCMC realization when compared to V_{1186} are extracted, and $\widehat{VaR}_\alpha(\mathbf{L}_{T+m})$ and $\widehat{ES}_\alpha(\mathbf{L}_{T+m})$ are extracted. When analyzing Table 10.3, a clear discrepancy between the estimations using different k's is noted; however, this is not surprising. Models with a higher number of dynamic PCs account for more variation of the original portfolio, which consequently increases VaR and ES.

	No. of PCs	Estimated $VaR_{0.05}$	Estimated ES
	4	−4.64%	−4.79%
One-day ahead	11	−5.65%	−5.91%
	36	−6.62%	−7.03%
	4	−5.31%	−5.85%
Five-day ahead	11	−7.55%	−8.26%
	36	−9.30%	−10.31%
	4	−6.01%	−6.85%
10-day ahead	11	−9.49%	−10.71%
	36	−11.45%	−13.08%
	4	−10.44%	−12.48%
50-day ahead	11	−16.31%	−19.37%
	36	−21.97%	−25.93%
	4	−13.26%	−16.06%
100-day ahead	11	−21.11%	−25.06%
	36	−28.37%	−33.65%

Table 10.3. *Estimated 1-, 5-, 10-, 50- and 100-day ahead $VaR_{0.05}$ and ES when taking $k = 4, k = 11$ and $k = 36$ dynamic PCs. The percentages reflect the estimated fluctuations from the last observed value of the portfolio, i.e. V_{1186}*

In the following section, the different models will be put to the test by comparing them with actual future values and checking the performance between different dynamic PCs.

10.6. Measuring predictive ability

Since the main aim of the analysis here is to find a model that can adequately predict future risks, we need to evaluate the predictive ability of the Bayesian models fitted. This was done by applying a method that mimics the idea of cross-validation methods popularly applied in non-time series statistical models. You may recall from the previous section that we fitted the different models on a portfolio whose assets were observed between September 10, 2015 and September 10, 2020. We shall refer to these series as the training set. The observations between September 11, 2020 and May 4, 2021 will be used as the validation set, where all assets in the portfolio were simultaneously observed for a total of 135 days. The models for $k = 4, k = 11$ and $k = 36$ shall be forward-tested and compared. The models fitted are used to obtain simulated paths, denoted by $\widehat{\mathbb{V}} = \{\widehat{\mathbf{V}}_{1186+1}, \dots, \widehat{\mathbf{V}}_{1186+135}\}$, and these are compared to the actual values making up the validation set, denoted by $\mathbf{V} = \{V_{1186+1}, \dots, V_{1186+135}\}$. Figure 10.3 shows $\widehat{\mathbb{V}}$ and $\mathbf{V}$ for all models.

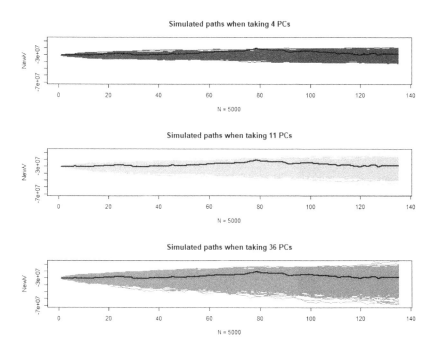

Figure 10.3. *The red, blue and green colored paths represent the 5,000 simulated paths forecasted until May 4, 2021 when taking $k = 4, k = 11$ and $k = 36$ dynamic PCs. The black path represents the true value of the given portfolio from September 10, 2020 to May 4, 2021. For a color version of this figure, see www.iste.co.uk/ dimotikalis/data3.zip*

	4 PCs	11 PCs	36 PCs
log PsML	−2338.27	−2210.67	−2213.38

Table 10.4. *Displaying the log PsML for the model when taking $k = 4, k = 11$ and $k = 36$ dynamic PCs*

Using the terminology given in Gelfand et al. (1992), the posterior probability of observing V_{1186+m} is referred to as the conditional predictive ordinate (CPO). We can denote the CPO as $p(V_{1186+m}|\widehat{V}_{1186+m})$ for $m = 1, ..., 135$. Higher CPO values are an indication of a better predictive ability. To measure the predictive ability of the entire model, Congdon (2007) suggests looking at the product of the CPOs $\hat{p}(\mathbf{V}) = \prod_{m=1}^{135} p(V_{1186+m}|\widehat{V}_{1186+m})$. This is referred to as the pseudomarginal likelihood (PsML). It may sometimes be easier to calculate the log PsML, given by $\log \hat{p}(\mathbf{V}) = \sum_{m=1}^{135} \log p(V_{1186+m}|\widehat{V}_{1186+m})$ where the larger the log PsML, the better the predictive ability. By comparing the spread of the paths when taking different PCs in Figure 10.3, we note that the more PCs we take, the more conservative the model becomes, with the paths taking on a larger spread. As a result, during stable market conditions, we should expect a lower PC model to still perform well. Table 10.4 shows the log PsML for the different models. Since the log PsML is lowest when four PCs are taken, we may conclude that it has the worst predictive ability. The fact that the four PCs model performed the worst on the validation set (not used in the model fit) even though the value of the portfolio did not experience any extreme variation allows us to conclude that not enough variation of the original dataset is being accounted for when taking few PCs. Interestingly, the 11 PC model slightly outperforms the 36 PC model, when compared to the true observations. While this may simply be due to the fact that the 135 observation validation set does not represent any unstable market conditions, it is a possibility that the additional PCs did not represent a significant source of variation and may have therefore caused only a slight detrimental effect to the model. However, it must also be noted that the difference between log PsML when $k = 11$ and log PsML when $k = 36$ is marginal, compared to the considerably inferior log PsML when $k = 4$ case. Of course, this result is valid only for this particular validation set, and considering different time periods and different portfolios may yield different outcomes. However, it is encouraging that we may still get higher predictive ability with a much-reduced dimension.

10.7. Conclusion

In this study, a Bayesian approach to measuring the risk on portfolios with many assets is taken. The idea behind this study is to adopt a dimension reduction approach whereby the orthogonal series can be modeled independently, rather than dealing with the dependency dynamics of multivariate approaches that can become unwieldy when processing a large number of assets. Inevitably, however, when dealing with a model in reduced dimension, some of the variation of the original portfolio may be lost. We have seen that this may not necessarily lead to an inferior model; indeed, it was found that for the validation dataset, the best predictive ability was that of the model considering 11 dynamic PCs. The model considering 36 dynamics PCs, on the contrary, was only marginally inferior. Furthermore, the MCMC algorithm was found to be less stable when modeling dynamic PCs of a higher order, although this was not expected to have a major impact on the results, as higher-order PCs account for a very small proportion of the variation. Further research in this direction that can be undertaken is to consider Bayesian models (of the GARCH type or otherwise) that take into account asymmetry in the distribution when it comes to positive and negative shocks, as the Bayesian GARCH(1,1) does not, and to examine whether the above methodology of modeling many assets can be extended to the portfolio optimization problem.

10.8. Acknowledgments

We would like to thank Mr. George Camilleri, a risk management professional, for his contributions to this study.

10.9. References

Alexander, C. (2003). Principal component models for generating large GARCH covariance matrices. *Economic Notes*, 31, 337–359. doi: 10.1111/1468-0300.00089.

Alexander, C. (2008). *Market Analysis III: Pricing, Hedging and Trading Financial Instruments*. John Wiley & Sons, New York.

Ardia, D. (2008). *Financial Risk Management with Bayesian Estimation of GARCH Models: Theory and Applications*. Springer-Verlag, Berlin, Heidelberg.

Ardia, D. and Hoogerheide, L. (2010). Bayesian estimation of the GARCH(1,1) model with student-t innovations. Tingbergen Institute Discussion Papers, 2. doi: 10.32614/RJ-2010-014.

Artzner, P., Delbaen, F., Jean-Marc, E., Heath, D. (1999). Coherent measures of risk. *Mathematical Finance*, 9, 203–228. doi: 10.1111/1467-9965.00068.

Bollerslev, T. (1987). A conditionally heteroskedastic time series model for speculative prices and rates of return. *The Review of Economics and Statistics*, 69(3), 542–547. doi: 10.2307/1925546.

Bonello, S., Suda, D., Borg Inguanez, M. (2022). Supplementary material for paper. A Bayesian approach to measuring risk on portfolios with many assets [Online]. Available at: https://github.com/davidsuda80/bonello_suda_inguanez [Accessed 5 July 2022].

Brillinger, D.R. (1975). *Time Series: Data Analysis and Theory*. Society for Industrial and Applied Mathematics, Philadelphia.

Brillinger, D.R. (1981). *Time Series: Data Analysis and Theory*, expanded edition. Holden-Day, New York.

Brockwell, P.J. and Davis, R.A. (1991). *Time Series: Theory and Methods*, 2nd edition. Springer-Verlag, Berlin, Heidelberg.

Congdon, P. (2007). *Bayesian Statistical Modelling*. John Wiley & Sons, New York.

Galeano, P. and Ausín, C. (2010). The gaussian mixture dynamic conditional correlation model: Parameter estimation, value at risk calculation, and portfolio selection. *Journal of Business & Economic Statistics*, 28, 559–571. doi: 10.1198/jbes.2009.07238.

Gelfand, A., Dey, D., Chang, H. (1992). Model determination using predictive distributions with implementation via sampling-based methods. In *Bayesian Statistics: Proceedings of the Fourth Valencia International Meeting*, April 15–20, 147–167.

Hoogerheide, L. and van Dijk, H.K. (2010). Bayesian forecasting of value at risk and expected shortfall using adaptive importance sampling. *International Journal of Forecasting*, 26(2), 231–247. doi: 10.1016/j.ijforecast.2010.01.007.

Hörmann, S. and Kidziński, Ł. (2022). Package 'freqdom'. CRAN. doi: 10.1111/rssb.12076.

Hörmann, S., Kidziński, Ł., Hallin, M. (2015). Dynamic functional principal components. *Journal of the Royal Statistical Society, Series B (Statistical Methodology)*, 77(2), 319–348. doi: 10.17877/DE290R-4881.

Orskaug, E. (2009). Multivariate DCC-GARCH Model: With various error distributions. Master's Thesis, Norwegian Computing Center, Accession Order No. SAMBA/19/09.

Tsay, R.S. (2010). *Analysis of Financial Time Series*. John Wiley & Sons, New York.

Virbickaite, A., Ausín, M.C., Galeano, P. (2015). Bayesian inference methods for univariate and multivariate garch models: A survey. *Journal of Economic Surveys*, 29(1), 76–96. doi: 10.1111/joes.12046.

11

Financial Management of Four Hellenic Public Health Units. Analysis and Evaluation through Numerical Indicators

The Covid-19 outbreak spread in 2020 to become the most severe pandemic in the last 100 years. The public health crisis has led to a major economic crisis, which will have serious consequences on individual and societal well-being, both now and in the future. Covid-19 has exposed latent healthcare system fragilities that existed before the outbreak. This chapter studies the financial results, operating costs and the production of services of four public hospitals, which are General Hospital of "Rhodes", General Hospital of "Chios", General Hospital of "Syros" and General Hospital of "Kythira". They all belong to island areas of Greece and are under the administrative control of the 2nd Regional Health Authority of Piraeus & North Aegean. The study covers the period of 2017–2020 and is carried out using financial ratios and the financial data of hospital financial statements. The main sources of data were hospital financial reports issued in the program "Diavgeia" on the above periodic basis, General Hospitals' websites, as well as Greek and foreign bibliography – articles. The purpose of the study is to interpret the skills of hospitals, during the period of adjustment from the crisis, to maintain necessary liquidity, generate profits and also the efficient use of human and material resources. The analyses results showed that public hospitals managed to survive through regular funding of the state and not from the delayed up to three years of compensation of the EOPYY (National Organization of Providing Health Services), to increase their performance and make more effective use of the available resources.

Chapter written by Maria SACHINIDOU and George MATALLIOTAKIS.

For a color version of all the figures in this chapter, see www.iste.co.uk/dimotikalis/data3.zip.

11.1. Introduction

The economic crisis, from the years 2008–2019, in which Greece presented huge deficits and external borrowing problems, catalyzed and inevitably affected the public health sector; in particular, the operation and efficiency of public hospitals. Consequences such as the limitation of available resources and costs, combined with a parallel increase in the demand for better quality and more efficient health services for citizens, led to the adoption of a series of structural changes in the NHS. The most important of these was the institutionalization of the National Organization for Health Care Services EOPYY, the purpose of which was the correct management of insurance contributions as a single insurance fund; later, this became the sole provider of the healthcare system, always supported by state funding.

Adding to this unstable economic environment was the migration crisis that affected the operations of hospitals, especially in island regions, and culminated in the emergence of the SARS-CoV-2 virus pandemic at the beginning of 2020; this contributed to the strengthening of financial difficulties of the healthcare system worldwide.

11.2. Theoretical framework

Numerators indicators are an important tool for the analysis of financial statements. According to the Presidential Decree 1123/1980, Official Gazette A 283/15.12.1980 of the General Chart of Accounts, "indicators are relationships between quantities of accounting or statistical origin" that aim to determine the actual position or efficiency of the economic unit, or in a more general context of the industry to which this unit belongs (Ministry of Finance and Trade and Coordination 1980). Essentially, it is a mathematical number that represents the ratio between two values and can be expressed as a ratio, percentage or fraction.

This is considered an excellent tool for studying and interpreting financial statements, helping all groups of stakeholders to gain knowledge about the financial situation and profitability of the financial unit, in order to make the necessary and correct decisions (Carmichael and Willingham 2000). At the same time, it is a key tool for analysts, depicts the numerical status of the economic unit, provides the possibility of identifying and correcting the weaknesses of the unit, and facilitates the comparison of information in relation to equivalent units with the previous period or the period as a whole (Andjelic and Vesic 2017).

11.3. Methodology

This chapter studies the financial results, operating costs and the production of services of four public hospitals, which are General Hospital of "Rhodes", General Hospital of "Chios", General Hospital of "Syros" and General Hospital of "Kythira". These all belong to island areas of Greece and are under the administrative control of the 2nd Regional Health Authority of Piraeus & North Aegean. Conclusions can be drawn about the effectiveness of management in these hospitals in the period of the economic crisis, the immigration crisis faced by the Aegean islands, and the incipient health crisis since the beginning of 2020, due to the emergence of the Covid-19 pandemic.

For the analysis of the financial statements, the published financial statements of the hospitals for a four-year period, specifically for the years 2017–2020, were used. Conclusions will be deduced concerning effectiveness from the analysis of the temporal trend of the indicators, both per hospital and for the average of the five hospitals selected in the sample, whilst it was chosen to perform a statistical analysis using measures of location (means) and dispersion (standard deviation). The analysis will be performed using the tool of numerators indicators, and the results will be presented both in the form of tables and with a diagrammatic display, so that there is also a visual image of the long-term trends, if and where they exist.

11.4. Research results

11.4.1. *Liquidity indicators*

11.4.1.1. *Indirect or general liquidity indicator*

According to the data in Table 11.1 and Figure 11.1, which show the intertemporal evolution of the indirect or general liquidity index over time, it is established that the general liquidity index has a value much higher than two, both in all the hospitals of the sample and in all of its study years. Therefore, with the existing liquidity, the short-term liabilities are satisfactorily met. However, the very high index of the General Hospital of Syros raises questions regarding the possible investment of existing funding in more productive sectors.

More specifically, in 2018, all hospitals show an increase in the prices of the index. This increase in the indicator trend is mainly influenced by the reduced short-term liabilities. At the same time, the indicators in all hospitals are interesting in 2019, where they show a large decrease compared to 2018, which is justified by the increase in hospital liabilities – most likely due to the outbreak of the Covid-19 pandemic at the beginning of 2020.

	Hospital/year	2017	2018	2019	2020	Average 2017–2020	Standard deviation
1	General Hospital of **Rhodes**	9.54	10.93	5.64	6.65	8.19	2.13
2	General Hospital of **Chios**	11.87	13.25	8.23	10.89	11.06	1.84
3	General Hospital of **Siros**	11.15	15.3	10.65	11.02	12.03	1.9
4	General Hospital – Health Center of **Kithira**	2.95	7.57	5.48	11.94	6.99	3.3
	General average	8.88	11.76	7.50	10.13	9.57	2.29

Table 11.1. *Current ratios*

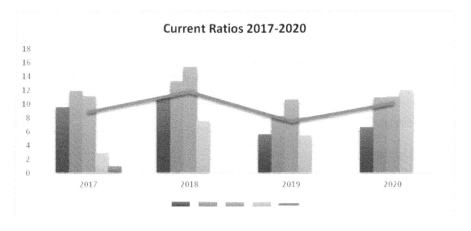

Figure 11.1. *Current ratios 2017–2020*

11.4.1.2. *Direct or special liquidity indicator*

Table 11.2 and Figure 11.2 show the intertemporal evolution of the direct or specific liquidity ratio over time, the meaning of which is limited to current assets that are liquidated faster (cash, deposits and debt securities) with the aim of repaying overdue liabilities.

At a quick glance at the sample hospitals, the indices appear quite satisfactory and much higher than the safety value of 1.75 for the public hospitals, with the prices average of the General Hospital of Syros showing the highest value (11.49) and the Kythera General Hospital the lowest (6.90), a fact that demonstrates the coverage of their short-term obligations with great ease. In addition, the high values of the index are considered as completely natural for the public hospitals which hold the majority of the assets in deposits and cash, while they do not show an investment portfolio (shares, bonds).

Particular interest is presented in 2019 where there is a decrease in the prices of the index in all hospitals with the largest change being recorded at the General Hospital of Rhodes by −94.8%, while in 2020, the majority of hospitals show an increasing trend.

	Hospital/year	2017	2018	2019	2020	Average 2017–2020	Standard deviation
1	General Hospital of **Rhodes**	9.15	10.54	5.41	6.45	7.89	2.37
2	General Hospital of **Chios**	11.5	12.95	7.95	10.5	10.73	2.11
3	General Hospital of **Siros**	10.56	14.66	10.24	10.49	11.49	2.12
4	General Hospital – Health Center of **Kithira**	4.79	6.98	4.88	10.93	6.9	2.87
	General average	9.00	11.28	7.12	9.59	9.25	2.37

Table 11.2. *Quick ratios*

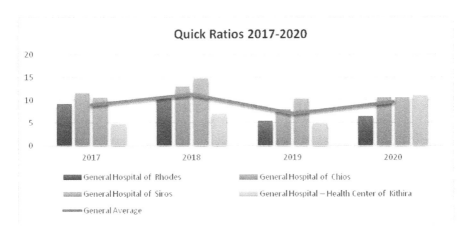

Figure 11.2. *Quick ratios 2017–2020*

11.4.1.3. *Cash liquidity indicator*

Table 11.3 and Figure 11.3 show the intertemporal evolution of the cash flow ratio, which helps to capture the ability of a hospital to repay its immediate liabilities in cash.

The lowest value of the index appears in the General Hospital of Chios (0.78) and the highest in the General Hospital of Kythera (5.55). Also, it is not a clear indication to support an inability to meet their short-term obligations, as this is due to the existence of requirements that far exceed the obligations. Finally, it is important that short-term liabilities are recycled and creditworthy entities are characterized by the credit limits they set in their partnerships with suppliers and banks.

Examining the period 2019–2020, it is found that the cash available shows a decrease in all hospitals – except the General Hospital of Kythira in relation to liabilities, which may be justified by the increase in claims from hospital insurance funds and the fact that hospitals did not receive the state grants until the end of 2019.

	Hospital/year	2017	2018	2019	2020	Average 2017–2020	Standard deviation
1	General Hospital of **Rhodes**	2.34	1.74	1.27	0.93	1.57	0.61
2	General Hospital of **Chios**	1.96	1.72	1.13	0.78	1.40	0.54
3	General Hospital of **Siros**	3.79	4.19	3.7	2.8	3.62	0.59
4	General Hospital – Health Center of **Kithira**	1.83	1.93	2.49	5.55	2.95	1.76
	General average	2.48	2.40	2.15	2.52	2.38	0.87

Table 11.3. *Cash ratios*

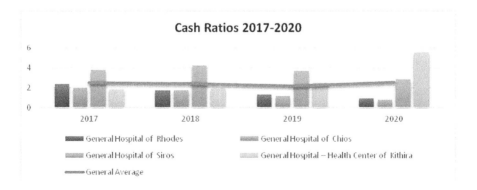

Figure 11.3. *Cash ratios 2017–2020*

11.4.2. *Activity ratios*

11.4.2.1. *Receivable turnover ratios and average collection period*

The rate of collection of receivables from services is a particularly important indicator for public hospitals, since the main buyer of their services is EOPYY, which makes them weak in forcing the institution to fixed payment policies.

As observed in Table 11.4 and Figure 11.4, the value of Receivable Turnover Ratio remains almost constant over time and around the sample average. In all of the sample hospitals for the period 2017–2020, the prices of the index are much lower than the unit, with the lowest price showing at the hospitals of Rhodes and Chios (0.35) and the highest the General Hospital of Syros (0.78).

However, observing Table 11.5 and Figure 11.5 showing the Average Collection Period, it is found that during the period 2017–2020, most hospitals are around the general sample average, which is 808.62 days.

The General Hospital of Kythera shows the fewest days of collection of receivables (654.29), while the General Hospital of Rhodes the most (942.11), approximately 2.6 years, a period that is considered excessive for the collection of revenues for the services provided.

	Hospital/year	2017	2018	2019	2020	Average 2017–2020	Standard deviation
1	General Hospital of **Rhodes**	0.35	0.41	0.43	0.37	0.39	0.04
2	General Hospital of **Chios**	0.43	0.40	0.43	0.35	0.40	0.04
3	General Hospital of **Siros**	0.78	0.52	0.46	0.40	0.54	0.17
4	General Hospital – Health Center of **Kithira**	0.75	0.43	0.50	0.68	0.59	0.15
	General average	0.58	0.44	0.46	0.45	0.48	0.10

Table 11.4. *Receivable turnover ratio 2017–2020*

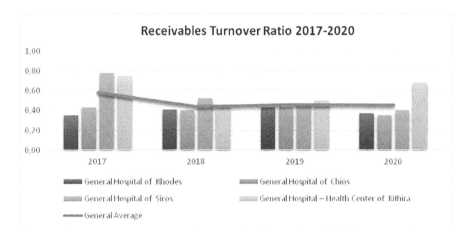

Figure 11.4. *Receivable turnover ratio 2017–2020*

	Hospital/year	2017	2018	2019	2020	Average 2017–2020	Standard deviation
1	General Hospital of **Rhodes**	1042.86	890.24	848.84	986.49	942.11	88.52
2	General Hospital of **Chios**	848.84	912.50	848.84	1042.86	913.26	91.46
3	General Hospital of **Siros**	467.95	701.92	793.48	935.90	724.81	196.45
4	General Hospital – Health Center of **Kithira**	486.67	848.84	744.90	536.76	654.29	171.24
	General average	711.58	838.38	809.02	875.50	808.62	136.92

Table 11.5. *Average collection period 2017–2020*

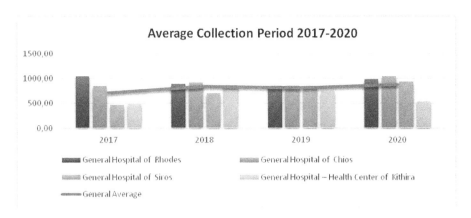

Figure 11.5. *Average collection period 2017–2020*

11.4.2.2. *Creditors payable turnover ratio and average payment period*

According to the data in Tables 11.6 and 11.7 and in Figures 11.6 and 11.7, there is a gradual annual increase of Creditors Payable Turnover Ratios (ATEBY) from 2017 to 2020 in the general average index of the four sample hospitals. However, while for the Payment Period, it shows some fluctuations between 2017 and 2020, in all years it is less than 90 days, a limit beyond which the outstanding liabilities are characterized as overdue. The General Hospital of Rhodes presents a long delay in the repayment of short-term liabilities in 2020, while the rest show better performance.

It is worth noting that the emerging improvement of the Creditors Payable Turnover Ratio is due to the ministerial decision 2/57103/DPG/29.06.2016 (Government Gazette B' 1932/29-06-2016), including its subsequent amendments related to the process of liquidation of overdue liabilities of hospitals and also to subsidizing them to repay their suppliers.

	Hospital/year	2017	2018	2019	2020	Average 2017–2020	Standard deviation
1	General Hospital of **Rhodes**	5.12	5.02	3.94	3.07	4.28	0.97
2	General Hospital of **Chios**	5.44	6.06	5.02	5.06	5.40	0.48
3	General Hospital of **Siros**	7.16	7.08	6.82	6.19	6.81	0.44
4	General Hospital – Health Center of **Kithira**	6.76	8.52	10.07	13.15	9.63	2.71
	General average	6.12	6.67	6.46	6.87	6.53	1.15

Table 11.6. *Creditors payable turnover ratios 2017–2020*

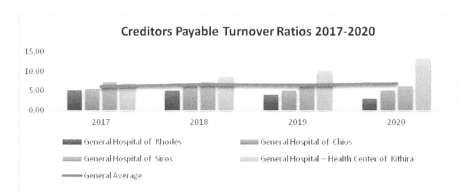

Figure 11.6. *Creditors payable turnover ratios 2017–2020*

At the same time, for the Average Payment Period, there is an increasing trend of the average of the four sample hospitals from 60.84 days in 2017 to 69.44 days in 2020 (14% increase).

By attempting a comparison of Tables 11.5 and 11.7 and the corresponding Figures 11.5 and 11.7, concerning the Average Collection Period and the Average Payment Period, it is initially observed that the Average Collection Period increased by 23% over the period considered 2017–2020, when the average of the Collection Period of the four sample hospitals increased from 711.58 days in 2017 to 875.50 days in 2020. The above data reflects the lack of required liquidity on the part of those involved for the operation of the financial system, such as businesses and households, in order to pay for the services provided, resulting in a continuous increase of the average credit periods.

	Hospital/year	2017	2018	2019	2020	Average 2017–2020	Standard deviation
1	General Hospital of **Rhodes**	71.29	72.71	92.64	118.89	88.88	22.25
2	General Hospital of **Chios**	67.10	60.23	72.71	72.13	68.04	5.79
3	General Hospital of **Siros**	50.98	51.55	53.52	58.97	53.76	3.64
4	General Hospital – Health Center of **Kithira**	53.99	42.84	36.25	27.76	40.21	11.07
	General average	60.84	56.83	63.78	69.44	62.72	10.69

Table 11.7. *Average payment period 2017–2020*

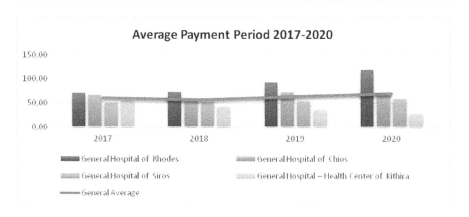

Figure 11.7. *Average payment period 2017–2020*

11.4.3. *Profitability ratios*

11.4.3.1. *Return on equity (ROE) ratios*

Table 11.8 and Figure 11.8 show the evolution of the return on equity (ROE) ratio over time, which in the case of public hospitals determines whether hospital management utilizes government funding provided by taxpayers' revenues. According to the data, the general average index does not show a specific trend; it shows large fluctuations from 2017 to 2020 while also showing a large standard deviation value (3.65).

	Hospital/year	2017	2018	2019	2020	Average 2017–2020	Standard deviation
1	General Hospital of **Rhodes**	1.84	8.29	−14.75	1.56	−0.77	8.51
2	General Hospital of **Chios**	4.61	10.24	11.3	7.13	8.32	2.63
3	General Hospital of **Siros**	8.25	7.43	5.93	3.29	6.23	1.89
4	General Hospital – Health Center of **Kithira**	1.08	−0.7	−2.6	1.34	−0.22	1.58
	General average	3.95	6.32	−0.03	3.33	3.39	3.65

Table 11.8. *Return on equity (ROE) ratios 2017–2020*

At the same time, in some sample hospitals, such as the General Hospital of Rhodes and Kythera, there are even negative values, which indicate problems of these hospitals in those time periods. These may be due to low productivity, inadequate management in terms of its response to adverse external economic conditions, and also to unproductive employment of capital.

The best average for all study years is observed at the General Hospital of Chios with a rate of 8.32%. Thus, although the price tends to be down after 2019, it is distinguished as the most efficient sample hospital that used the equity more effectively, while the hospitals of Rhodes and Kythera show negative prices.

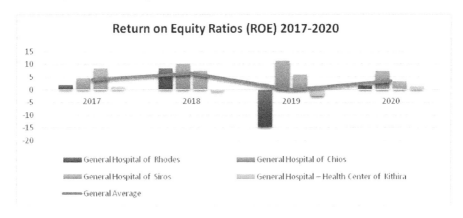

Figure 11.8. *Return on equity (ROE) ratios 2017–2020*

11.4.3.2. *Return on capital employed (ROCE)*

Studying the results of the Employee Capital Returns ratios of Table 11.9 and Figure 11.9, similar results are observed with the ROE ratios, such as negative values due to losses in some sample hospitals and large fluctuations of the ratios.

More specifically, the general hospital of Rhodes in 2019 shows a large negative value (−13.21); however, it recovers in 2020, presenting a satisfactory value of Return on Capital Employed (ROCE) of 1.39%, while the General Hospital of Kythira presents a declining trend with the average for the period 2017–2020 showing a negative value (−0.82%).

On the contrary, the General Hospital of Chios in 2019 presents an ideal value of ROCE of 10.2% due to proper investment of the management of total funds and the improvement of the use of employed capital, necessarily due to the pandemic outbreak of Covid-19.

	Hospital/year	2017	2018	2019	2020	Average 2017–2020	Standard deviation
1	General Hospital of **Rhodes**	1.71	7.79	−13.21	1.39	−0.58	8.92
2	General Hospital of **Chios**	4.28	9.55	10.2	6.58	7.65	2.75
3	General Hospital of **Siros**	7.76	6.94	5.38	2.99	5.77	2.10
4	General Hospital – Health Center of **Kithira**	1.02	−0.66	−2.42	−1.21	−0.82	1.43
	General average	3.69	5.91	−0.01	2.44	3.01	3.80

Table 11.9. *Return on capital employed (ROCE) ratios 2017–2020*

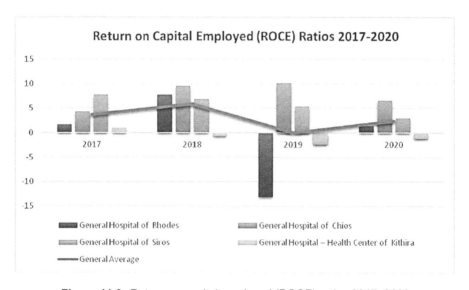

Figure 11.9. *Return on capital employed (ROCE) ratios 2017–2020*

11.4.4. *Capital adequacy and viability ratios*

11.4.4.1. *Debt-to-equity ratio*

This index aims to investigate an increased debt burden of a company or organization, which corresponds to the total funds used for operations and activities – in the present study, of hospitals.

Table 11.10 and Figure 11.10 show the evolution of the debt-to-equity ratios over time. According to the above data, in all of the examined hospitals throughout the four years, the Equity Funds exceed the Foreign Funds; therefore, the latter do not create problems in the hospitals. More specifically, the highest index is presented at the General Hospital of Kythera in 2020 (36.15), while the lowest is at the Hospital of Rhodes (8.73) at the same year.

The average of four hospitals for the four years is in all samples at quite high levels; however, in all hospitals in 2019, the indicators appear to have a downward trend, reducing the margin in Foreign Funds to cause insecurity to creditors for their repayment and showing credibility to shareholders. An exception is the General Hospital of Kythera, where it shows an increase of 69% in 2020.

The price of the general average sample from 2017 (18.12) to 2018 (18.70) remains at the same levels, although it fluctuates in the intermediate years. It is worth noting that all above prices show that the hospitals exceed their obligations multiple times, which is mainly due to the annual subsidies of the hospitals from the state budget, causing in turn an increase in their income or own funds, regardless of the accounting handling.

	Hospital/year	2017	2018	2019	2020	Average 2017–2020	Standard deviation
1	General Hospital of **Rhodes**	15.43	16.82	9.05	8.73	12.51	4.22
2	General Hospital of **Chios**	14.61	15.49	10.20	13.35	13.41	2.31
3	General Hospital of **Siros**	21.08	23.31	16.42	16.55	19.34	3.42
4	General Hospital – Health Center of **Kithira**	21.34	27.53	21.69	36.15	26.68	6.92
	General average	18.12	20.79	14.34	18.70	17.99	4.22

Table 11.10. *Dept-to-equity ratios 2017–2020*

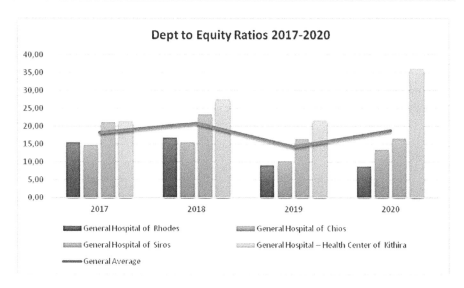

Figure 11.10. *Debt-to-equity ratios 2017–2020*

11.4.4.2. *Fixed assets cover ratios*

The Fixed Assets Cover Ratios provides information on how much hospital funds have been invested in their fixed assets. According to the calculations presented in Table 11.11 and Figure 11.11, the majority of Hospital Units show a positive result well above the unit, while the general average index appears to show an upward trend by 19.7% in 2018, and in 2020 remains at the same levels. The highest average index in the period 2017–2020 appears at the General Hospital of Chios with a price of 6.19, while the lowest price is held by Kythera (1.32).

	Hospital/year	2017	2018	2019	2020	Average 2017–2020	Standard deviation
1	General Hospital of **Rhodes**	2.6	3.17	2.77	3.14	2.92	0.28
2	General Hospital of **Chios**	5.64	6.89	5.58	6.65	6.19	0.68
3	General Hospital of **Siros**	2.2	2.61	2.33	2.51	2.41	0.18
4	General Hospital – Health Center of **Kithira**	1.37	1.46	1.23	1.32	1.35	0.10
	General average	2.95	3.53	2.98	3.41	3.22	0.31

Table 11.11. *Fixed assets cover ratios 2017–2020*

It is worth noting that the increased equity ratios of the Chios Hospital show that part of the working capital comes from equity and that the hospital has overinvested in fixed assets. However, they can also be due to government grants, where they increase equity or revenue. Finally, no hospital has a price lower than the unit, which means that none of them exceeds the Fixed Capital in relation to the Equity, so that their coverage requires the use of foreign capital.

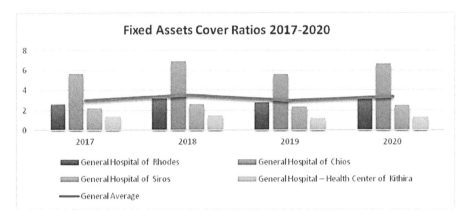

Figure 11.11. *Fixed assets cover ratios 2017–2020*

11.5. Conclusions

During the period under review, as before, a great effort was made to address chronic pathogens in Greece's National Health System (NSS) by enacting a variety of laws and regulations, while acting in parallel with the country's obligations to its creditors, creating horizontal funding cuts in the healthcare system. This fact, combined with the consequences of the refugee migration crisis, which acted as a catalyst in the hospitals of the island areas – aggravating their already difficult operating conditions – led the NSS to support a large number of citizens who no longer had insurance capacity.

According to the results of the financial analysis through financial ratios of the four public hospitals during the period 2017–2020, it is concluded:

– The majority of hospitals show a long-term tendency to improve Creditors Payable Turnover Ratios, a fact that may be due not only to government subsidies that acted positively on cash but also to the implementation of the ministerial decision on the process of liquidation of overdue liabilities falling below the legal 90 days, which deemed the debts overdue. In both cases, the dependent relationship between the Hospital Units with the state subsidy and the EOPYY is clearly visible.

– The very slow collection of receivables compared to the repayment time of their liabilities demonstrates the inefficiency of the administrations of the four hospitals in the sample in managing the credit policy, since an effective management should present the values of the two ratios approximately equal. As a result of all of the above, hospitals are being driven into financial straits and need additional government funding to cover the claims that have not been collected, which leads to a burden on the state budget.

– The Average Collection Period is much longer than the Average Payment Period of short-term liabilities; therefore, hospitals are forced to maintain large amounts of current asset as they are dependent on the credit policy of their suppliers. As a result, they have a reduced bargaining power, while in case of supply of suppliers, they present a risk of increasing production costs, acting as an urgent need for administrative actions in order to speed up the collection of receivables and to make overall scheduling of receivables – liabilities. Therefore, it is particularly important not only to ensure faster submission of hospitalizations to EOPYY but also for the management of EOPYY to take correct actions in order to pay the compensations to the hospitals faster.

11.6. References

Andjelic, S. and Vesic, T. (2017). The importance of financial analysis for business decision making. In *Finance, Banking and Insurance*. Faculty of Business Economics and Entrepreneurship, Belgrade.

Carmichael, D.R. and Willingham, J.J. (2000). *Auditing Concepts and Methods: A Guide to Current Auditing Theory and Practice*, 5th edition. McGraw-Hill, New York.

Greek Republic. Ministry of Finance and Trade and Coordination (1980). Definition of the Content and the Start Time of the Optional Application of the General Chart of Accounts. Ministry of Finance and Trade and Coordination, Athens.

Ministry of Health (n.d.). [Online]. Available at: https://www.moh.gov.gr/articles/newspaper/oikonomikes-katastaseis-nosokomeiwn/2h-ype.

Presidential Decree 1123/1980, Official Gazette A' 283/15.12.1980 of the General Chart of Accounts "Indicators are Relationships Between Quantities of Accounting or Statistical Origin" (FEK A' 283/15.12.1980).

Balance Sheet G.H RHODES 31/12/2017

Balance Sheet G.H RHODES 31/12/2018

Balance Sheet G.H RHODES 31/12/2019

Balance Sheet G.H RHODES 31/12/2020

Balance Sheet G.H CHIOS 31/12/2017

Balance Sheet G.H CHIOS 31/12/2018

Balance Sheet G.H CHIOS 31/12/2019

Balance Sheet G.H CHIOS 31/12/2020

Balance Sheet G.H SYROS 31/12/2017

Balance Sheet G.H SYROS 31/12/2018

Balance Sheet G.H SYROS 31/12/2019

Balance Sheet G.H SYROS 31/12/2020

Balance Sheet G.H KITHIRA 31/12/2017

Balance Sheet G.H KITHIRA 31/12/2018

Balance Sheet G.H KITHIRA 31/12/2019

Balance Sheet G.H KITHIRA 31/12/2020

PART 4

Health Services

12

Lean Management as an Improvement Factor in Health Services. The Case of Venizeleio General Hospital of Crete, Greece

In recent years, the issue of lean management has been of great concern to the health sector, as its previous application in other sectors has shown how significant the benefits it can bring are for the organizations that adopt it. The work examines the degree of application of the simple management in the health units of Greece and specifically in the Venizeleio General Hospital of Heraklion, Crete, examining the views of the employees.

The research sample consisted of 83 employees of the Venizeleio General Hospital of Heraklion, Crete, who were selected according to the convenient sampling. The research method used was quantitative and the research tool used was the questionnaire. The research data were analyzed according to the SPSS statistical package.

The results of the research showed that the Venizeleio General Hospital of Heraklion, Crete, has adopted and applies the principles of simple management to a significant degree. It was also found that employees have knowledge of simple management issues, while understanding the benefits of its implementation. In addition, the hospital staff are positive about acquiring additional knowledge about simple management.

Chapter written by Eleni GENITSARIDI and George MATALLIOTAKIS.

For a color version of all the figures in this chapter, see www.iste.co.uk/dimotikalis/data3.zip.

12.1. Introduction

In the 21st century, the health sector has faced a multitude of fiscal problems: as the demand for health services increases, so does their cost (Toussaint and Berry 2013). The rapid increase in health expenditures, combined with the stagnation observed at the level of resources, have consequences of the financial exhaustion and the inability of hospitals to meet the demand for health services. The above situation in turn leads to a reduction in the quality of health services (Blackmore et al. 2013).

The provision of immediate and quality health services to patients is considered to be a key concern of every health system as it ensures the continuous improvement of the level of efficiency and productivity of health services. The application of austere management and more generally of the austere philosophy in the provision of health services aims to restructure the existing health status, without additional financial aid or new investment approaches in the field of health (Tsasis and Bruce-Barrett 2008; Machado and Leitner 2010).

Lean management interventions in the health sector seek to change the procedures provided by each hospital, to ensure that the provision of health services that will be distinguished by a high level of safety, quality, efficiency and suitability (Trägardh and Lindberg 2004; Ballé and Rénier 2007). In no case does austere management coincide with the restriction of employees, but aims, with the existing or less resources, to achieve as many better results as possible (Poksinska 2010).

The present research aims to examine whether and to what extent the simple management is applied in the health units of the Greek state and specifically in the Venizeleio General Hospital of Heraklion, Crete. The ultimate goal of the work is to demonstrate whether the employees of Venizeleio understand the meaning and content of simple management and whether they believe that it contributes to improving the level of efficiency, effectiveness and cost of health organizations.

12.2. Theoretical framework

Lean management refers to the process aiming to achieve as much as possible, with the least possible effort, the least equipment, space and time, to ensure the maximum ability of customers to obtain the products they want (Womack and Jones 2003). The starting point of simple management is considered to be the elimination of unnecessary expenses so that the work performed has a positive impact on the value of the business and the satisfaction of customers' needs. The main axis of application of simple management is the identification of those actions that, if implemented, will add value to the business, as well as the identification of those actions that do not offer value (Institute for Healthcare Improvement 2005; Lavalle 2011).

According to the literature on simple management, it is based on a framework of five principles, which are the following (Womack and Jones 2003): a) determination of value by end customers; b) mitigation of actions that do not have value; c) actions that contribute to value and must be carried out continuously so that the product reaches the customer smoothly; d) the product and service are produced for the customer; and e) the pursuit of perfection through continuous improvement. In addition to the five values mentioned, simple management is based on the subtraction of actions, which lead to the consumption of resources, but without producing value, resulting in waste. In the context of simple management, the eight types of waste that should be avoided which are: a) defects, b) overproduction, c) transport, d) waiting, e) stocks, f) traffic, g) overwork and h) nonuse of cognitive of capital (Graban 2011).

From the time of the introduction of lean management, strategies aimed at developing value and reducing the spending for each business began to emerge. One of the most popular tools used by simple management is "value stream mapping". The instrument graphically represents all of the responsibilities that occur within the value stream that concern either a product or a service (Womack and Jones 2003). Also, one of the most well-known strategies of simple management concerns the continuous and gradual improvement. This strategy refers to a set of actions that occur over a period of four to five days, aiming to make significant changes in the body (Lavalle 2011). A very common strategy of simple management is that of "5S" that refers to five Japanese words beginning with the letter "S". Specifically, it is the word Seiri, which refers to the sorting of the tools and accessories considered as important for the working environment and respectively for the removal of what is not necessary. The second word is Seiton, which refers to the identification and arrangement of tools and media so that they can be easily used. The third word is Seiso, which refers to the existence of a clean working environment. The fourth word is Seiketsou, which is associated with the creation and development of those processes that aim to ensure the improvements of the above three steps. The fifth word is Shitsuke, which refers to the acquisition of habits so that the realization of the four above-mentioned steps takes place (Womack and Jones 2003). The 5S strategy can occur in warehouses where there are tools, medicines or accessories, for example, a hospital unit (Lavalle 2011).

Visual inspection is another widely used tool, as it has been proven to be useful in the field of health. Essentially, all of the tools, components, productive activities and performance indicators of each system are placed in common view so that all employees can understand the state of the system at a glance (Womack and Jones 2003; Lavalle 2011).

Many scientists point out that the application of lean management in the health sector is considered to be necessary and imperative as it allows health units to improve (Leggat et al. 2015), enabling them to become more flexible (Neufeld et al. 2013).

The application of lean management in the health sector aims to orient the health units in a specific framework of changes, which must be made when clinical care is provided so that there is continuous improvement in quality, productivity, efficiency, safety and suitability of patient–client services (Houchens and Kim 2013). Within this field, lean management offers a specific regulatory framework that determines which of the actions that an organization, a hospital, will perform are "Value-Added" actions and which are "Non-Value-Added" actions.

The 5S has been proposed as the most appropriate strategy for simple management in the health sector, as it leads to the reduction of excessive spending, while improving the workplace in terms of organization and visual management. The "5S" in the case of hospitals refer to the following terms: Sort, Standardize, Store, Shine, Sustain (Machado and Leitner 2010).

The systematic application of lean management has shown that hospitals in a short period of time have had a much better patient flow and improved staff mobility (Tsasis and Bruce-Barrett 2008; Houchens and Kim 2013). It improves the level of systematic application of patient care (Houchens and Kim 2013) and the level of employee satisfaction (Graban 2011). Regional activities of hospitals are improving, such as administrative services, laboratory controls and logistics infrastructure (Edwards et al. 2012). There is also a significant improvement in the flow of patients who were emergencies, especially in terms of their waiting time and the correct use of surgical instruments (Edwards et al. 2012). Through the application of simple management, the defects of the organism can be understood and eliminated (Adamson and Kwolek 2008). Any non-added value or action that is considered redundant is eliminated. The consequence of all of the above is that procedures applied in the hospital are distinguished by efficiency and effectiveness, focusing on the benefit of the patient (Ben-Tovim et al. 2007).

Research has shown that the application of lean management in health facilities can reduce injuries, infections and even deaths. It is not a magic solution, but it helps to eliminate many mistakes, in order to change the mentalities of the employees and to limit those mistakes that can be predicted (May 2007). Graban (2011) emphasized that the application of lean management achieves fast and good results in terms of hospital laboratories, disinfection, sterilization of hospitals, reduction of infections and waiting times, increasing hospital revenues.

In addition, through the implementation of simple management, there is an improvement in the financial performance of hospitals, as costs are reduced and at the same time patient satisfaction is improved both in terms of results and in terms of the flexibility of health units. Lean management also improves the policies followed by health units at the level of healthcare, while increasing cost control. Quantitative assessment of the results of lean management can also lead to a further improvement in the quality of services provided. Employees are more wary of waste and their productivity increases, as problematic situations in the workplace are resolved. At the same time, the stress of the employees is reduced, while they themselves become more flexible in the performance of their duties. Through their training and participation in simple management processes, they also make a decisive contribution to the provision of high-quality health services (Plsek and Greenhalgh 2001).

Lean management helps to transmit an organizational culture to healthcare units, which leads to easier acceptance of the reforms that need to take place in healthcare. The organizational culture of austere management can have a decisive effect on employee performance, greater job satisfaction, commitment to work and to patients (Ross-Baker 2014).

However, in order for lean management to be implemented in the health sector, a number of important obstacles must cease to exist. First of all, it is necessary to convince the human resources of the hospital unit of the importance of the implementation of the simple management and to proceed with its implementation. Many employees believe that simple management involves reductions and layoffs, with the result that due to the above perception they do not want to apply it because they believe that they or their colleagues may lose their jobs (Houchens and Kim 2013).

Apart from the issue of limited time and the accumulated practical experience of implementing simple management, the nondevelopment of methods that suit the specifics of the industry, such as issues of complexity and value associated with them, also acts as a deterrent to its effective implementation on health organizations (Plsek and Greenhalgh 2001).

In addition, it is observed that most hospitals are organized in functional silos so that they can take advantage of the benefits of specialization, making it difficult to create coherent and uninterrupted patient flows and to observe conflicts at the level of roles and ambiguity regarding the duties of employees (Perrow 1986). In addition to the above obstacles, it should be noted that hospital units depend on the coordination of institutions from different professions (Plsek and Wilson 2001). The complexity of the health sector explains to some extent why it is difficult to implement lean management in relation to other sectors.

In conclusion, an important obstacle in using the application of lean management correctly and effectively is the existing perception of the concept of its value. The hospital context can hardly determine the value in a strict context, as the nursing staff focusing on care understands the value differently to the medical staff focusing on treatment and the administrative staff focusing on the hospital performance and its value to the community (Young and McClean 2008).

12.3. Purpose of the research

The purpose of this research is to investigate the application of simple management in the case of the Greek health reality, with reference to the Venizeleio General Hospital of Heraklion, Crete. The work seeks to demonstrate that the staff of the aforementioned health unit understands the meaning and content of simple management and how it believes that it can lead to the provision of effective and efficient health services.

12.4. Methodology

A quantitative method and specifically a questionnaire were used to conduct the research (Creswell 2016). The questionnaire of the present survey consists of 23 questions, of which the first 8 refer to the demographic data of the respondents (gender, age, marital status, education, field of work, etc.), while the rest concern the issue of simple management. The combination of different types of questions was chosen, as it was considered that this would contribute to the conduct of the research more effectively, since its results would be better codified and quantified. More specifically, the questions in the research were dichotomous, Likert-scale questions, multiple choice questions and short answer questions (Babbie 2013). The sample of the research consisted of 82 employees at the Venizeleio General Hospital of Heraklion, Crete, who were asked to fill in electronically the questionnaire created on the Google Forms platform. The survey was conducted from May 12 to June 10, 2021. The results were analyzed according to the statistical package SPSS-27 (Sahlas and Mpersimis 2017).

12.5. Research results

The survey sample consisted of 82 participants, of which 79.3% were women and 20.7% were men. Of the participants, 46% were aged between 36 and 45 years, while 76.3% were graduates of higher education.

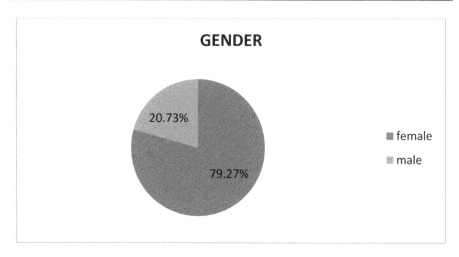

Figure 12.1. *Gender*

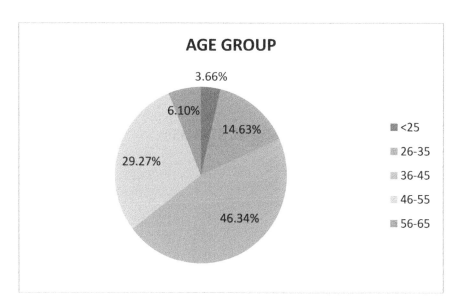

Figure 12.2. *Age group*

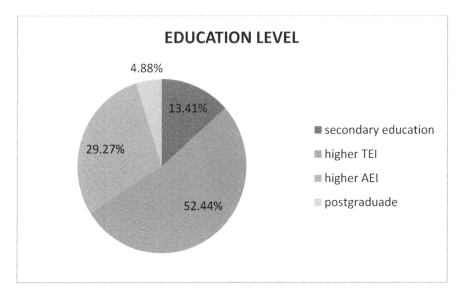

Figure 12.3. *Educational level*

Of the participants, 82.9% were married, almost one in two worked as nurses at the Venizeleio Hospital, while 50% had previous service from 16 to 27 years.

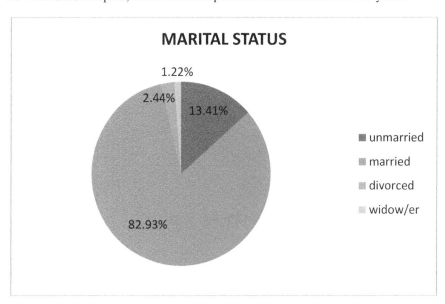

Figure 12.4. *Marital status*

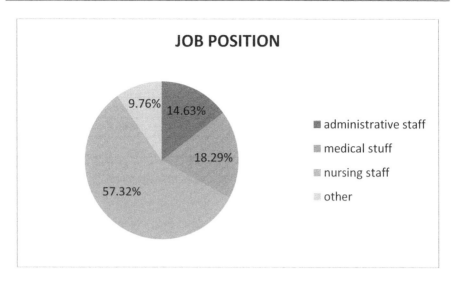

Figure 12.5. *Job position in the hospital unit*

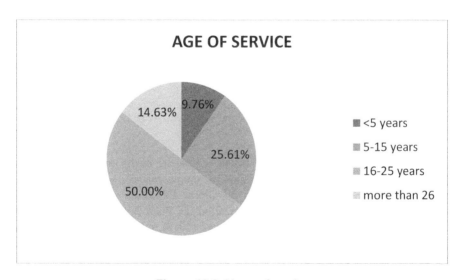

Figure 12.6. *Years of service*

It should be mentioned that in the minds of the participants in the research, simple management is understood in combination of a reduction of excessive costs, the number of employees, a constant control of the production process, and a system of organization of the organization's management.

		Frequency	Percent	Valid percent	Cumulative percent
Valid	1	10	12.2	12.2	12.2
	2	3	3.7	3.7	15.9
	3	3	3.7	3.7	19.5
	4	7	8.5	8.5	28.0
	5	59	72.0	72.0	100.0
	Total	82	100.0	100.0	

Table 12.1. *How to define simple management*

Of the respondents, 84.1% answered that the organization that works systematically applies simple management techniques. It is therefore concluded that Venizeleio has adopted and applied the principles of simple management, which is confirmed through its vision and mission (General Hospital Venizeleio-Pananeio 2021).

		Frequency	Percent	Valid percent	Cumulative percent
Valid	Yes	69	84.1	84.1	84.1
	No	13	15.9	15.9	100.0
	Total	82	100.0	100.0	

Table 12.2. *Do you think that simple management is systematically applied to the health organization you work for?*

Another fact established by the research is that the health organization, in its effort to introduce some of the principles of simple management to employees, emphasizes the training of its human resources. Education is a key factor in promoting lean management in an organization, as Plsek and Greenhalgh (2001) found. This view is also endorsed by Poksinska (2010), who stated that training in simple management issues helps employees to understand the waste and proceed to reduce it in the context of the implementation of simple management.

The most common technique of simple management in the health unit is that of "5S". The above technique is the most common technique of simple management (Womack and Jones 2003; Lavalle 2011), which shows that the health organization has specialized knowledge on the issue of simple management. Another common technique is progress monitoring meetings. Techniques that seem to be less developed are visual inspection and design to limit/avoid mistakes.

	N	Minimum	Maximum	Mean	Standard deviation	Variance
ε13_1	82	1	2	1.93	.262	.069
ε13_2	82	1	2	1.26	.439	.193
ε13_3	82	1	2	1.11	.315	.099
ε13_4	82	1	2	1.10	.299	.089
ε13_5	82	1	2	1.28	.452	.204
ε13_6	82	1	2	1.67	.473	.224
ε13_7	82	1	2	1.44	.499	.249
ε13_8	82	1	2	1.57	.498	.248
ε13_9	82	1	2	1.90	.299	.089
ε13_10	82	1	2	1.09	.281	.079
Valid N (listwise)	82					

Table 12.3. *Indicate whether each of the following simple management techniques applies to the organization you work for*

The most important reasons that led the organization to apply some simple management techniques, according to the respondents, were the adaptation to modern management techniques, the improvement of security and the reduction of errors/mistakes. The reasons for the incentive to adopt lean management techniques are consistent with the results of previous research that concluded that lean management contributes to better management of the organization, improving its level of security and reducing the mistakes made (Golden 2006; Kim et al. 2006; Graban 2011; Houchens and Kim 2013; Hasle et al. 2016).

	N	Minimum	Maximum	Mean	Standard deviation	Variance
ε14_1	82	1	5	4.21	1.003	1.006
ε14_2	82	1	5	4.37	1.000	1.000
ε14_3	82	1	5	3.24	1.117	1.248
ε14_4	82	1	5	4.21	.939	.882
ε14_5	82	1	5	4.00	.943	.889
ε14_6	82	1	5	2.79	.842	.710
ε14_7	82	1	5	3.70	.812	.659
ε14_8	82	1	5	4.22	1.031	1.062
ε14_9	82	1	5	4.26	1.184	1.403
ε14_10	82	1	5	4.41	1.133	1.283
ε14_11	82	1	5	4.49	1.057	1.117
ε14_12	82	1	5	3.20	.881	.776
Valid N (listwise)	82					

Table 12.4. *Reasons that led the health organization to implement lean management*

Based on the results of the survey, most respondents answered that austerity management cannot be easily implemented, due to the refusal of employees due to fear of change, due to the refusal of employees, due to lack of knowledge of the principles and benefits of austerity management and due to lack of proper training. The reasons presented as obstacles to the application of the simple management of the present research are in line with the results of the research of Zidel (2006) and Hummer and Daccarett (2009) who had reached the same conclusions. Therefore, it can be observed that the obstacles that have been in place for more than 15 years in the implementation of simple management still exist in 2021.

	N	Minimum	Maximum	Mean	Standard deviation	Variance
ε15_1	82	2	5	4.54	.789	.622
ε15_2	82	1	5	4.43	.861	.741
ε15_3	82	2	5	4.62	.641	.411
ε15_4	82	1	5	4.62	.696	.485
ε15_5	82	1	5	2.17	1.303	1.699
ε15_6	82	1	5	2.01	1.138	1.296
ε15_7	82	1	5	1.89	.994	.988
ε15_8	82	1	5	2.01	1.171	1.370
ε15_9	82	1	5	2.78	.802	.643
ε15_10	82	1	5	3.32	.887	.787
ε15_11	82	1	5	4.61	.766	.587
ε15_12	82	2	5	4.54	.905	.820
ε15_13	82	2	5	4.59	.785	.616
Valid N (listwise)	82					

Table 12.5. *Barriers to the implementation of simple management*

The research also distinguishes the main forms of excessive spending pointed out by the employees of the Venizeleio Hospital in Heraklion. They mentioned the defects as the most important waste, while the unused knowledge as the least. According to Graban (2011), defects are the main causes of waste in a health organization, something that is confirmed in this case as well.

Concluding the discussion of the research results, the research presents the main benefits that the respondents consider to be obtained by a health organization from the application of simple management. As evidenced by the answers given, the most important benefits were the reduction of the cost of the provided services, the improvement of the level of care and safety of the patients (Locock 2003; Leggat et al. 2015) and the improvement of the level of patient satisfaction and staff. Benefits such as staff mobility and overcrowding are achieved less often. Respondents' views converge with the results of previous research by Thompson et al. (2003), Graban (2011) and Houchens and Kim (2013), Kraebber (2014), who had reached exactly the same conclusions in investigations conducted.

It is understood from the above that the Venizeleio General Hospital of Heraklion, Crete, seeks the application of the principles of simple management in the context of the services it offers to patients, which shows that the health units in Greece have understood the importance and benefits for its operation and also for patients. It was also found that the participants have a basic knowledge framework for simple management, although there should be further training, something that they point out themselves. A very positive perspective for the implementation of lean management was the fact that the respondents knew the content of the concept of lean management and correctly identified the benefits that the organization derives from its implementation. The above-mentioned positions of the employees can work encouragingly for the universal application of the simple management in the health units, as the correct knowledge of the content of the concept both in theory and in practice removes from misconceptions and stereotypes about it, which can work by discouraging its implementation.

12.6. Conclusions

Simple management is a practice that, with appropriate adjustments, can be applied in the health sector and has very positive results. Particularly in the case of Greece, the health sector is plagued by a multitude of problems associated with misconceptions, limited resources, mismanagement, etc. The application of simple management could bring substantial solutions and give a new breath of modernization to health facilities. The need to implement lean management in the Greek public health system also seems more urgent than ever if public health units want to compete on an equal footing with the rapidly growing private health sector, as well as the international health systems that systematically seem to apply lean management.

However, in order for simple management to be implemented properly, it is necessary for healthcare workers to be informed about the content of its implementation and to be properly trained. Only under the above conditions will they stop demonizing the simple management and have misconceptions about it, as the perception still prevails that its implementation is associated with staff and resource cuts in health facilities.

The Venizeleio hospital, as can be seen from what is mentioned in its vision and mission, has understood that it is important to implement the simple management, in order to be functional and to provide the best and highest quality health services to patients. The above perception seems to permeate the employees of the health unit who have understood the importance of its implementation. It is particularly encouraging that a regional hospital seeks to modernize and follow the international European trends of the time in the health sector, as the disposition of the Greek health system becomes more efficient and effective.

The results of the present research showed that the simple management can and should be applied in the Greek health units, as there is suitable ground and disposition in this direction. The Greek state, for its part, must "exploit" this disposition and develop policies in this direction, as well as incentives for the health units, in order to adopt it and implement it systematically.

Further research on the issue of austere management and the evaluation of the existing picture it presents in the health units will help significantly in this direction, as in this way it will be possible to overcome the obstacles that hinder its implementation and to develop the prospects so that it can be a reference point for the Greek health institutions.

12.7. References

Adamson, B. and Kwolek, S. (2008). Strategy, leadership and change: The North York general hospital transformation journey. *Healthcare Quarterly*, 11(3), 50–53.

Babbie, E. (2013). *Entry Into Social Research*. Critique, Athens.

Ballé, M. and Rénier, A. (2007). Lean as a learning system in a hospital ward. *Leadership in Health Services*, 20, 33–41.

Ben-Tovim, D.I., Bassham, J.E., Bolch, D., Martin, M.A., Dougherty, M., Szwarcbord, M. (2007). Lean thinking across a hospital: Redesigning care at the Flinders Medical Centre, *Australian Health Review*, 31(1), 10–15.

Blackmore, C.C., Bishop, R., Luker, S., Williams, B.L. (2013). Applying lean methods to improve quality and safety in surgical sterile instrument processing. *Joint Commentary Journal of Quality of Patient Safety*, 39(3), 99–105.

Creswell, J. (2016). *Research in Education*. Ion, Athens.

Edwards, K., Nielsen, A., Jacobsen, P. (2012). Implementing lean in surgery – Lessons and implications. *International Journal of Technology Management*, 57(1/2/3), 4–17.

Golden, B. (2006). Change: Transforming healthcare organizations. *Healthcare Quarterly*, 10, 10–19.

Graban M. (2011). *Lean Hospitals: Improving Quality, Patient Safety, and Employee Satisfaction*, 2nd edition. CRC Press, New York.

Hasle, P., Nielsen, A., Edwards, K. (2016). Application of lean manufacturing in hospitals the need to consider maturity, complexity, and the value concept. *Human Factors and Ergonomics in Manufacturing*, 26(4), 430–442.

Houchens, N. and Kim, C. (2013). The application of lean in the healthcare sector: Theory and practical examples. In *Lean Thinking for Healthcare*, Wickramasinghe, N., Al-Hakim, L., Gonzalez, C., Tan, J. (eds). Springer, New York, 43–53.

Hummer, J. and Daccarett, C. (2009). Improvement in prescription renewal handling by application of the lean process. *Nursing Economy*, 27(3), 197–201.

Institute for Healthcare Improvement (2021). Going Lean in Health Care. IHI Innovation Series White Paper [Online]. Available at: http://www.ihi.org/IHI/Results/WhitePapers/GoingLeaninHealthCare.htm [Accessed 8 June 2021].

Kraebber, K. (2014). Lean in healthcare. In *Management Engineering: A Guide to Best Practices for Industrial Engineering in Health Care*, Larson, J.A. (ed.). CRC Press, New York.

Lavalle, D. (2011). Improve patient safety with lean techniques. In *Error Reduction in Health Care: A Systems Approach to Improving Patient Safety*, Spath, P.L. (ed.). John Wiley & Sons, San Francisco.

Leggat, S.G., Bartram, T., Stanton, P., Bamber, G.J., Sohal, A.S. (2015). Have process redesign methods, such as lean, been successful in changing care delivery in hospitals? A systematic review. *Public Money & Management*, 35(2), 161–168.

Locock, L. (2003). Healthcare redesign: Meaning, origins and application. *Quarterly Safety and Health Care*, 12, 53–58.

Machado, V. and Leitner, U. (2010). Lean tools and lean transformation process in health care. *International Journal of Management Science and Engineering Management*, 5(5), 383–392.

May, M.E. (2007). *The Elegant Solution: Toyota's Formula for Mastering Innovation*. Free Press, New York.

Neufeld, N.J., Hoyer, E.H., Cabahug, P., González-Fernández, M., Mehta, M., Walker, N.C., Mayer, R.S. (2013). A lean six sigma quality improvement project to increase discharge paperwork completeness for admission to a comprehensive integrated inpatient rehabilitation program. *American Journal of Medical Quality*, 28(4), 301–307.

Perrow, C. (1986). *Complex Organizations – A Critical Essay*. McGraw-Hill, New York.

Plsek, P.E. and Greenhalgh, T. (2001). Complexity science – The challenge of complexity in health care. *British Medical Journal*, 323, 625–628.

Poksinska B. (2010). The current state of Lean implementation in health care: Literature review. *Quality Management in Health Care*, 4(19), 319–329.

Ross-Baker, G. (2014). Improving healthcare using lean processes. *Healthcare Quarterly*, 17(2), 18–19.

Sahlas, A. and Mpersimis, S. (2017). *Applied Statistics Utilizing IBM SPSS Statistics 23: Focusing on Health Sciences*. Tziola Publications, Athens.

Thompson, D.N., Wolf, G.A., Spear, S.J. (2003). Driving improvement in patient care: Lessons from Toyota. *Journal of Nursing Administration*, 33(11), 585–595.

Toussaint, J. and Berry, L. (2013). The promise of lean in health care. *Mayo Clinic Proceedings*, 88(1), 74–82.

Trägardh, B. and Lindberg, K. (2004). Curing a meagre health care system by lean methods – Translating "chains of care" in the Swedish health care sector. *The International Journal of Health Planning and Management*, 19(4), 383–398.

Tsasis, P. and Bruce-Barrett, C. (2008). Organizational change through lean thinking. *Health Services Management Research*, 21(3), 192–198.

Venizelio Pananio General Hospital (2021). [Online]. Available at: https://www.venizeleio.gr/ [Accessed 8 June 2021].

Womack, J.P. and Jones, D.T. (2003). *Lean Thinking. Banish Waste and Create Wealth in Your Corporation*. Free Press, New York.

Young, T.P. and McClean, S.I. (2008). A critical look at lean thinking in healthcare. *Quality and Safety in Health Care*, 17(5), 382–386.

Zidel, T.G. (2006). A lean toolbox – Using lean principles and techniques in healthcare. *JHQ*, 28(1), W1–7.

13

Satisfaction of Employees in Primary and Secondary Healthcare Structures During the Pandemic Period in the Prefecture of Magnesia

The pandemic period brought about changes in the levels of job satisfaction and burnout in healthcare professionals. The aim of this study is to examine the satisfaction and burnout levels of healthcare professionals as well as how their perceptions have been affected based on their demographic and occupational profile. The relationship between job satisfaction and burnout has also been studied.

The methodology of the survey was based on a quantitative survey, primary, correlative between and within the groups using valid, highly reliable questionnaires ($\alpha \geq 0.708$). The research involved 120 healthcare professionals working at the General Hospital of Magnesia, the majority of nurses and other healthcare professionals, women who are middle-aged (46 years old), married with one to two children and have 14 years of service in this unit. The analysis was performed at a significance level of 5%, using the independent samples t-test, Mann–Whitney, ANOVA, Kruskal–Wallis and Spearman.

The conclusions of the study are that healthcare professionals at this hospital felt moderate to high personal achievement, low emotional exhaustion and very low depersonalization during the Covid-19 period. The more emotionally exhausted healthcare professionals are, the less satisfied they are with the supervision, the operating conditions and the communication in the unit they serve as well as the nature of the work. The feeling of personal achievement is achieved by the nature of

Chapter written by Sofia TRIKALLIOTI and George MATALLIOTAKIS.

work and relationships with colleagues and supervisors; however, it creates increased demands. Bad interpersonal relationships and dissatisfaction with the nature of work create depersonalization in employees, which is reinforced by high wages.

13.1. Introduction

In December 2019, a new coronavirus was isolated from three patients treated for pneumonia at a hospital in Wuhan. As of January 2, 2020, 41 hospitalized patients had been identified as having a laboratory-confirmed Covid-19 infection. As of March 1, 2020, there were 87,137 reported cases worldwide with a case fatality rate of 2.3%. As of March 29, 2020, there were 713,171 confirmed cases worldwide (De Wit et al. 2020).

While measures had been taken to mitigate transmission, the impact of these measures on the temporal and geographic distribution of infection in the population was unpredictable. The dilemma facing healthcare workers was twofold: first, the expected overload of the healthcare system's ability to respond to this pandemic with an appropriate flow of equipment, and second, the high risk to healthcare workers on the front line and their family members as a result of continuous exposure (Sasangohar et al. 2020).

13.2. The Covid-19 pandemic and its effects

The 2019 coronavirus (Covid-19) pandemic had become the most important health crisis in the world at the time of writing as it does not discriminate between countries, socio-economic status or races and has spread to most countries in the world (Bulut and Kato 2020; Lai et al. 2020).

Covid-19 has caused an unprecedented global crisis, involving millions of lives lost, public health systems in panic, and economic and social disruption, disproportionately affecting the most vulnerable. As of April 2021, there were over 140 million confirmed cases and over 3 million deaths from Covid-19 worldwide. While vaccination programs have been carried out in many countries, new cases and mutations of the virus continue to emerge.

Fear and panic about Covid-19 can lead to experiences of stigmatization and social exclusion of confirmed patients, their families and others associated with the disease, which can cause an increased risk of developing mental health problems such as adjustment disorder and depression (Zhang et al. 2020). It is a fact that uninfected people have reported fearing contact with people infected with Covid-19 (Li et al. 2020).

The pandemic has exposed the limitations of many health systems, including some previously classified as high-performing and resilient and has revealed many issues related to current processes and established practices. More importantly, the lack of established policies for pandemic triage, equipment ordering and emergency management has led to inefficiencies throughout the health system and increased the burden on healthcare workers. While new protocols were put in place in response to the pandemic, they were seen as complex and, in some cases, premature (Sasangohar et al. 2020).

Covid-19 has pushed the global economy to the brink of or into a major recession. Modifications of population dispersion (social distancing) and quarantine protocols, as well as the complete shutdown of large parts of the economy, have led to unprecedented general social stress (Sasangohar et al. 2020). It is also well documented that uncertainty about future occupational stability (job security) is also associated with worsening mental well-being (Sasangohar et al. 2020).

Pandemics of this scale occur about every 100 years, with more localized or less severe cases in between. Humanity may have learned from them, but has yet to devote enough of its public resources to providing adequate supplies (Sasangohar et al. 2020).

13.3. Job satisfaction of healthcare professionals

Job satisfaction is important to ensure the growth of any organization. For many years now, employee satisfaction has been a key area of research among psychologists. Job satisfaction is of great importance to the well-being of employees and helps them reach their full potential (Rathi and Muhammad 2021).

In the healthcare field, the literature has widely highlighted that high physician job satisfaction benefits physicians' physical and mental health. Indeed, it can be a protective factor against burnout, intention to leave, absenteeism and turnover intention. Healthcare professional satisfaction is an important indicator of service quality as well as a work resource issue that affects their psychological well-being (Capone et al. 2022).

Healthcare professionals may be one of the most important groups affected by the pandemic, experiencing one of the great paradoxes of the current pandemic: while the general population had to stay at home and avoid social contact, healthcare professionals had to continue to perform their care in direct contact with the virus and constantly exposed to it. This, together with the lack of personal protective equipment, has made them one of the most contaminated groups (Greenberg et al. 2020).

Furthermore, healthcare professionals must provide healthcare while also making extensive ethical decisions (Xiang et al. 2020). They are thus exposed to a high level of suffering from the patients they care for in an overburdened healthcare system (Brooks et al. 2020), which is exacerbated by the uncertainty surrounding the disease, the severity of symptoms and the fear of death (González-Silva et al. 2020). All of these situations can create a series of symptoms in healthcare professionals, such as fear, insecurity and anxiety (Xiang et al. 2020), which manifest in the form of irritability, reluctance to rest and signs of psychological distress (Chen et al. 2020).

In some healthcare settings, such as intensive care units and emergency departments, or in health crises such as the case of the Covid-19 pandemic, professionals may suffer from high levels of anxiety, stress and burnout and their satisfaction may decrease (Alharbi et al. 2020). Healthcare workers' desire to act to relieve others' pain may exceed their ability to provide in some situations, which may cause them to experience emotional distress (Nolte et al. 2017). Healthcare professionals suffering from burnout may experience feelings of fear or dread when interacting with the patients they care for, which can lead to avoidant behaviors in professional–patient relationships (Sabo 2011), thereby reducing the quality of care they provide.

13.4. Healthcare professionals and the burnout syndrome

The current pandemic, from the highly contagious new coronavirus called SARS-CoV-2, has spread rapidly around the world. This critical situation was faced by healthcare workers on the front lines of Covid-19, who were directly involved in the treatment, diagnosis and care of patients with SARS-CoV-2. The increasing daily number of confirmed and suspected cases, the overwhelming workload, the lack of personal protective equipment and the lack of effective treatment contribute to the physical and psychological burden of these healthcare professionals.

Health workers on the frontline of Covid-19 have reported more severe symptoms of anxiety, depression and stress than those not on the frontline (Lai et al. 2020). The emergency work literature has focused on the effects of crisis work, especially burnout, as it poses a risk to healthcare workers (Zhang et al. 2018). Thus, the prevalence of burnout, as an adverse outcome of the pandemic, among healthcare workers has increased significantly during the Covid-19 pandemic.

As a concept, burnout refers to the emotional feeling associated with feelings of frustration and helplessness that develop in professionals' negative attitudes at work (Algunmeeyn et al. 2020). People working in healthcare services have been identified as a group at high risk for burnout and employees who have symptoms of this syndrome are less satisfied with their work activities than others (Heath et al. 2020). In a recent study of this population, more than 62% of workers experienced a moderate degree of burnout (Liu et al. 2020).

Burnout syndrome has the following stages: emotional exhaustion, depersonalization and a low sense of personal fulfillment. Its prevalence is high among different groups of healthcare professionals and is usually higher among doctors.

The clinical picture appears in various ways and can include psychosomatic, psychological and behavioral symptoms among professionals and have negative consequences at the individual, professional, family and social level. In the context of health institutions, this implies a reduction in the efficiency and quality of services (França et al. 2012). Burnout syndrome is an important psychosocial problem that affects professionals from different fields (Rojas and Grisales 2011).

Emotional exhaustion, characterized by a lack of energy or a feeling of exhaustion and a lack of professional motivation, is generally caused by personal conflict in relationships and a heavy workload. Depersonalization is a psychological state of emotional detachment where the impersonal treatment of people in the workplace can cause a hostile attitude, self-centered behavior, alienation, anxiety, irritability and frustration. Reduced career success is characterized by an employee's tendency to evaluate themselves negatively, which leads them to feel less capable and successful and therefore dissatisfied with their performance (Cañadas-Dela Fuente et al. 2015).

Research in different countries has identified individual (behavioral, demographic and personality-related), organizational as well as societal determinants of burnout among physicians. Physicians rarely seek help for their illnesses from other healthcare professionals and when they do, often after a long delay, their health status has worsened (Fridner et al. 2012). Further individual risk factors are two personality types, neuroticism and perfectionism, which may play an important role in the development of burnout through the development of maladaptive coping mechanisms for work stress (Swider and Zimmerman 2010). Among demographic factors, age, dependent care demands such as large number of children and elderly in the family requiring care, and gender have been identified as important determinants of burnout.

The role of gender in the development of burnout has been extensively studied. While the results are inconclusive, in general, women score higher on emotional exhaustion and men higher on depersonalization and personal accomplishment. This trend has also been described by physicians (Linzer et al. 2002). Among workplace characteristics, high job demands, role conflict, low job resources and lack of workplace support have been identified as key risk factors for burnout among general practitioners and physicians (Robinson 2003). In addition, studies have shown that psychosocial stress affects the mental well-being of doctors and contributes to an increase in the prevalence of burnout, anxiety and depression (Vićentić et al. 2010).

Since the future of the Covid-19 pandemic is unpredictable, the epidemic situation has been prolonged and health workers are facing tough working conditions. Health policy makers should place special emphasis on the mental health of healthcare personnel.

13.5. Research purpose

Job satisfaction is the most important factor that greatly affects the efficiency and productivity of human resources. In addition, the success of healthcare programs also depends on the commitment and job satisfaction of health personnel. Healthcare workers not only provide health promotion, epidemic prevention activities but also provide treatments, rehabilitation and palliative care (Thai et al. 2021). The study of the professional burnout (burnout) of healthcare professionals, related to the satisfaction of healthcare professionals, gives a substantial understanding of the causes that create it, thus contributing to the disclosure of daily issues related to their physical and mental state (Umann et al. 2014).

13.6. Research methodology

The present research is primary, quantitative and correlational between and within groups, using Likert-scale questionnaires. Primary research is considered appropriate for direct assessment of research participants (Cohen et al. 2007). Quantitative research is expected to be used to study the levels of satisfaction and burnout of healthcare professionals, concepts which are measurable; therefore, they can be measured objectively with Likert-scale questionnaires (Creswell 2013), while correlational research is the right design when it is required to study interactions between variables, using statistical techniques on numerical data (Muijs 2011). Professional burnout and professional satisfaction are considered to be dependent variables, while demographic characteristics are independent. The target population concerns 120 healthcare professionals of all specialties who worked in Secondary

Healthcare structures during the pandemic period in the Prefecture of Magnesia using the convenience sampling method.

To measure job satisfaction, the Spector (1985) questionnaire was used, which includes 36 questions on a six-point Likert scale. The questionnaire by Maslach and Jackson (1981) was used to measure burnout, which includes 22 questions on a seven-point Likert scale. In addition, a demographic information questionnaire was used regarding gender, age, marital status, number of children and educational level and a professional information questionnaire regarding specialty and years of service in the specific unit. The statistical analysis was carried out in the statistical program IBM SPSS 24, while the reliability of the questionnaire was checked with the Cronbach alpha index where values above 0.7 are considered as satisfactory (McLeod 2007).

Factor	Questions	Cronbach alpha
Emotional exhaustion	C(8-16)	0.874
Personal achievement	C(17-24)	0.892
Depersonalization	C(25-29)	0.838
Salary	D(30,39R,48R,57)	0.748
Promotion	D(31R,40,49,62)	0.726
Supervision	D(32,41R,50R,59)	0.796
Privileges–benefits	D(33R,42,51,58R)	0.757
Rewards	D(34,43R,52R,61R)	0.795
Operating conditions	D(35R,44,53R,60R)	0.769
Colleagues	D(36,45R,54,63R)	0.723
Nature of work	D(37R,46,56,64)	0.708
Contact	D(38,47R,55R,65R)	0.777

Table 13.1. *Results of reliability analysis*

13.7. Research conclusions

Healthcare professionals at Magnesia General Hospital felt moderate to high personal achievement, low emotional exhaustion and very low depersonalization during the Covid-19 period.

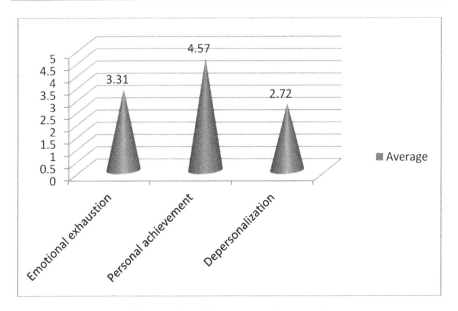

Figure 13.1. *Mean values for burnout*

	Average	95% lower limit CI	95% upper limit CI
Emotional exhaustion	3.31	3.08	3.53
Personal achievement	4.57	4.32	4.82
Depersonalization	2.72	2.47	2.96

CI = Confidence intervals

Table 13.2. *Mean values and 95% CI for burnout*

Factors such as gender, age, marital status, educational level and years of service affected the emotional exhaustion of employees. According to the statistical analysis of the data, women and older professionals with more experience in the unit experienced more emotional exhaustion. However, older participants showed a higher percentage of personal achievement. Also, widowers showed more emotional exhaustion than married, single and divorced workers as well as people with a higher educational level.

The available literature is consistent with the results of this study regarding high personal achievement (O'Connor et al. 2018; El-Menyar et al. 2021) and low depersonalization (El-Menyar et al. 2021), in contrast to emotional exhaustion which occurs at high levels (Chen et al. 2013; O'Connor et al. 2018; El-Menyar et al.

2021). It is likely that in this hospital, there was less pressure during the pandemic period which did not lead to an increase in the levels of emotional exhaustion.

Job satisfaction was studied through nine different elements, which are salary, promotion, supervision, perks-benefits, rewards, working conditions, colleagues, nature of work and communication.

Factors	Average	95% lower limit CI	95% upper limit CI
Salary	2.86	2.63	3.08
Promotion	3.10	2.89	3.31
Supervision	4.56	4.33	4.78
Privileges–benefits	2.73	2.51	2.95
Rewards	3.31	3.09	3.52
Operating conditions	3.15	2.93	3.36
Colleagues	3.93	3.72	4.14
Nature of work	4.03	3.83	4.22
Contact	3.72	3.51	3.92

Table 13.3. *Mean values and 95% CI for professional satisfaction*

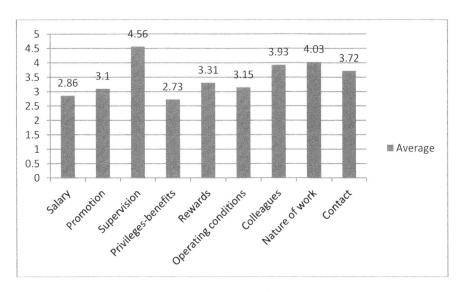

Figure 13.2. *Mean values for professional satisfaction*

Healthcare professionals expressed high satisfaction with the supervisor and moderate to high satisfaction with the nature of the work. More specifically, they somewhat agreed that they often feel that their work has meaning and that they are proud of doing this work. As also highlighted by Ford, Bammer and Becker (2008), organizational support in the workplace enhances role self-esteem, perceived knowledge and feelings of empowerment among healthcare professionals.

Satisfaction with colleagues, communication, working conditions, rewards and promotion were moderate. In contrast, Thai and colleagues (2021), observed a lower level of satisfaction in working conditions and contingent rewards and a high level in communication.

Levels of satisfaction with pay and benefits were low, with participants reporting that they are not paid enough for the work they do and that raises are minimal and disproportionate, a finding consistent with the study by Thai et al. (2021).

Educational level is a characteristic that affects the job satisfaction of the respondents. Healthcare professionals who have graduated from secondary education are more satisfied with the nature of work and communication in the organization. Master's degree holders were less satisfied with promotion conditions; however, together with university graduates, they expressed greater satisfaction with relationships with colleagues. Other healthcare professionals are less satisfied with promotion from their job. It is likely that the educational level is associated with increased responsibilities and a subsequent increase in burnout that implies reduced satisfaction (Adam et al. 2018), especially when they feel that they are not rewarded enough for the services they offer.

Healthcare professionals with more years of service in the unit were less satisfied with relationships with colleagues. Accordingly, Vandenbroeck et al. (2017) linked the job satisfaction of healthcare professionals mainly to their relationships with their colleagues.

With reference to the relationship between professional satisfaction and burnout, it was shown that the most emotionally exhausted healthcare professionals are less satisfied with the supervision, operating conditions and communication in the unit they serve as well as with the nature of the work. The higher the employees rated personal achievement, the less satisfied they were with their salary, benefits and working conditions in the unit they serve. Conversely, the more highly they rated personal achievement, the more satisfied they were with the supervision in the unit they serve, their colleagues and the nature of their work. Most likely, the feeling of personal achievement is achieved by the nature of work (Busis et al. 2017; O'Connor et al. 2018; El-Menyar et al. 2021) and relationships with colleagues and superiors (Thai et al. 2021), but this leads to increased demands.

Finally, the greater the levels of depersonalization in healthcare professionals, the more satisfied they are with their salary, with the conditions for promotion, with the working conditions as well as with the privileges–benefits in the unit they serve. At the same time, the higher the levels of depersonalization in healthcare professionals, the less satisfied they were with the supervision in the unit they serve, with their colleagues and with the nature of their work. It appears that poor interpersonal relationships and lack of satisfaction with the nature of work creates depersonalization in employees, a fact that is reinforced by high wages.

There is some controversy about all of the variables that moderate levels of burnout, and further research is needed to improve understanding of this phenomenon. Also, psychological factors have been considered less relevant, despite the fact that many studies have highlighted that some personality characteristics could develop the syndrome and others may protect against burnout (Geuens et al. 2017).

13.8. References

Adam, S., Mohos, A., Kalabay, L., Torzsa, P. (2018). Potential correlates of burnout among general practitioners and residents in Hungary: The significant role of gender, age, dependent care and experience. *BMC Family Practice*, 19(1), 1–10.

Algunmeeyn, A., El-Dahiyat, F., Altakhineh, M.M., Azab, M., Babar, Z.U.D. (2020). Understanding the factors influencing healthcare providers' burnout during the outbreak of Covid-19 in Jordanian hospitals. *Journal of Pharmaceutical Policy and Practice*, 13(1), 1–8.

Alharbi, J., Jackson, D., Usher, K. (2020). The potential for Covid-19 to contribute to compassion fatigue in critical care nurses. *Journal of Clinical Nursing*, 29(15–16), 2762–2764.

Brooks, S.K., Webster, R.K., Smith, L.E., Woodland, L., Wessely, S., Greenberg, N., Rubin, G.J. (2020). The psychological impact of quarantine and how to reduce it: Rapid review of the evidence. *The Lancet*, 395(10227), 912–920.

Bulut, C. and Kato, Y. (2020). Epidemiology of Covid-19. *Turkish Journal of Medical Sciences*, 50, 563–570.

Busis, N.A., Shanafelt, T.D., Keran, C.M., Levin, K.H., Schwarz, H.B., Molano, J.R., Cascino, T.L. (2017). Burnout, career satisfaction, and well-being among US neurologists in 2016. *Neurology*, 88(8), 797–808.

Cañadas-De la Fuente, G.A., Vargas, C., San Luis, C., García, I., Cañadas, G.R., Emilia, I. (2015). Risk factors and prevalence of burnout syndrome in the nursing profession. *International Journal of Nursing Studies*, 52(1), 240–249.

Capone, V., Borrelli, R., Marino, L., Schettino, G. (2022). Mental well-being and job satisfaction of hospital physicians during Covid-19: Relationships with efficacy beliefs, organizational support, and organizational non-technical skills. *International Journal of Environmental Research and Public Health*, 19(6), 3734.

Chen, K.Y., Yang, C.M., Lien, C.H., Chiou, H.Y., Lin, M.R., Chang, H.R., Chiu, W.T. (2013). Burnout, job satisfaction, and medical malpractice among physicians. *International Journal of Medical Sciences*, 10(11), 1471.

Chen, Q., Liang, M., Li, Y., Guo, J., Fei, D., Wang, L., Zhang, Z. (2020). Mental health care for medical staff in China during the Covid-19 outbreak. *The Lancet Psychiatry*, 7, e15–e1.

Cohen, L., Manion, L., Morrison, K. (2007). *Research Methods in Education*. Routledge Falmer, New York.

Creswell, J.W. (2013) *Research Design: Qualitative, Quantitative, and Mixed Methods Approaches*, 4th edition. SAGE Publications, Inc., London.

De Wit, K., Worster, A., Chan, T., Wallner, C., Barbic, D., Kemplin, K., Mercuri, M. (2020). Impact of the Covid-19 pandemic on emergency physician work and well-being. *Morbidity and Mortality Weekly Report*, 69, 699–704.

El-Menyar, A., Ibrahim, W.H., El Ansari, W., Gomaa, M., Sathian, B., Hssain A., Al-Thani, H. (2021). Characteristics and predictors of burnout among healthcare professionals: A cross-sectional study in two tertiary hospitals. *Postgraduate Medical Journal*, 97(1151), 583–589.

Ford, R., Bammer, G., Becker, N. (2008). The determinants of nurses' therapeutic attitude to patients who use illicit drugs and implications for workforce development. *Journal of Clinical Nursing*, 17(18), 2452–2462.

França, F.M.D., Ferrari, R., Ferrari, D.C., Alves, E.D. (2012). Burnout and labour aspects in the nursing teams at two medium-sized hospitals. *Revista latino-americana de enfermagem*, 20, 961–970.

Fridner, A., Belkic, K., Marini, M., Gustafsson Sendén, M., Schenck-Gustafsson, K. (2012). Why don't academic physicians seek needed professional help for psychological distress? *Swiss Medical Weekly*, 142(2930).

Geuens, N., Van Bogaert, P., Franck, E. (2017). Vulnerability to burnout within the nursing workforce – The role of personality and interpersonal behaviour. *Journal of Clinical Nursing*, 26(23–24), 4622–4633.

González-Silva, Y., Bahíllo Marcos, E., Martín Gutiérrez, R., Merino, M.M. (2020). Clinical involvement and symptoms of patients older than 65 years with Covid-19. *Atencion Primaria*.

Greenberg, N., Docherty, M., Gnanapragasam, S., Wessely, S. (2020). Managing mental health challenges faced by healthcare workers during Covid-19 pandemic. *The British Medical Journal*, 368.

Heath, C., Sommerfield, A., von Ungern-Sternberg, B.S. (2020). Resilience strategies to manage psychological distress among healthcare workers during the Covid-19 pandemic: A narrative review. *Anaesthesia*, 75(10), 1364–1371.

Lai, J., Ma, S., Wang, Y., Cai, Z., Hu, J., Wei, N., Hu, S. (2020). Factors associated with mental health outcomes among health care workers exposed to coronavirus disease 2019. *JAMA Network Open*, 3(3), e203976.

Li, J., Wang, L., Guo, S., Xie, N., Yao, L., Cao, Y., Sun, D. (2020). The data set for patient information-based algorithm to predict mortality cause by Covid-19. *Data in Brief*, 30, 105619.

Linzer, M., McMurray, J.E., Visser, M.R., Oort, F.J., Smets, E., De Haes, H.C. (2002). Sex differences in physician burnout in the United States and The Netherlands. *Journal of the American Medical Women's Association (1972)*, 57(4), 191–193.

Liu, Y., Lu, L., Wang, W.X., Liu, S., Chen, H.R., Gao, X., Huang, M.-Y., Liu, Y.-N., Ren, Y.-M., Wang, C.-C. (2020). Job burnout and occupational stressors among Chinese healthcare professionals at county-level health alliances. *International Journal of Environmental Research and Public Health*, 17(6), 1848.

Maslach, C. and Jackson, S.E. (1981). The measurement of experienced burn-out. *Journal of Occupational Behaviour*, 2, 99–113.

McLeod, S.A. (2007). *What is Reliability?* Simply Psychology, London.

Muijs, D. (2011). *Doing Quantitative Research in Education with SPSS*. SAGE, London.

Nolte, A.G., Downing, C., Temane, A., Hastings-Tolsma, M. (2017). Compassion fatigue in nurses: A metasynthesis. *Journal of Clinical Nursing*, 26(23–24), 4364–4378.

O'Connor, K., Neff, D.M., Pitman, S. (2018). Burnout in mental health professionals: A systematic review and meta-analysis of prevalence and determinants. *European Psychiatry*, 53, 74–99.

Rathi, S.R. and Muhammad, N. (2021). Interpersonal conflict and job satisfaction: A comparative study on workers of grocery shop and super shop, *IOSR Journal of Business and Management (IOSR-JBM)*, 23(6), 1–4.

Robinson, G.E. (2003). Stresses on women physicians: Consequences and coping techniques. *Depression and Anxiety*, 17(3), 180–189.

Rojas, B.M.L. and Grisales, R.H. (2011). Burnout syndrome in professors from an academic unit of a Colombian university. *Investigación y Educación en Enfermería*, 29(3), 427–434.

Sabo, B. (2011). Reflecting on the concept of compassion fatigue. *Online Journal of Issues in Nursing*, 16(1), 1

Sasangohar, F., Jones, S.L., Masud, F.N., Vahidy, F.S., Kash, B.A. (2020). Provider burnout and fatigue during the Covid-19 pandemic: Lessons learned from a high-volume intensive care unit. *Anesthesia and Analgesia*, 131(1), 106–111.

Spector, P.E. (1985). Measurement of human service staff satisfaction: Development of the job satisfaction survey. *American Journal of Community Psychology*, 13(6), 693–713.

Swider, B.W. and Zimmerman, R.D. (2010). Born to burnout: A meta-analytic path model of personality, job burnout, and work outcomes. *Journal of Vocational Behavior*, 76(3), 487–506.

Thai, T.T., Le, T.A.T., Truong, L.T.T., Le, N.H., Huynh, Q.N.H., Van Nguyen, T., Tran, H.G.N. (2021). Care for the careers: An evaluation of job satisfaction of community healthcare workers in charge of infectious disease prevention and control in vietnam. *Risk Management and Healthcare Policy*, 14, 2831.

Umann, J., Guido, L.D.A., Silva, R.M.D. (2014). Stress, coping and presenteeism in nurses assisting critical and potentially critical patients. *Revista da Escola de Enfermagem da USP*, 48, 891–898.

Vićentić, S., Jovanović, A., Dunjić, B., Pavlović, Z., Nenadović, M., Nenadović, N. (2010). Professional stress in general practitioners and psychiatrists: The level of psychologic distress and burnout risk. *Vojnosanitetski pregled*, 67(9), 741–746.

Xiang, Y.T., Yang, Y., Li, W., Zhang, L., Zhang, Q., Cheung, T., Ng, C.H. (2020). Timely mental health care for the 2019 novel coronavirus outbreak is urgently needed. *The Lancet Psychiatry*, 7(3), 228–229.

Zhang, Y., Han, W.L., Qin, W., Yin, H.X., Zhang, C.F., Kong, C., Wang, Y.L. (2018). Extent of compassion satisfaction, compassion fatigue and burnout in nursing: A meta-analysis. *Journal of Nursing Management*, 26(7), 810–819.

Zhang, J., Wu, W., Zhao, X., Zhang, W. (2020). Recommended psychological crisis intervention response to the 2019 novel coronavirus pneumonia outbreak in China: A model of West China Hospital. *Precision Clinical Medicine*, 3(1), 3–8.

14

A Parametric Analysis of OpenFlow and P4 Protocols Based on Software Defined Networks

A software defined network (SDN) is a network approach that intelligently manages, centrally controls and programs using software applications. This helps to improve network performance and monitoring, making it more like cloud computing than traditional network management. This is beneficial to network operators as it allows network management, regardless of the underlying network technology. There are various protocols that are used to enable a software-define network to function optimally. These protocols are OpenFlow and Programming Protocol-independent Packet Processors (P4). There is a need for P4 that can constantly verify information between the controller and the data plane. It is essential to have a P4 that can detect inconsistencies by checking reports between its control and data plane. These reports must be the same for the network to be operational. The moment the reports are not the same, the network will suffer the consequences. This research work analyses a comparison between OpenFlow and P4 protocols on an SDN. This SDN decouples the control logic from the network device (switch or a router). The control intelligence is centralized in an SDN controller, which controls the infrastructure elements. This leaves the network architecture with a three-layer plane in the application, control and infrastructure.

This research work performed a parametric analysis of the OpenFlow and P4 protocols. For this purpose, firstly, an OpenFlow process and the data using flow tables have been explained. Also, when the packet does not match any conditions on the flow entries, it is sent back to the controller to decide whether to discard the packet or create new rules. Most of the decisions rest with the controller when using

Chapter written by Lincoln S. PETER, Hlabishi I. KOBO and Viranjay M. SRIVASTAVA.

OpenFlow. OpenFlow switches have no intelligence like routing capabilities, hence a fixed chip. The P4 assists in overcoming these challenges. The P4 switches are programmable and network administrators can make changes on the data plane without having to do the same for the controllers. Another critical aspect of P4 is that packet processing is done at the data and control plane. Before any packets can be processed, P4 performs a pre-security check. When a link failure occurs, P4 will automatically route the traffic onto the available path. This has proven that P4 is much better than the OpenFlow protocol.

14.1. Introduction

A software defined network (SDN) separates the controlling element from the network device (switch or router). The control intelligence is centralized in an SDN controller that controls the infrastructure elements (Hakiri et al. 2014; Kreutz et al. 2015). This leaves the network architecture with a three-layer plane in the application, control and infrastructure. The controller is a very critical component of the SDN because it also links the application layer with the infrastructure layer. These layers are communicated through northbound and southbound APIs. The northbound interface connects the application layer with the controller. The southbound interface connects the infrastructure and control layer. The most prevalent northbound interfaces are Simple Object Access Protocol (SOAP), Web Service Description Language (WSDL), Representational State Transfer (RESTful) and Application Programming Interface (APIs), with the RESTful interfaces being the most commonly used in SDNs (Braun and Menth 2014; Kaljic and Maric 2019). OpenFlow was a de facto protocol on the southbound interfaces for many years until the introduction of P4.

The SDN has a standard protocol used in real applications (Hu et al. 2014). The OpenFlow protocol has made it very simple to implement the SDN on both hardware and software platforms. The OpenFlow protocol relies on ports and switches to manage the flow of tables. The SDN controller manages a group of switches. The controller manages switches that are layer 2 devices via the OpenFlow protocol (Farhady et al. 2015; Xia et al. 2015; Peter and Srivastava 2021). This OpenFlow switch contains an OpenFlow channel, a group table and several flow tables. Every flow table has its own entries, which are communicated to the controller.

Initially, the routing table of the routing devices will be empty. The routing table inside the OpenFlow routing devices has packet fields such as destination, as well as the action field that contains codes of every action that needs to be taken by the routing device. The routing table is populated as the packets are incoming and forwarded to the destination port. A new packet with no matching conditions in the data flow table is passed through the controller to be processed (Cox et al. 2017). The controller is tasked with managing decisions; either that packet is dropped or a new policy is added to the controller on how to manage such packets in the future.

In the SDN architecture, the routing table is generated in the control plane. The data plane uses that routing table to see where the packet should go. The OpenFlow protocol is very simple, and some data centers have used it in their operations. It is easy to manage large networks using the OpenFlow protocol and SDN (Alsmadi and Xu 2015; Ali et al. 2020). The OpenFlow protocol architecture has three important components:

– *Switches*: the OpenFlow switch has the authority to change the flow tables on other layers 2 devices. This OpenFlow switch contains flow tables, communication channels and the OpenFlow protocol. The flow tables have an action field that relates to each flow entry. The communication channel links the controller and the OpenFlow switch so that packets can be transmitted. The OpenFlow protocol enables the OpenFlow switches to communicate with the controller.

– *Controllers*: continuously update the flow entries on the flow tables and add or delete routes. The controller must be configured to dynamically update the routes. This helps to ease the flow of data.

– *Flow entries*: each entry has an action to be undertaken. OpenFlow switches send the flows to a certain port. Then it encapsulates the packet and passes it through the controller, which drops the packets if there is no matching entry.

There are several OpenFlow standard iterations, and the version is 1.5. The first version was from 1.0 to 1.1; this version had only a single flow table. There was no flexibility due to limited matching capabilities. The second version 1.1, in 1.2, extended the type length value to allow more fields to be added (Chang and Lin 2015). This also allowed the controllers to be added to the network to assist with failover options. This means that once the primary controller fails, it is then handed over to the standby controller. This is to make sure that the network is resilient to any node that falls on the network. The third version, from 1.2 to 1.3, introduced the quality of service; it is important for any network to differentiate what traffic is important so that we mitigate the effects of delays. The fourth version 1.3 to 1.4 introduced the scalability of the network. This allows the network to keep up with the demand for network resources. The last version, from 1.4 to 1.5, extended flow entries' grouping and scheduling time. This also made sure that data processing was faster than in the previous versions.

To overcome these issues, there is a need for P4 that can constantly verify the information to the data and controller plane. Authors have presented this point in clear terms in the following two scenarios. It is important to have a P4 that can detect inconsistencies by checking reports between its control and data plane. These reports must be the same for the network to operate. The network will suffer the consequences when the reports are not the same.

This chapter has been organized as follows. Section 14.2 provides the motivation for this work and its basic terminology. Section 14.3 discusses the challenges to the current models. Finally, section 14.4 concludes the work and recommends the future aspect of this work.

14.2. Motivation

The P4 language is just a normal programming language that enhances the concept of SDN (Wang et al. 2019). Initially, it could only configure SDN-enabled switches with a fixed switch chip supporting limited protocols. The P4 is mainly based on the forwarding model named the protocol-independent switch architecture. PISA consists of high packet processing (Wazirali et al. 2021). The P4 switch does not have any understanding of a protocol unless it is programmed, and hence protocol independent. The P4 language has two versions, namely $P4_{14}$ and $P4_{16}$. Figure 14.1 shows the $P4_{16}$ packet processing pipeline. Here, six blocks have been used: programmable ingress parser, ingress match action, ingress deparser, egress parser, egress match action and egress deparser. In addition, two blocks that are non-programmable, i.e. packet replication engine (PRE) and buffer queuing engine (BQE) have been modified.

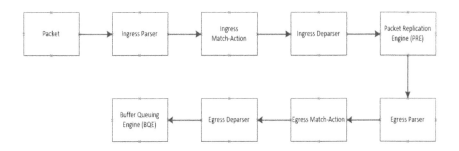

Figure 14.1. *P4 packet processing pipeline*

P4 pipeline: The ingress parser receives the packet and transforms it from binary representation to headers (Hu et al. 2014). After that, a decision would be taken on how to process the packet by the ingress match action. Then, the ingress deparser will queue the packet for processing. The packet will then be passed to the egress match action. The egress deparser indicates how packets are deparsed from the headers into a binary representation. A P4 program is generated using $P4_{16}$. Once generated, it is sent to the P4 compiler and then deployed onto the P4 switch. The match action rules are inserted in the matching table inside the P4 switch (Wang et al. 2019). An important issue about the P4 protocol is that it can be used on SDN switches and non-SDN switches, whereas OpenFlow can only be used on SDN switches.

The authors have analyzed the P4Consist using two practical examples of mismatch in the data and control planes that normally occur on a network.

Example 1: Configuring more than one configuration channel. This is illustrated in Figure 14.2 as an example of inconsistencies between control-data planes. The P4 program is installed by the SDN controller and then propagated to the P4 runtime and API. The packets are supposed to be routed through paths S1-S3-S2-S4. If the network administrator, by mistake, updates the rules on S1 via the command-line interface (CLI), then traffic will be routed on the path S1-S2-S4, which then bypasses the firewall on S3. This exposes the server to malware that can cause severe damage to the network. In this case, there was no message notifying the SDN controller of the changes in the CLI. This indicates that there were inconsistencies on the planes.

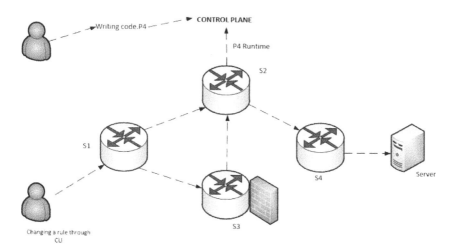

Figure 14.2. *P4 switches. For a color version of this figure, see www.iste.co.uk/dimotikalis/data3.zip*

Example 2: In a case whereby there is no runtime exception inside the P4 switch. Once the P4 switch is disturbed, it is difficult for it to locate a fault at runtime. If the packet is not initialized in the header field, it has the potential to cause the P4 switch to behave abnormally. This could result in the P4 switch dropping a packet. Packets that the P4 switch cannot identify could result in inconsistencies between it and the SDN controller.

14.3. Challenges to the existing models

The current OpenFlow standard relies on centralized control. This means that the single controller handles the flow tables for all these switches. Indeed, this is applicable for a very small-scale network. When the network grows and more switches are added to the network, it becomes difficult for a single controller to manage that. This is especially true if wireless media is also used to connect far sites (Kobo et al. 2017). A single controller is a single point of failure and poses a threat to the network.

Another challenge with OpenFlow is that when the network expands, it becomes flooded and begins to discard packets as it cannot cope with high data processing. This is because of the memory limitations in OpenFlow. OpenFlow works on fixed chip switches and is strictly for SDN (Seeber et al. 2015). The fixed chip switches are not sustainable as these only allow a certain amount of data to be processed on the network and do not cater to any network expansion. OpenFlow cannot work with any switch that is non-SDN.

OpenFlow cannot configure QoS dynamically, as is demanded by the network. This can only be done manually on the OpenFlow switches. In any communication network, security and privacy are very important (Benabbou et al. 2019). This becomes impossible to protect when using OpenFlow, as it brings security challenges due to virtual network management.

14.3.1. *A comparison with OpenFlow*

The data plane programmability is an important feature of the SDN. Network administrators can configure how packets can be processed inside the pipelines on the switch hardware. The P4 switch can achieve this. P4 allows packets to be processed through the pipelines onto the data plane. The packet headers are processed through match + action tables, and the P4 program will describe how these packet headers are parsed (Shukla et al. 2020).

The P4 switch programmers can control the packet headers that are operated on the user-defined headers. P4 switches aggregate small packets and combine them into large packets (Paolucci et al. 2021). On the other transmission end, these packets are then disaggregated back into their original small packets.

The P4 switches cannot manipulate the payload but can manipulate packet headers. The packet payload is treated as different headers, which helps the P4 switch to be able to aggregate and disaggregate the payload inside the pipelines (Shu et al. 2016; Perepelkin and Tsyganov 2019). The P4 protocol can process data more quickly than OpenFlow. It does not operate on a fixed chip switch. The P4 protocol is even compatible with non-SDN switches.

14.3.2. *System: P4Consist*

The name P4Consist is derived from the consistency of P4. This continuously checks for mismatches on the data and control planes (Peter and Srivastava 2021). Figure 14.3 illustrates the P4Consist flowchart that identifies the role of each module. First, the input traffic generator will send the traffic to the data plane module. All switches will push the data to the header stack (Chang and Lin 2015). As the traffic propagates towards its destination, it samples the packets. The control plane module generates the network graph. The analyzer traverses the graph to generate all possible paths between the source and destination (Shukla et al. 2020). Finally, the analyzer will generate a packet with a header similar to that of the previous one. The actual report is then simulated and forwarded through the returned paths. The symbolic execution then returns the status of each path; this is to ensure that consistencies are detected. The analyzer will then analyze the standing of the actual report with the results (Shukla et al. 2020). The P4 consists of 4 modules on a high level with the following:

– the control plane module assists the SDN controller with all information related to the topology and configuration of the network;

– the input traffic generator generates traffic that flows from the source–destination pair;

– the data plane module assists with routing the given packet header from the source–destination pair;

– the analyzer is the brain of P4Consist as it detects inconsistencies between the data and the control plane by comparing the expected and actual report on both planes.

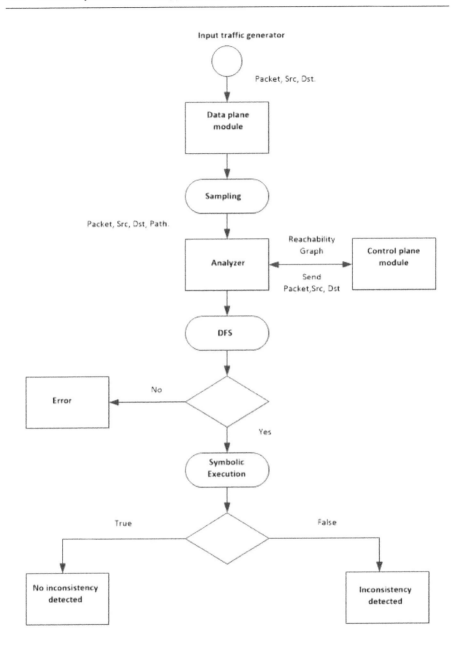

Figure 14.3. *P4Consist flow diagram*

14.4. Conclusions and future recommendations

This chapter is a parametric study between the OpenFlow and P4 protocols. We have explained how OpenFlow processes the data using flow tables. Also, when the packet does not match any conditions on the flow entries, it is sent back to the controller to decide whether to discard the packet or create new rules. Most of this decision is made by the controller when using OpenFlow. OpenFlow switches have no intelligence-like routing capabilities, hence a fixed chip. The P4 helps us overcome these challenges. P4 switches are programmable, and network administrators can make changes on the data plane without having to do so on the controllers.

Another important aspect of P4 is that packet processing is performed in both the data and control plane. Before any packets can be processed, P4 performs a pre-security check. When a link failure occurs, P4 will automatically route traffic to the available path. This has shown that P4 is much better than the OpenFlow protocol.

Future research will gain the process to enhance the P4 interface with other emerging technologies, such as Virtual Extensible Local Area Network (VXLAN) and Software-Defined Wireless Area Network (SDWAN). The P4 intelligence has to be more capacitated to make sure that packets with no matching conditions must be discarded at that level, without being passed through to the controller. Another future aspect that needs to be explored is the security mechanism so that the protocol is more secured.

14.5. References

Ali, J., Lee, G.M., Roh, B.H., Ryu, D.K., Park, G. (2020). Software defined networks approaches for link failure recovery: A survey. *Sustainability*, 12(10), 1–28.

Alsmadi, I. and Xu, D. (2015). Security of software defined networks: A survey. *Computers & Security*, 53, 79–108.

Benabbou, J., Elbaamrani, K., Idboufker, N. (2019). Security in OpenFlow-based SDN, opportunities and challenges. *Photonic Network Communications*, 37(1), 1–23. doi: 10.1007/s11107-018-0803-7.

Braun, W. and Menth, M. (2014). Software-defined networking using openflow: Protocols, applications and architectural design choices. *Future Internet*, 6(2), 302–336. doi: 10.3390/fi6020302.

Chang, C.H. and Lin, Y.D. (2015). OpenFlow version roadmap. *Dept. of Computer Science, National Chiao Tung University*, 1–15.

Cox, J.H., Chung, J., Donovan, S., Ivey, J., Clark, R.J., Riley, G., Owen, H.L. (2017). Advancing software defined networks: A survey. *IEEE Access*, 5, 25487–25526.

Farhady, H., Lee, H.Y., Nakao, A. (2015). Software-defined networking: A survey. *Computer Networks*, 81, 79–95.

Hakiri, A., Gokhale, A., Berthou, P., Schmidt, D.C., Gayraud, T. (2014). Software-defined networking: Challenges and research opportunities for future internet. *Computer Networks*, 75(PartA), 453–471. doi: 10.1016/j.comnet.2014.10.015.

Hu, F., Hao, Q., Bao, K. (2014). A survey on software-defined network and OpenFlow: From concept to implementation. *IEEE Communications Surveys and Tutorials*, 16(4), 2181–2206. doi: 10.1109/COMST.2014.2326417.

Kaljic, E. and Maric, A. (2019). A survey on data plane flexibility and programmability in software-defined networking. *IEEE Access*, 7, 47804–47840. doi: 10.1109/Access.2019. 2910140.

Kapil, B. (2013). Considerations for software define network (SDN): Approaches and use cases. *IEEE Aerospace Conference*, Big Sky, MT, 1–8.

Kobo, H.I., Abu-Mahfouz, A.M., Hancke, G.P. (2017). A survey on software-defined wireless sensor networks: Challenges and design requirements. *IEEE Access*, 5. Institute of Electrical and Electronics Engineers Inc., 1872–1899. doi: 10.1109/ACCESS.2017. 2666200.

Kreutz, D., Ramos, F.M.V., Verissimo, P.E., Rothenberg, C.E., Azodolmolky, S., Uhlig, S. (2015). Software-defined networking: A comprehensive survey. *Proceedings of IEEE*, 103(1), 14–76. doi: 10.1109/JPROC.2014.2371999.

Paolucci, F., Cugini, F., Castoldi, P., Osinski, T. (2021). Enhancing 5G SDN/NFV edge with P4 data plane programmability. *IEEE Network*, 35(3), 154–160. doi: 10.1109/MNET.021. 1900599.

Perepelkin, D. and Tsyganov, I. (2019). Development and implementation of an improved segmentation algorithm in software defined networks. *International Conference on Software, Telecommunications and Computer Networks (SoftCOM)*, Split, Croatia, 19–21, 1–5.

Peter, L.S. and Srivastava, V.M. (2021). High speed and secured network connectivity for higher education institution using software define networks. *19th International Conference of the Applied Stochastic Models and Data Analysis (ASMDA)*, Athens, Greece.

Seeber, S., Stiemert, L., Rodosek, G.D. (2015). Towards an SDN-enabled IDS environment. *IEEE Conference on Communications and Network Security* (CNS), Florence, 751–752. doi: 10.1109/CNS.2015.7346918.

Shu, Z., Wan, J., Li, D., Lin, J., Vasilakos, A.V., Imran, M. (2016). Security in software defined network: Threats and counter measures. *Mobile Networks and Applications*, 21, 764–776.

Shukla, A., Fathalli, S., Zinner, T., Hecker, A., Schmid, S. (2020). P4Consist: Toward consistent P4 SDNs. *IEEE Journal on Selected Areas in Communications*, 38(7), 1293–1307. doi: 10.1109/JSAC.2020.2999653.

Wang, S.Y., Wu, C.M., Lin, Y.B., Huang, C.C. (2019). High-speed data-plane packet aggregation and disaggregation by P4 switches. *Journal of Network and Computer Applications*, 142, 98–110. doi: 10.1016/j.jnca.2019.05.008.

Wazirali, R., Ahmad, R., Alhiyari, S. (2021). SDN-openflow topology discovery: An overview of performance issues. *Applied Sciences*, 11(15), doi: 10.3390/app11156999.

Xia, W., Wen, Y., Foh, C.H., Niyato, D., Xie, H. (2015). A survey on software defined network. *IEEE Communications Surveys & Tutorials*, 17(1), 27–43.

15

A Dynamic Neural Network Model for Accurate Recognition of Masked Faces

Neural networks have become prominent and widely engaged in algorithmic-based machine learning networks. They are perfect in solving day-to-day issues to a certain extent. Neural networks are computing systems with several interconnected nodes. One of the numerous areas of application of neural networks is object detection. A neural network model can be adequately trained and fortified to become an object detector. Object detection techniques are used in the area of detection of face masks and recognition of masked faces in this work. This is a prominent area due to the coronavirus disease (Covid-19) pandemic and the post-pandemic phases. This pandemic has made facial biometrics the safest authentication and access control choice because other biometric means are contact-based. Experts are of the opinion that universities/colleges can only fully reopen if adequate protection and prevention means are judiciously observed.

One of these examples is wearing face masks in public places. However, wearing face masks can bring about compromises in security and safety. This necessitates the need to develop a robust and efficient model for detecting face masks on peoples' faces for compliance checks, and recognizing the faces behind the face masks for authentication, access control and safety surveillance. There have been some breakthroughs in face mask detection and masked faces recognition using neural networks. The existing neural network models are characterized by their black-box nature and large dataset requirement. The highlighted challenges have compromised the performance of the existing models. This focuses on developing a neural network model that is suitable for detecting face masks and recognizing masked faces of various complexions. The developed model also has the capacity for unsupervised object detection and detection of objects from partially captured images. The performance of the neural network model has been evaluated.

Chapter written by Oladapo T. Ibitoye and Viranjay M. Srivastava.
For a color version of all the figures in this chapter, see www.iste.co.uk/dimotikalis/data3.zip.

15.1. Introduction

Face mask detection is a crucial component of security and surveillance systems, particularly in the pandemic period in 2019. Applications such as facial security checks and face mask compliance checks now require an effective face mask detection and identification system. Studies on Covid-19 proved that wearing face masks limits the spread of the deadly virus. This made most organizations implement a "no mask, no entry" policy, but then it is difficult to manually monitor and ensure the use of face masks in public places (Mheidl et al. 2020; Said 2020; Ibitoye 2021).

The field of computer vision has recently become interested in research on face mask detection. Deep learning applications for digital image processing have been developed as a result of research into establishing automatic face mask detection and recognition of faces obscured by masks (Ibitoye 2021). According to Said (2020), deep learning is the ability of a "deep neural network" with multiple layers to learn directly from incoming data. The Convolutional Neural Network (CNN) is a deep learning technology primarily used for object detection and image processing. The field of masked face recognition has seen an increase in research articles and datasets, but when applied to people with various complexions, the effectiveness of such systems is quite poor. This research is in line with the Sustainable Development Goal (SDG) on good health and well-being, which was adopted by the United Nations General Assembly in September 2015 (Morton et al. 2017).

The development of face mask detection and masked faces recognition systems takes place in stages. Image acquisition is usually the first stage for every object detection system, followed by image pre-processing. The third stage is face mask detection. There are other stages, especially for systems that are meant to further analyze the detected faces with masks. Such stages can include, but are not limited to: masked faces identification, gender identification and mask position (to determine whether the mask is properly worn). Figure 15.1 shows the typical masked faces detection system discussed.

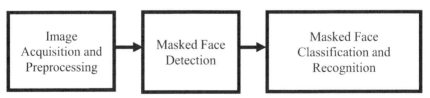

Figure 15.1. *Typical masked faces detection system (Qin and Li 2020; Chowdary et al. 2021; Ibitoye 2021)*

Preparation of the acquired images for accurate detection by the detector requires some image pre-processing techniques. Hariri (2022) applied a cropping filter, which is done to ensure that only the useful regions of faces wearing masks are obtained. To achieve this, normalization of the images was carried out by resizing the images into 240×240 pixels. The images were later split into blocks with a range of uniform square sizes. The non-masked region was included only in the blocks that were removed. Using the Dlib-ml open-source software, the face's rotation was adjusted by Chowdary et al. (2021) to remove the masked area effectively.

Face detection is one of the most important and challenging tasks in object detection. There are three types of face detection:

– boost-based face detection, which makes use of normalized pixels difference, and boosted cascade Haar features;

– deformable part model, simulating faces' deformation;

– convolutional neural network (CNN) technology, which directly learns the features from the input image (Shitala et al. 2021).

Ge et al. (2017) combined CNN with locally linear embedding. They also presented the 30811 Internet photos from the masked faces dataset. Each image in the collection has at least one face that is obscured by a variety of masks, including faces that are hidden by hands or other objects. Loey et al. (2021) proposed a detector model that combined ResNet-50 for feature extraction and detection with the You Only Look Once (YOLO) version 2 (v2) architecture. Multitask Cascaded (MT) CNN and VGG-16 were suggested as a novel framework by Qiting (2018) for the detection of masked faces. A fully convolutional neural network was used by Jang et al. (2019) to identify numerous faces in a picture. Numerous face identification methods using single-stage and double-stage methodologies have been developed in prior related publications. These methods are ineffective for masked faces detection.

To detect faces, Li et al. (2021) used YOLO v3 and a deep learning architecture called darknet-19. To train the model, they used the wider face and Celebi datasets. The SRCNet classification network was used to create a face mask identification system by Qin and Li (2020). The system evaluation indicates a 98.7% accuracy rate for classifying facial images into three groups, with the first group consisting of individuals wearing appropriate face masks, the second group including individuals wearing inappropriate face masks, and the third group including individuals not wearing face masks. For the purpose of detecting face masks in public settings, Shashi (2020) presented a single-shot multi-box detector. The Microsoft common objects in the context dataset was used to pre-train the single-shot model for object detection. A single-shot multi-box detector was also proposed by Nagrath et al. (2020) as a face detector, while using the MobilenetV2 architecture as a framework for the classifier.

A deep learning model built on the InceptionV3 architecture was proposed by Chowdary et al. (2021). Due to a lack of suitable datasets, the authors used picture augmentation techniques for performance and "training data variety" enhancement. In Hariri's (2022) article, the VGG-16 face CNN descriptor was used to extract deep features from masked faces. The model was developed using approximately 14 million pictures and 1000 class ImageNet datasets. There are 16 layers in the VGG-16 architecture. Convolutional, max pooling, activation and fully connected make up its layers. Ejaz et al. (2019) used principal component analysis to construct a traditional machine learning method for distinguishing between masked and unmasked faces. According to the system evaluation, the approach is effective for recognizing faces without masks, while when used on covered faces, the effectiveness falls. Generative adversarial network was used by a novel network that was proposed by Din et al. (2020) to eliminate mask objects from facial photos. The network used two discriminants: the first extracts the masked face's overall structure, while the second extracts the region that is absent.

Shitala et al. (2021) introduced a system known as MaskedFaceNet. This was a collection of fixed-size bounding boxes and scores that are computed for each instance of a detected item type. The predictions were transmitted to the non-maximum suppression layer for the final detection computation. A CNN model for the detection of faces using masks was put forth by Madhura and Mehendale (2020). The proposed model's straightforward design comprises a convolution layer, an activation layer, a pooling layer, a fully connected layer and a softmax layer. The method was created to recognize individual masked faces and detect face masks. The masked face detection dataset, which is a publicly accessible dataset, was used to train the model. The Convolutional Long Short-Term Memory (ConvLSTM) algorithm and fully convolutional networks were combined in a system that was proposed by Wang et al. (2019). The model makes use of the temporal correlation in video clips and operates on a per-sequence basis.

A CNN-based cascade framework was created in papers by Bu et al. (2017), Adithya and Jismi (2020) and Lin et al. (2020) that comprises of three meticulously constructed convolutional neural networks to recognize masked faces. The system cannot be efficiently implemented in real time due to the architecture's use of three layers for just two blocks, which causes the inference time to be relatively slow (Ibitoye 2021). Shortening the inference time by using SSDLite for the detector will speed up the system and make it more robust for real-time applications. Convolutional neural network VGG-16 was used to create a face mask detection system (MIT 2018; Meenpal et al. 2019; Ngan et al. 2020; Mandal et al. 2021; Ryumina et al. 2021). For segmentation, the VGG-16 architecture of a convolutional neural network and a fully convolutional network were both used. With its 16 layers, the VGG-16 network performs better on systems that are solely GPU-based. A better network is needed to make the system work on a CPU-based system.

A hybrid technique for the automatic detection and recognition of the presence (or absence) of a protective mask on a human's face was introduced in the papers by Mahore and Tripathi (2018), Ngan et al. (2020) and Ryumina et al. (2021). The method combines image histograms, which provide information on pixel intensity, with visual features derived using a CNN. The authors took into account a number of pre-trained models for creating feature extraction systems, employing a CNN and several kinds of image histograms. Cross-corpus analysis was done on two more databases, Real-World Masked Face Dataset (RMFD) and Masked Faces (MAFA), as well as the Medical Mask Dataset test, the method RMFD. The CNN network's several spatial compressions led to a significant level of system complexity. Without sacrificing efficiency, a less complicated network would minimize the complexity of the whole system. Wang et al. (2019), Batagelj et al. (2021), Wang and Deng (2021) and Ziwei et al. (2022) created a face mask extractor from video clips. The assessment demonstrates how ineffective the real-time operation of the system is. Some other basic neural networks were realized in works by Ebhota et al. (2018, 2019).

To enhance such a system, a real-time still picture extractor from the video is needed. The majority of the datasets used in the literature on masked face identification were not implemented in real time. The existing works also use a dataset of fair-skinned individuals. Therefore, a real-time system that is trained on a dataset of persons with various complexions is required; this system will be valuable and relevant worldwide. This chapter has been organized as follows. Section 15.2 discusses the methodology. The findings are provided and discussed in section 15.3. Finally, section 15.4 concludes the work and recommends the future aspects.

15.2. Methodology

Acquiring face images is the first step in the model training phase. Next, the images are prepped for additional augmentation, and finally, the model is trained and validated. Acquisition of face images precedes image pre-processing to detect face masks in the model testing phase. After detection of the face mask, the face images would be processed again for effective recognition of the face behind the mask using template matching techniques. The last stage in the implementation phase is the storage of the recognized faces extracted in a database. The system flowchart is shown in Figure 15.2.

In the created system, both hardware and software components were utilized. The images used in the training and validation phase were taken with a camera that features dual pixel 12MP auto focus, a 1/2.55" sensor size and a resolution of 1080×680 pixels. The photographs were taken during the implementation phase using an Internet Protocol-enabled camera with a dual pixel 12MP, 1/2.55" sensor size and a resolution of 1080×720 pixels. The frameworks and libraries for the system's software were housed on a laptop running 64-bit version of Microsoft Windows 10 Pro (intel core i5 CPU at 2.7 GHz, installed 16 GB memory and 256 GB solid-state drive). Anaconda Navigator IDE was utilized to develop the codes. Visualization of the training and testing results of the developed system was carried out using a Jupyter notebook.

15.2.1. *Data collection and preprocessing*

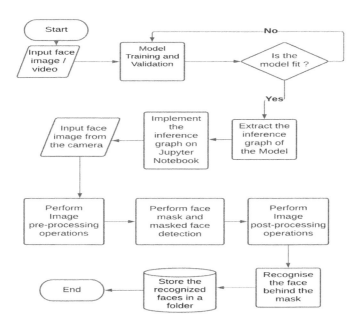

Figure 15.2. *System flowchart*

Using a mobile phone camera set to RGB format and placed one foot apart from the subjects, a total of 1000 photographs of skin faces with masks (positive images), and 1000 images of skin faces without masks (negative images) were taken. According to equation [15.1], the photos were resized at a certain ratio to create uniformity:

$$Ratio = W/H \qquad\qquad [15.1]$$

where W is the width and H is the height. To only gain the useful parts of the masked faces, a cropping filter was applied. This streamlined computing and accelerated network processing. The cropping was accomplished by normalizing all face photos to 240×240 pixels.

15.2.2. Model training and validation

Faster-RCNN with the Inception V3 architecture was modeled, as shown in Figure 15.3. Convolutions in the original model were more effective in terms of computational complexity because of the employment of clever "factorization techniques". The Inception V3 model factorizes a convolution of 7×7 and uses an additional classifier to propagate information about labels. The network's performance improved as a result of convolution factorization. For instance, a 3×3 convolution with the same number of filters is computationally 49/9 = 5.44 times more expensive than a 7×7 convolution over a grid with "n" filters and "m" filters.

Utilizing a momentum optimizer, the faster-RCNN Inception V3 model was trained. Here, 250 images were used to validate the model, after 750 images were used to train the model. To speed up computation and increase localization accuracy over R-CNN and Fast R-CNN, Region Proposal Network (RPN) was added to the faster R-CNN architecture. The RPN received its input from the final convolution layer of the CNN. Regression box differences with regards to anchors were predicted by the RPN, together with objectness. To produce proposals, these offsets were positioned alongside the anchors. The ROI Align layer, followed by the classifier and bbox regressor, received the RPN proposal. The architecture of faster R-CNN is shown in Figure 15.3.

The ROI max-pooling method used in the original faster R-CNN divides the ROI window into grids, before max-pooling the values in each sub-window. Each feature map channel underwent independent pooling. Numerous quantization procedures must be performed to map the generated proposal to precise indexes during ROI pooling implementation. These quantization operations introduce misalignments between the ROI and extracted features. This, however, has some negative impact on object detection. To address the misalignment issue, ROI align was used to remove all possible quantization operations in the network.

After successfully aligning the ROI, the convolution layer was used to extract features from the input face image. The convolution would use the input image to calculate the dot product and produce a feature map of a smaller scale as output. The output feature from the convolution layer was used by the fully connected layer to detect and predict the bounding box score for the input face image.

An adaptive gradient algorithm was used to support the optimizer; this adapted the learning rate during the model training. Furthermore, early stopping was used to stop the training when there was no noticeable improvement for some time; this would reduce the risk of model overfitting and long training time. Upon successful training, the inference graph of the model was generated.

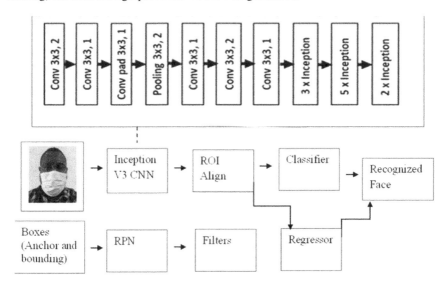

Figure 15.3. *Faster R-CNN model on the Inception V3 backbone*

15.2.3. *System implementation*

The inference graph generated after successful model training was implemented on the Jupyter notebook, an open-source web application that permits the creation and implementation of documents that contain codes, algorithms, visualizations and narrative texts. The implemented faster R-CNN detector was used in this research for face mask detection and mask face recognition. In order to achieve good results from the detector, the extracted masked face images were further subjected to image processing. Scale uniformity through rescaling of the extracted images was performed using a suitable equation. Image binarization was also performed using a suitable equation to remove a certain number of unwanted details from the extracted masked face images.

15.2.4. *System evaluation*

The accuracy of training and validation processes was obtained from the accuracy-epochs curves generated by the model. These were engaged in the evaluation of the trained model. Training and validation losses were also computed by the model. These losses amount to the trained model classification loss, which is a measure of the predictive inaccuracy of the model. The overall loss function of the model is obtained from the model classification loss. After a successful training procedure, the system was tested in real time with 250 random faces with masks and 250 random faces without masks. The system's overall accuracy was calculated using equation [15.2], and the values obtained from the confusion matrix are presented in Table 15.1.

$$\text{Overall Accuracy} = (TP + TN)/(TP+TN+FP+FN) \qquad\qquad [15.2]$$

		True class	
		Masked	**Non-masked**
Predicted classes	**Masked**	True positive	False negative
	Non-masked	False positive	True negative

$$\left(m_t, r_t \right) = \left(j, l \right)$$

Table 15.1. *Two-class confusion matrix*

The ratios between the expected and actual classes are shown in the confusion matrix table. The true positive (TP) value represents the proportion of positive samples (masked faces) correctly classified; the false positive (FP) value represents the proportion of positive samples incorrectly classified. The true negative (TN) value represents the proportion of negative samples incorrectly classified, and the false negative (FN) value represents the proportion of negative samples falsely classified.

15.3. Results and discussion

15.3.1. *Training accuracy*

Training accuracy measured the trained model classification ability using the given datasets during training procedures. The model prediction was used to automatically compute training accuracy per epoch curve to depict the model's response to the training datasets. Figure 15.4 shows a plot of accuracy against epochs. It is evident from the plot that the highest accuracy for best fit was recorded at the 16th epoch, where an accuracy of 0.94 has been achieved.

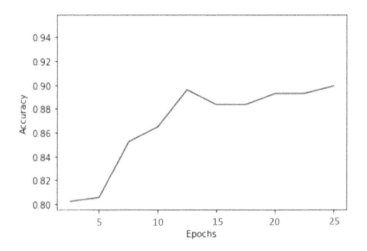

Figure 15.4. *Computed plot of training accuracy*

15.3.2. *Validation accuracy*

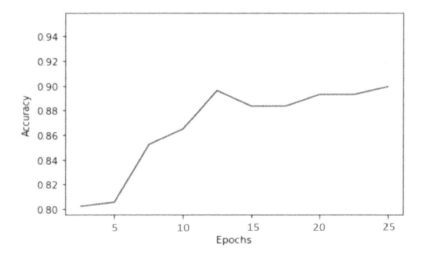

Figure 15.5. *Computed plot of validation accuracy*

Validation accuracy is the measure of the trained model classification ability during the model training procedure using the given datasets. The model prediction was used to automatically compute validation accuracy per epoch curve to depict the response of the model to the validation datasets. Figure 15.5 shows a plot of accuracy against epochs. It is evident from the plot that the highest accuracy for best fit was recorded at the 25th epoch, where accuracy of about 0.90 has been achieved.

15.3.3. *Training loss*

Training loss is an indication of how excellent the trained model is fitting the training dataset. It is measured during an individual epoch. Figure 15.6 shows a plot of loss against epochs. It is evident from the plot that minimal training loss for best fit was recorded at the 17th epoch, where a loss of about 0.14 has been achieved.

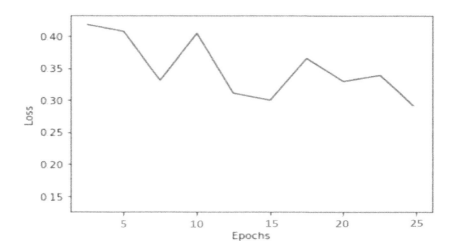

Figure 15.6. *Computed plot of training loss*

15.3.4. *Validation loss*

Validation loss indicates how well the trained model fits the validation dataset. Unlike training loss, validation loss is measured after an individual epoch. Figure 15.7 shows a plot of loss against epochs. It is evident from the plot that minimal validation loss for best fit was recorded at the 25th epoch, where a loss of about 0.28 has been achieved.

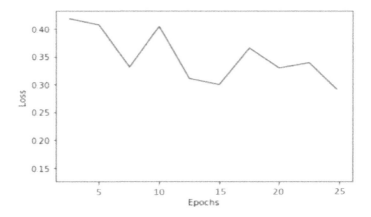

Figure 15.7. *Computed plot of validation loss*

15.3.5. *Overall accuracy*

In this research, the overall accuracy is the ratio of the number of accurate predictions to the number of all predictions. Equation [15.2] and the values obtained in the confusion matrix in Table 15.2 have been used to compute the overall accuracy value.

		True class	
		Masked	**Non-masked**
Predicted classes	**Masked**	TP (244)	FN (6)
	Non-masked	FP (10)	TN (240)

Overall accuracy = (TP + TN)/(TP+TN+FP+FN)
Overall accuracy = (244+240)/(244+10+240+6)
Overall accuracy = 484/500 = 0.97

Table 15.2. *Results of the two-class confusion matrix*

15.4. Conclusions and future recommendations

This study presented a face mask detection system using the FasterRCNN model with the InceptonV3 architecture. A Python-based integrated development environment such as Anaconda navigator was utilized for the implementation of the development algorithms and system. The face mask detector developed in this study is capable of determining whether someone wears a face mask or not. The system is developed such that it can perfectly detect a face mask on people's faces regardless of gender, skin color and the color of the mask. This system can be adapted for use anywhere in the world to enforce usage of face masks, especially in the era of the respiratory-related pandemic.

Future research and development in face mask detection system could include an automated system that can be positioned strategically to access a person's compliance levels with respect to wearing the face mask. Such a system could further be developed to send an SMS or place a call to security personnel the moment a defaulter is detected. Another area worthy of further research is the development of a deep learning framework capable of working on different classes, such that the system can detect not only face mask and non-face mask faces, but also faces with improperly worn face masks.

15.5. References

Adithya, K. and Jismi, B. (2020). A review on face mask detection using convolutional neural network. *International Research Journal of Engineering and Technology*, 7(11), 1302–1304.

Batagelj, B., Peer, P., Štruc, V., Dobrisek, S. (2021). How to correctly detect face-masks for COVID-19 from visual information. *Applied Science*, 11(2070), 1–24.

Bu, W., Xiao, J., Zhou, C., Yang, M., Peng, C. (2017). Detection, a cascade framework for masked face. *IEEE 8th International Conference on CIS & RAM*, Ningbo. doi: 10.1109/ICCIS.2017.8274819.

Chowdary, G.J., Punn, N.S., Sonbhadra, S.K., Agarwal, S. (2021). Face mask detection using transfer learning of inception V3. *Lecture Notes in Computer Science*, Springer, 12581, 1–10.

Din, N.U., Javed, K., Bae, S., Yi, J. (2020). A novel GAN-based network for unmasking of masked face. *IEEE Access*, 8, 44276–44287.

Ebhota, V.C., Isabona, J., Srivastava, V.M. (2018). Improved adaptive signal power loss prediction using combined vector statistics based smoothing and neural network approach. *International Journal on Progress in Electromagnetics Research C*, 82, 155–169.

Ebhota, V.C., Isabona, J., Srivastava, V.M. (2019). Environment-adaptation based hybrid neural network predictor for signal propagation loss prediction in cluttered and open urban microcells. *Wireless Personal Communication*, 104(3), 935–948.

Ejaz, M.S., Islam, M.R., Sifatullah, M., Sarker, A. (2019). Implementation of principal component analysis on masked and non-masked faces recognition. *1st International Conference on Advances in Science, Engineering and Robotics Technology (ICASERT)*. doi: 10.1109/ICASERT.2019.8934543.

Ge, S., Li, J., Ye, Q., Luo, Z. (2017). Detecting masked faces in the wild with LLE-CNNs. *IEEE Conference on Computer Vision and Pattern Recognition (CVPR)*, Honolulu, HI, 426–434.

Hariri, W. (2022). Efficient masked face recognition method during the Covid-19 pandemic. *Signal, Image and Video Processing*, 16, 605–612.

Ibitoye, O. (2021). A brief review of convolutional neural network techniques for masked face recognition. *IEEE Concurrent Processes Architectures and Architectures and Embedded Systems Virtual Conf. (COPA)*, San Diego, 1–4.

Jang, Y., Gunes, H., Patras, I. (2019). Registration-free face-SSD: Single-shot analysis of smiles, facial attributes, and affect in the wild. *Computer Vision and Image Understanding*, 182, 19–29.

Li, Y., Guo, K., Lu, Y., Liu, L. (2021). Cropping and attention-based approach for masked face recognition. *Applied Intelligence*, 51, 3012–3025.

Lin, K., Zhao, H., Lv, J., Li, C. (2020). Face detection and segmentation based on improved mask R-CNN. *Discrete Dynamics in Nature and Society*, 1–11.

Loey, M., Manogaran, G., Taha, M.N., Khalifa, N.E.M. (2021). Fighting against COVID-19: A novel deep learning model based on YOLO v2 with ResNet-50 for medical face mask detection. *Sustainable Cities and Society*, 65.

Madhura, I. and Mehendale, N. (2020). Real-time face mask identification using facemasknet deep learning network. *SSRN*, Preprint, 1–7. doi: 10.2139/ssrn.3663305.

Mahore, A. and Tripathi, M. (2018). Detection of 3D Mask in 2D face recognition system using DWT and LBP. *IEEE 3rd International Conference on Communication and Information System*. doi: 10.1109/ICOMIS.2018.8644807.

Mandal, B., Okeukwu, A., Theis, Y. (2021). Masked face recognition using ResNet-50. Preprint. doi: 10.48550/arXiv.2104.08997.

Meenpal, T., Balakrishnan, A., Verma, A. (2019). Facial mask detection using semantic segmentation. *IEEE 4th International Conference on Computing, Communication and Security*. doi: 10.1109/CCCS.2019.8888092.

Mheidl, N., Fares, M., Zalzale, H., Fares, J. (2020). Effects of face masks on interpersonal relatioshionships during COVID 19 pandemic. *Frontiers in Public Health*, 8, 1–6.

MIT (2018). Study finds gender and skin-type bias in commercial artificial-intelligence systems. *MIT News*, USA.

Morton, S., Pencheon, D., Squires, N. (2017). Sustainable development goals (SDGs), and their implementation: A national global framework for health, development and equity needs a systems approach at every level. *British Medical Bulletin*, 124, 81–90.

Nagrath, P., Jain, R., Madan, A., Arora, R., Kataria, P., Hemanth, J. (2021). A real time DNN-based face mask detection system using single shot multibox detector and MobileNetV2. *Sustainable Cities and Society*, 66, 1–11.

Ngan, M., Grother, P., Hanaoka, K. (2020). Face recognition accuracy with masks using pre-COVID-19 algorithms. NIST Pubs Report. NISTIR 8311, Gaithersburg, MD.

Qin, B. and Li, D. (2020). Identifying facemask-wearing condition using image super-resolution with classification network to prevent COVID-19. *Sensors*, 20(18), 1–23.

Qiting, Y. (2018). Masked face detection via a novel framework. *International Conference on Mechanical, Electronic, Control and Automation Engineering*. doi: 10.2991/mecae-18.2018.137.

Ryumina, E., Ryumin, D., Ivanko, D., Karpov, A. (2021). A novel method for protective face mask detection using convolutional neural networks and image histograms. *4th International Workshop on Photogrammetric & Computer Vision Techniques for Video Surveillance, Biometrics And Biomedicine*. doi: 10.5194/isprs-archives-XLIV-2-W1-2021-177-2021.

Said, Y. (2020). Pynq-YOLO-Net: An embedded quantized convolutional neural network for face mask detection in COVID-19 pandemic era. *International Journal of Advanced Computer Science and Applications*, 11(9), 100–106.

Shashi, Y. (2020). Deep learning-based safe social distancing and face mask detection in public areas for Covid-19 safety guidelines adherence. *International Journal for Research in Applied Science & Engineering Technology*, 8(7), 1368–1375.

Shitala, P., Li, Y., Lin, D., Sheng, D. (2021). MaskedFaceNet: A progressive semi-supervised masked face detector. *IEEE/CVF Winter Conf. on Applications of Computer Vision (WACV)*, Waikoloa, HI, 3388–3397.

Wang, M. and Deng, W. (2021). Deep face recognition: A survey. *Neurocomputing*, 429, 215–244.

Wang, S.Y., Luo, B., Shen, J. (2019). Face masks extraction in video. *International Journal of Computer Vision*, 127, 625–641.

Ziwei, S., Kristie, N., Tien, N., Catherine, C., Jerry, G. (2022). Spartan face mask detection and facial recognition system. *Healthcare*, 10(1), 1–24.

16

An Action-based Monitoring Tool for Processes Subject to Multiple Quality Shifts

Two usual key assumptions in the statistical process control (SPC) literature are: (i) the implementation of a process investigation whenever an out-of-control signal occurs and (ii) the process investigation is perfect and defines with certainty the process state. Nevertheless, in many real cases, a thorough process investigation may not be error-free and is not always a cost-efficient option. To this effect, a process monitoring tool, designed under an action-oriented framework, is developed. The proposed model is based on Markov chain theory and considers processes subject to multiple assignable causes. A benchmark of examples has been generated to demonstrate the performance of the monitoring scheme and a comparison to simpler approaches is presented.

16.1. Introduction

In the manufacturing sector, the need for viable, acceptable and stable levels of quality, aligned with the modern quality standards requirements, is ever-increasing, thereby, necessitating new, effective approaches to fault diagnosis. It is well known that many intangible and poor-quality costs, including inter alias, inventory, lost production and personnel costs, are hidden in unplanned downtime, and their elimination is a milestone commitment and challenge for quality (Woodall and

Chapter written by Konstantina Tsiota and Konstantinos A. Tasias.

For a color version of all the figures in this chapter, see www.iste.co.uk/dimotikalis/data3.zip.

Faltin 2019). The use of appropriate machine performance metrics to develop statistical models could eliminate the unplanned downtime and the excessive poor-quality costs that impact a company's bottom line. Scaling-up process lines have led industries to adopt automation, process learning and sensor implementation, to handle the high probability of obtaining false alarms from multiple testing (Sall 2018; Woodall and Faltin 2019).

The evaluation of alarms and the identification of patterns can become a powerful capability for failure prediction, according to Adams et al. (1992), who carried out a detailed study on false alarm handling. The interpretation of alarms and trends combined with historical data and failure reoccurrence tracking can: a) classify the severity of the alarms; b) predict the potential failure trouble areas; and c) suggest the proper replacement achieving high restoration rates (Aytaçoğlu et al. 2021).

Nevertheless, two key assumptions widely implemented in the statistical process control (SPC) literature pertain to the following hypotheses: a) every alarm issued by the control chart, regardless of being true or false, necessitates a process investigation. Therefore, the process may be unnecessarily charged with an additional cost and face an increased downtime. b) The investigation is perfect, revealing with certainty the process state.

Consequently, the above-mentioned simplistic assumptions raise the following questions: is the process investigation worth it? Is the probability of an out-of-control (OOC) operation high enough to justify a process halt for investigation? Is the process investigation always perfect?

In real-world applications, the process investigation may not be an efficient or even feasible, option. Specifically, an error-free investigation of a process subject to multiple quality disruptions prerequisites the one-by-one examination of all potential causes to identify the process state, which is a time and/or cost-prohibitive procedure for many practical applications. Moreover, potential causes of process quality deterioration may include components and spare parts, which must be sent to another facility for their operational condition to be evaluated, thereby resulting in even larger time and cost requirements. In the conventional SPC literature, a relatively large investigation cost and/or required time would result in a no-SPC policy to minimize the number of investigations, and so, avoid a very costly monitoring procedure. Either way, such a thorough and error-free process investigation may not be the optimal decision.

To this effect, this study presents a different SPC approach, where the control scheme is separated into action zones. Online process monitoring is implemented, indicating signals if any disruption has probably impacted the process. Nonetheless, in the proposed approach, the process investigation step is omitted, and the value of the chart statistic directly defines the proper restoration plan, thereby aiming at reducing the economic impact of overcounted false alarms by redesigning the typical Shewhart control chart.

For ease of presentation, and without any loss of generality, a process affected by two assignable causes that lead to defined mean shifts is considered to evaluate the performance of the proposed approach. The process is restored from an OOC state to the in-control (IC) state by the implementation of specific restoration actions. The Markov chain theory has been used to model the operation of the proposed control scheme, and a source code developed in MATLAB defines the optimal design parameters for each approach.

This study is structured as follows: section 16.2 presents the problem definition and introduces the model assumptions. In section 16.3, a presentation of the conventional SPC approach and the proposed SPC approach is provided. In section 16.4, the Markov chain models are presented. The formulation of the optimization problem is given in section 16.5. In section 16.6, a numerical investigation is provided and a comparison of the proposed approach against the conventional approach is made. Finally, conclusions and future research directions are given in section 16.7.

16.2. Problem definition and assumptions

Let us consider a process that operates indefinitely, and its quality is fully defined by a critical-to-quality characteristic X, a continuous, normally distributed random variable. The process has a perfect initial setup, i.e. starts with the mean and standard deviation coinciding with their target values (μ_0, σ_0).

Two possible assignable causes may occur at random times, affecting the process mean, and so, shifting the process from the IC state to an OOC operation state (OOC_1, OOC_2). Assignable cause 1 shifts the process mean by a multiple d_1 of the standard deviation ($\mu_1 = \mu_0 + d_1 \sigma_0$), and assignable cause 2 by a d_2 ($\mu_2 = \mu_0 + d_2 \sigma_0$) ($d_2 > d_1 > 0$). To increase the applicability of the model, the occurrence of assignable cause 1 does not impede the occurrence of assignable cause 2, which further deteriorates the process performance. The standard deviation (σ_0) is assumed to remain constant and unaffected by the assignable causes. The process is not self-correcting and so, at each sampling interval of duration h (see Figure 16.1), only transitions to inferior states may occur without the implementation of restoration actions (see Figure 16.2). The process may be restored to the IC state from an OOC state (OOC_1, OOC_2), through different restoration actions, i.e. action A for OOC_1 and action B for OOC_2.

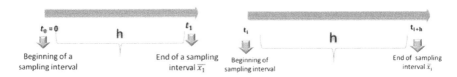

Figure 16.1. *Process setup: sampling interval*

The time until the occurrence of each assignable cause is assumed to be an exponentially distributed random variable.

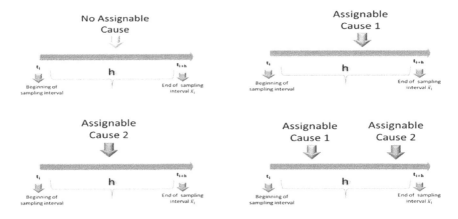

Figure 16.2. *Possible scenarios during a sampling interval*

The notations used to formulate the model are presented in Table 16.1.

Notation	Description+
X	Critical to quality characteristic
μ_0	In-control process mean
σ_0	In-control standard deviation
μ_i	Out-of-control mean when assignable cause i has occurred
d_i	Magnitude of the shift in the process mean due to assignable cause i
n	Sampling size
h	Sampling interval
OOC_1	Out-of-control operating state due to assignable cause 1
OOC_2	Out-of-control operating state due to assignable cause 2
m_t	Current state of the process at t^{th} inspection
r_t	Decision made based on the chart statistic at t^{th} inspection
k_i	Action limit (i = 1,2)
k	Control limit
λ_{ij}	Occurrence rate of assignable cause j when the process is already under the effect of assignable cause i
v_i	Transition rate to any inferior state of the process, when it is already under the effect of assignable cause i
γ_{ij}	Probability of occurrence of assignable cause j when the process is already under the effect of assignable cause i
b	Fixed cost per sampling
c	Sampling cost per unit
L_0	Cost of a process investigation
L_i	Cost of process restoration from state OOC_i (i = 1,2)
M_i	Cost per time unit for operation under the effect of state OOC_i (i = 1,2)
Q_0	Expected OOC operation cost for IC state being the initial state of an interval
Q_i	Expected OOC operation cost for OOC_i being the initial state of an interval
T_0	Time required for a process investigation
T_i	Time required for a process restoration from state OOC_i
$p_{ij \atop kl}$	Transition probabilities from state $\left(m_{t-1}, r_{t-1} \right) = \left(i, k \right)$ to state $\left(m_t, r_t \right) = \left(j, l \right)$ during a sampling interval
$\pi_{(mt,rt)}$	Steady-state probabilities

Table 16.1. *Notations*

16.3. Conventional versus proposed SPC approach

16.3.1. *Conventional SPC approach*

In the classic SPC approach, at each sampling point, the mean of the quality characteristic is evaluated and compared with a defined control limit k. Every time the control chart issues an OOC signal, i.e. the plotted statistic exceeds the control limit k, a process investigation is activated, revealing, with certainty, either a false alarm or the effect of an assignable cause that has caused quality deterioration. The control chart used in the conventional SPC approach is shown in Figure 16.3.

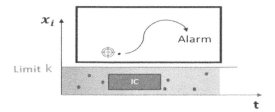

Figure 16.3. *Conventional SPC approach control chart*

In the latter case, the process is restored from the OOC state to the IC state by specific restoration actions which restrain the process performance degradation. On the other hand, in case of a false alarm, the investigation charges the process with a cost that could be potentially avoided.

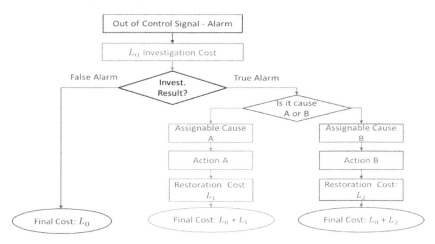

Figure 16.4. *Graphical representation of the economic model of conventional SPC approach*

The following cost categories are associated with this approach (Lorenzen and Vance (1986): inspection, investigation, restoration and OOC operation.

A graphical representation of the economic model of the conventional SPC approach is shown in Figure 16.4. It should be noted that both the conventional and proposed approaches are correspondingly affected by the inspection and OOC operation costs, and so, are not presented in the graph, aiming to highlight the differences between the two approaches.

16.3.2. Proposed SPC approach

In the proposed SPC approach, the control chart is separated into action zones, delimited by one limit for each possible quality disruption, which will be hereafter denoted as action limits. Consequently, in the present study, where two assignable causes may affect the process, two action limits, k_1 and k_2 ($k_1 < k_2$), are considered as design parameters, along with the sample size n and sampling interval h, of the proposed control scheme (see Figure 16.5).

In case the sample mean is plotted below k_1, the process is considered IC, and no action is taken. If the sample mean lies between k_1 and k_2, we would suspect that assignable cause 1 has occurred, and so, restoration action A is implemented. Finally, a sample mean that outreaches k_2 indicates that assignable cause 2 is present and restoration action B must be implemented to eliminate the shift and restore the process. Consequently, this approach proposes a modified interpretation of the value of each chart statistic, as compared to the conventional SPC approach, by directly dictating the appropriate restoration action for every signal. The above-mentioned policy is shown in Figure 16.5.

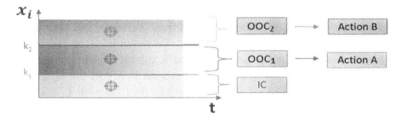

Figure 16.5. *Proposed SPC approach control chart*

Regarding the economic model of the proposed SPC approach, as already mentioned, the inspection and OOC operation costs are embedded in a similar manner compared to the conventional SPC approach. On the other hand, the investigation cost is not considered because the investigation step is omitted, and the restoration costs are, subsequently, modified. A graphical presentation of the economic model of the proposed SPC approach is presented in Figure 16.6.

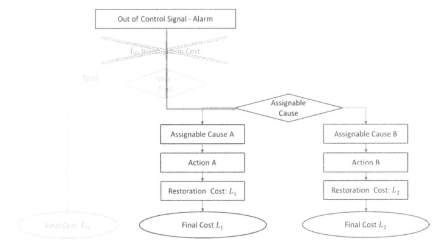

Figure 16.6. *Graphical presentation of the economic model of the proposed SPC approach*

16.4. Markov chain models

16.4.1. *Transition probability matrix*

The process state, at t^{th} inspection, is defined by the following parameters: a) the actual state of the process (m_t), which equals 0 if the process operates IC, 1 if the operates in the OOC_1 state and 2 if the process is in the OOC_2 state; b) the decision made at each sampling interval based on the collected inspection data (r_t). As already mentioned, the decision policy differs between the two approaches. Regarding the conventional approach, r_t has two possible values: equals 0, if the chart statistic lies below the control limit, and 2, otherwise. On the other hand, the possible decisions in the proposed SPC approach are: 0, in case the sample mean lies below the action limit k_1, 1, if the chart statistic lies between k_1 and k_2, and 2, otherwise.

A visual representation of the parameters that define the process state, along with their possible values for each approach, is presented in Figure 16.7.

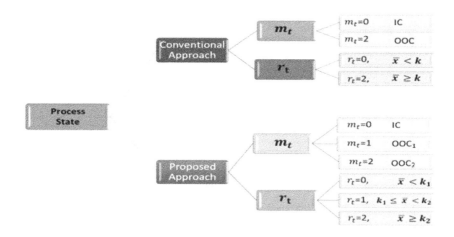

Figure 16.7. *Process state definition for conventional and proposed SPC approaches*

Therefore, the state space in the conventional model includes six (3x2) possible states, whereas the state space for the proposed model includes nine (3x3) possible states. The transition probability matrix of the Markov chain for the classic and proposed SPC approach is presented in Tables 16.2 and 16.3, respectively.

Conventional Approach		End of sampling interval process state					
		(0,0)	(0,2)	(1,0)	(1,2)	(2,0)	(2,2)
P / Beginning of sampling interval process state	(0,0)	p_{00}^{00}	p_{02}^{00}	p_{00}^{01}	p_{02}^{01}	p_{00}^{02}	p_{02}^{02}
	(0,2)	p_{20}^{00}	p_{22}^{00}	p_{20}^{01}	p_{22}^{01}	p_{20}^{02}	p_{22}^{02}
	(1,0)	p_{00}^{10}	p_{02}^{10}	p_{00}^{11}	p_{02}^{11}	p_{00}^{12}	p_{02}^{12}
	(1,2)	p_{20}^{10}	p_{22}^{10}	p_{20}^{11}	p_{22}^{11}	p_{20}^{12}	p_{22}^{12}
	(2,0)	p_{00}^{20}	p_{02}^{20}	p_{00}^{21}	p_{02}^{21}	p_{00}^{22}	p_{02}^{22}
	(2,2)	p_{20}^{20}	p_{22}^{20}	p_{20}^{21}	p_{22}^{21}	p_{20}^{22}	p_{22}^{22}

Table 16.2. *Transition probability matrix for the conventional approach*

Proposed Approach		End of sampling interval process state								
		(0,0)	(0,1)	(0,2)	(1,0)	(1,1)	(1,2)	(2,0)	(2,1)	(2,2)
P / Beginning of sampling interval process state	(0,0)	p^{00}_{00}	p^{00}_{01}	p^{00}_{02}	p^{01}_{00}	p^{01}_{01}	p^{01}_{02}	p^{02}_{00}	p^{02}_{01}	p^{02}_{02}
	(0,1)	p^{00}_{10}	p^{00}_{11}	p^{00}_{12}	p^{01}_{10}	p^{01}_{11}	p^{01}_{12}	p^{02}_{10}	p^{02}_{11}	p^{02}_{12}
	(0,2)	p^{00}_{20}	p^{00}_{21}	p^{00}_{22}	p^{01}_{20}	p^{01}_{21}	p^{01}_{22}	p^{02}_{20}	p^{02}_{21}	p^{02}_{22}
	(1,0)	p^{10}_{00}	p^{10}_{01}	p^{10}_{02}	p^{11}_{00}	p^{11}_{01}	p^{11}_{02}	p^{12}_{00}	p^{12}_{01}	p^{12}_{02}
	(1,1)	p^{10}_{10}	p^{10}_{11}	p^{10}_{12}	p^{11}_{10}	p^{11}_{11}	p^{11}_{12}	p^{12}_{10}	p^{12}_{11}	p^{12}_{12}
	(1,2)	p^{10}_{20}	p^{10}_{21}	p^{10}_{22}	p^{11}_{20}	p^{11}_{21}	p^{11}_{22}	p^{12}_{20}	p^{12}_{21}	p^{12}_{22}
	(2,0)	p^{20}_{00}	p^{20}_{01}	p^{20}_{02}	p^{21}_{00}	p^{21}_{01}	p^{21}_{02}	p^{22}_{00}	p^{22}_{01}	p^{22}_{02}
	(2,1)	p^{20}_{10}	p^{20}_{11}	p^{20}_{12}	p^{21}_{10}	p^{21}_{11}	p^{21}_{12}	p^{22}_{10}	p^{22}_{11}	p^{22}_{12}
	(2,2)	p^{20}_{20}	p^{20}_{21}	p^{20}_{22}	p^{21}_{20}	p^{21}_{21}	p^{21}_{22}	p^{22}_{20}	p^{22}_{21}	p^{22}_{22}

Table 16.3. *Transition probability matrix for the proposed approach*

16.4.2. *Transition probabilities*

The general expression of the transition probabilities, based on Markov chain theory, is defined as follows:

$$p_{\substack{ij \\ kl}} = P\left[m_t = j, r_t = l \mid m_{t-1} = i, r_{t-1} = k \right], \; i,j,k,l = 0,1,2 \quad [16.1]$$

For the sake of brevity, only the 81 transition probabilities for the proposed SPC approach are analytically presented. The transition probabilities regarding the conventional SPC approach are derived by following the same rationale:

$$p_{\substack{00 \\ 0l}} = p_{\substack{00 \\ 1l}} = p_{\substack{00 \\ 2l}} = p_{\substack{10 \\ 1l}} = p_{\substack{20 \\ 2l}} = \exp\left(-\left(\lambda_{01} + \lambda_{02}\right)\cdot h\right)\cdot \begin{cases} \Phi(k_1) & l = 0 \\ \left(\Phi(k_2) - \Phi(k_1)\right) & l = 1 \\ \left(1 - \Phi(k_2)\right) & l = 2 \end{cases} \quad [16.2]$$

$$
p_{01 \atop 0l} = p_{01 \atop 1l} = p_{01 \atop 2l} = p_{11 \atop 1l} = p_{21 \atop 2l} = \frac{\lambda_{01}}{v_0 - v_1} \cdot \left(\exp(-v_1 \cdot h) - \exp(-v_0 \cdot h) \right) \cdot \begin{cases} \Phi\left(k_1 - d_1 \cdot \sqrt{n}\right) & l = 0 \\ \begin{pmatrix} \Phi\left(k_2 - d_1 \cdot \sqrt{n}\right) - \\ -\Phi\left(k_1 - d_1 \cdot \sqrt{n}\right) \end{pmatrix} & l = 1 \\ \left(1 - \Phi\left(k_2 - d_1 \cdot \sqrt{n}\right)\right) \, l = 2 \end{cases} \qquad [16.3]
$$

$$
p_{02 \atop 0l} = p_{02 \atop 1l} = p_{02 \atop 2l} = p_{12 \atop 1l} = p_{22 \atop 2l} = \begin{pmatrix} \dfrac{\lambda_{02}}{v_0} \cdot \left(1 - \exp(-v_0 \cdot h)\right) + \\ + \dfrac{\lambda_{01} \cdot \lambda_{12}}{v_1 \cdot v_0} \cdot \left(1 - \exp(-v_0 \cdot h)\right) - \\ - \dfrac{\lambda_{01} \cdot \lambda_{12}}{v_1 \cdot (v_0 - v_1)} \cdot \exp(-v_1 \cdot h) \cdot \\ \cdot \left(1 - \exp\left(-(v_0 - v_1)\right) \cdot h\right) \end{pmatrix} \cdot \begin{cases} \Phi\left(k_1 - d_2 \cdot \sqrt{n}\right) & l = 0 \\ \begin{pmatrix} \Phi\left(k_2 - d_2 \cdot \sqrt{n}\right) - \\ -\Phi\left(k_1 - d_2 \cdot \sqrt{n}\right) \end{pmatrix} & l = 1 \\ \left(1 - \Phi\left(k_2 - d_2 \cdot \sqrt{n}\right)\right) l = 2 \end{cases} \qquad [16.4]
$$

$$
p_{11 \atop 0l} = p_{11 \atop 2l} = \exp(-\lambda_{12} \cdot h) \cdot \begin{cases} \Phi\left(k_1 - d_1 \cdot \sqrt{n}\right) & l = 0 \\ \left(\Phi\left(k_2 - d_1 \cdot \sqrt{n}\right) - \Phi\left(k_1 - d_1 \cdot \sqrt{n}\right)\right) l = 1 \\ \left(1 - \Phi\left(k_2 - d_1 \cdot \sqrt{n}\right)\right) & l = 2 \end{cases} \qquad [16.5]
$$

$$
p_{12 \atop 0l} = p_{12 \atop 2l} = \left(1 - \exp(-\lambda_{12} \cdot h)\right) \cdot \begin{cases} \Phi\left(k_1 - d_2 \cdot \sqrt{n}\right) & l = 0 \\ \left(\Phi\left(k_2 - d_2 \cdot \sqrt{n}\right) - \Phi\left(k_1 - d_2 \cdot \sqrt{n}\right)\right) l = 1 \\ \left(1 - \Phi\left(k_2 - d_2 \cdot \sqrt{n}\right)\right) & l = 2 \end{cases} \qquad [16.6]
$$

$$
p_{22 \atop 0l} = p_{22 \atop 2l} = \begin{cases} \Phi\left(k_1 - d_2 \cdot \sqrt{n}\right) & l = 0 \\ \left(\Phi\left(k_2 - d_2 \cdot \sqrt{n}\right) - \Phi\left(k_1 - d_2 \cdot \sqrt{n}\right)\right) l = 1 \\ \left(1 - \Phi\left(k_2 - d_2 \cdot \sqrt{n}\right)\right) & l = 2 \end{cases} \qquad [16.7]
$$

$$
p_{ij \atop kl} = 0, \ \forall \left(0 < j < i\right) \cap \left(k \neq i\right) \qquad [16.8]
$$

For a further review of formulas deriving the transition probabilities under multiple assignable causes, the reader should refer to Nenes et al. (2015).

The steady-state probabilities, which represent the long-term probability for the process operating under each possible state (m_t, r_t), denoted by $\pi_{(m_t, r_t)}$, are computed by solving the following system of linear equations:

$$\sum_{m_t=0}^{2}\sum_{r_t=0}^{2}\pi_{(m_t, r_t)} = 1 \text{ and } \pi_{(m_t, r_t)} = \sum_{m_{t-1}=0}^{2}\sum_{r_{t-1}=0}^{2} P_{\substack{m_{t-1}m_t \\ r_{t-1} r_t}} \cdot \pi_{(m_{t-1}, r_{t-1})} \qquad [16.9]$$

16.4.3. Expected cost per time unit

The expected cost per time unit defines the optimal design parameters of the process monitoring tools and is used as a key performance indicator for the two approaches. It is denoted by ECT_c and ECT_p for the conventional and proposed SPC approach, respectively, and equals the ratio of the expected cost of a transition step over its expected duration.

16.4.3.1. Expected OOC operation cost

The computation of the expected cost of a transition step for the two approaches, EC_c and EC_p, necessitates the evaluation of the OOC operation cost. The following three equations ([16.10]–[16.12]) are used to compute the OOC operation cost when a sampling interval begins with the process being in the IC state, in the OOC_1 state and in the OOC_2 state, respectively.

If the process operates IC at the beginning of the sampling interval, the following alternative scenarios should be considered: a) no assignable cause occurs, and so, the process continues operating IC. Apparently, in such case, the process is not charged with an OOC operation cost; b) assignable cause 1 occurs, and so, the OOC_1 state is the initial state of the remainder of the sampling interval; c) assignable cause 2 occurs and the process operates in the OOC_2 state for the remainder of the interval. Therefore, the expected OOC operation cost in case the IC state is the initial state of the interval equals:

$$Q_0 = \int_0^h \lambda_{01} \cdot \exp(-v_0 \cdot t) \cdot Q_1(h-t) dt + \int_0^h \lambda_{02} \cdot \exp(-v_0 \cdot t) \cdot Q_2(h-t) dt \quad [16.10]$$

If the process operates in the OOC_1 state at the beginning of the sampling interval, two possible scenarios may occur: a) assignable cause 2 does not occur, and so, the process operates in OOC_1 state for the whole interval; b) assignable cause

2 occurs, and the process further deteriorates to the OOC_2 state. The expected OOC operation cost is formulated as:

$$Q_1 = M_1 \cdot \left(h \cdot \exp(-\lambda_{12} \cdot h) + \frac{1 - \lambda_{12} \cdot h \cdot \exp(-\lambda_{12} \cdot h) - \exp(-\lambda_{12} \cdot h)}{\lambda_{12}} \right) +$$
$$+ M_2 \cdot \left(h \cdot (1 - \exp(-\lambda_{12} \cdot h)) - \frac{1 - \lambda_{12} \cdot h \cdot \exp(-\lambda_{12} \cdot h) - \exp(-\lambda_{12} \cdot h)}{\lambda_{12}} \right) \qquad [16.11]$$

Finally, if the process is under the effect of assignable cause 2 at the beginning of the sampling interval, then, given the assumption that the process is not self-correcting, it will operate in the OOC_2 state for the whole interval:

$$Q_2 = M_2 \cdot h \qquad [16.12]$$

16.4.3.2. ECT in conventional SPC approach

EC_c equals the weighted average of the expected cost of all possible states of the Markov chain (Table 16.2), and is computed from the following expression:

$$EC_c = b + c \cdot n + \sum_{i=0}^{2} \pi_{i0} \cdot Q_i + \sum_{i=1}^{2} \pi_{i2} \cdot (Q_0 + L_0 + L_i) + \pi_{02} \cdot (Q_0 + L_0) \qquad [16.13]$$

Similarly, ET_c indicates the weighted average of durations associated with each state of the Markov chain:

$$ET_c = h + \sum_{i=1}^{2} \pi_{i2} \cdot (T_0 + T_i) + \pi_{02} \cdot T_0 \qquad [16.14]$$

Consequently, the long-run average cost per time unit (ECT_c), which equals the ratio of EC_c to ET_c, is given from the following expression:

$$ECT_c = \frac{EC_c}{ET_c} = \frac{b + c \cdot n + \sum_{i=0}^{2} \pi_{i0} \cdot Q_i + \sum_{i=1}^{2} \pi_{i2} \cdot (Q_0 + L_0 + L_i) + \pi_{02} \cdot (Q_0 + L_0)}{h + \sum_{i=1}^{2} \pi_{i2} \cdot (T_0 + T_i) + \pi_{02} \cdot T_0} \qquad [16.15]$$

16.4.3.3. ECT in the proposed SPC approach

The ECT in the proposed SPC approach (ECT_p) is evaluated by following the same rationale described in section 16.4.3.2.

EC_p is computed as the weighted average of the expected cost of each possible state of the Markov chain (Table 16.3) and is given by:

$$EC_p = b + c \cdot n + \sum_{i=0}^{2} \pi_{i0} \cdot Q_i + \sum_{i=0}^{1} \pi_{i1} \cdot (Q_0 + L_1) +$$

$$+ (\pi_{02} + \pi_{22}) \cdot (Q_0 + L_2) + \pi_{12} \cdot (Q_1 + L_2) + \pi_{21} \cdot (Q_2 + L_1) \qquad [16.16]$$

Regarding ET_p, it is evaluated from the following equation:

$$ET_p = h + \sum_{i=0}^{2} \sum_{j=1}^{2} \pi_{ij} \cdot T_j \qquad [16.17]$$

Consequently, ECT_p is computed by the following function:

$$ECT_p = \frac{EC_p}{ET_p} = \frac{b + c \cdot n + \sum_{i=0}^{2} \pi_{i0} \cdot Q_i + \sum_{i=0}^{1} \pi_{i1} \cdot (Q_0 + L_1) + (\pi_{02} + \pi_{22}) \cdot (Q_0 + L_2) + \pi_{12} \cdot (Q_1 + L_2) + \pi_{21} \cdot (Q_2 + L_1)}{h + \sum_{i=0}^{2} \sum_{j=1}^{2} \pi_{ij} \cdot T_j} \qquad [16.18]$$

16.5. Optimization problem

As already stated, ECT is set as the objective function for the two approaches. The optimization problem is solved through a source code developed in MATLAB, which defines the minimum value of ECT through successive iterations of the design parameters, and is formulated as follows:

	Conventional approach	Proposed approach
Objective function	$\min ECT_c$	$\min ECT_p$
Constraints	$n, h, k > 0$	$n, h, k_1, k_2 > 0$
	$n \in \mathbb{Z}^+$	$n \in \mathbb{Z}^+$
		$k_1 < k_2$

Table 16.4. *Optimization problem for the conventional and proposed approach*

16.6. Numerical analysis

16.6.1. *Numerical examples*

To compare the performance of the two approaches, i.e. conventional and proposed, the economic impact of each of them is evaluated for an extended benchmark of scenarios. The goal of this study is to examine the superiority of each approach as a function of the process characteristics. To this effect, a wide benchmark of cases with different parameters has been examined. For the sake of brevity, a small fraction of these sets is indicatively presented in Table 16.5. The whole dataset is available upon request from the authors.

$\lambda_{01}=0.10$ $\lambda_{02}=0.15$ $\lambda_{12}=0.20$	$d_1=0.125$ $d_2=0.250$	Parameters										
			L_i			T_i		M_i		ECT		Comparison
Scenario		c	L_0	L_1	L_2	T_0	T_1	T_2	M_1	M_2	ECT_c	ECT_p	$ECT_{comparison}$
1		200	100	150	200	50	100	150	1000	500	1.613	1.647	-0.69
2		10	100	200	300	150	300	600	300	150	6.586	22.582	-2.469
3		150	100	300	350	15	30	60	20	500	1.976	1.479	0.251
4		60	100	300	450	200	400	600	400	550	1.906	0.312	0.836
5		20	100	350	500	150	60	50	3000	1500	0.784	6.104	-195.558
6		20	100	400	550	150	65	25	20	500	2.305	2.045	0.113
7		50	100	450	1000	100	40	9500	4500	2000	0.425	0.131	0.629
8		50	100	500	600	100	40	9500	4500	2000	2.149	0.350	0.837
9		50	100	550	750	100	40	9500	4500	2000	2.347	0.377	0.839
10		40	100	600	300	20	400	600	400	500	1.813	0.272	0.850
11		40	100	600	200	20	400	600	400	500	1.693	0.244	0.855
12		150	100	650	1000	15	30	60	20	500	3.050	2.718	0.109
13		50	100	650	800	100	40	9500	4500	2000	2.437	0.364	0.851
14		150	100	700	800	15	30	60	20	500	2.775	1.806	0.349
15		150	100	750	950	15	30	60	20	500	3.011	2.243	0.254
16		10	100	800	750	450	200	400	600	400	2.603	0.435	0.833
17		10	100	850	1000	450	200	400	600	400	0.439	0.154	0.651
18		60	100	900	700	200	400	350	1500	1000	2.391	0.043	0.982
19		10	100	950	800	450	250	150	1500	3000	2.513	0.158	0.936
20		200	100	1000	950	50	100	150	1000	500	2.781	6.18	-1.22

Table 16.5. *Set parameters and results*

16.6.2. *Performance comparisons*

The percentage difference of ECT between the conventional and proposed SPC approach, is computed as follows:

$$ECT_{comparison} = \frac{ECT_c - ECT_p}{ECT_c}$$

[16.19]

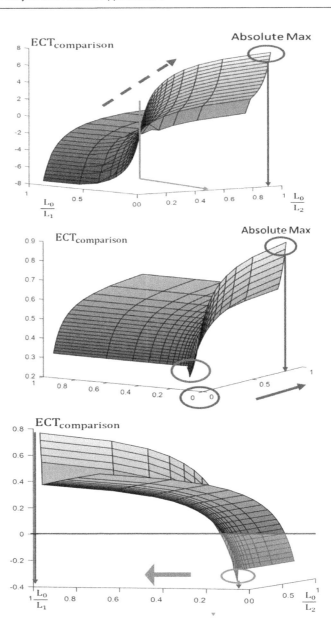

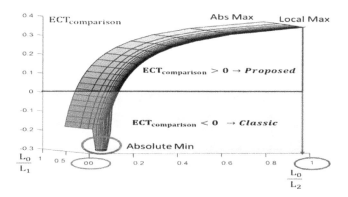

Figure 16.8. *3D surface plots for economic comparison between the classic and proposed approach*

The *ECTs* of the two approaches are compared side by side for the same set of parameters by the means of 3D surface plots with contour, as shown in Figure 16.8. The 3D surface plots allow visually appealing and customizable 3D visualization of the one-dimensional $ECT_{comparison}$ output with the two-dimensional input of the ratios L_0/L_1 and L_0/L_2. The investigation and restoration costs are the distinguishing features in the cost model of each approach, and so, are selected as indicators to identify the relative performance among the conventional and the proposed approach. The ratio L_0/L_1 denotes the indicator on the X-axis, whereas the ratio L_0/L_2 is the indicator on the Y-axis.

It is noteworthy that the Z-axis takes both positive and negative values indicating cases where the conventional approach outreaches the proposed one and vice versa. The area shaded in blue corresponds to negative values, i.e. $ECT_c < ECT_p$.

The global minimum of the function is negative, with the ratios associated with that point being closer to 0. Consequently, if the restoration costs are much greater than the investigation cost, the value of $ECT_{comparison}$ is negative, signifying that, in such case, the conventional approach has a better economic performance compared to the proposed one. On the other hand, the global maximum has a positive value and the ratios that correspond to this point are closer to 1; thus, relatively low restoration costs result in significant cost savings by the implementation of the proposed SPC approach. Regarding the intermediate points of the comparison function, the proposed approach has better economic results for most ratio values, as shown in Figure 16.8.

It should be emphasized that in the examined cases, the values of ratios L_0/L_1 and L_0/L_2 range from zero to unity, and so, from relatively large restoration costs to restoration costs at most equal to the investigation cost. Nonetheless, it is safe to conclude that if the restoration costs are lower than the investigation cost, thus resulting in ratios greater than 1, the proposed approach is expected to have an even better economic performance compared to the conventional one.

16.7. Conclusions

A different approach to statistical control of processes subject to multiple assignable causes, with unfeasible and/or costly investigation of their operation state, is proposed. To clarify the control policy of the developed approach, the simple case of two possible assignable causes is considered, albeit greater cost savings are expected with a larger number of possible quality disruptions. The economic performance of the proposed model is examined for several different scenarios. A side-by-side economic comparison between the proposed and the conventional approach has been conducted through 3D surface plots, concluding a better performance of the developed model for several process parameter sets.

16.8. References

Adams, B.M., Woodall, B.M., Lowry, C.A. (1992). The use (and misuse) of false alarm probabilities in control chart design. *Frontiers in Statistical Quality Control*, 4, 155–168.

Aytaçoğlu, B., Driscoll, A.R., Woodall, W.H. (2021). Controlling the conditional false alarm rate for the MEWMA control chart. *Journal of Quality Technology*, 54(5), 487–502.

Lorenzen, T.J. and Vance, L.C. (1986). The economic design of control charts: A unified approach. *Technometrics*, 28(1), 3–10.

Nenes, G., Tasias, A.K., Celano, G. (2015). A general model for the economic-statistical design of adaptive control charts for processes subject to multiple assignable causes. *International Journal of Production Research*, 53(7), 2146–2164.

Sall, J. (2018). Scaling-up process characterization. *Quality Engineering*, 30(1), 62–78.

Woodall, W.H. and Faltin, F.W. (2019). Rethinking control chart design and evaluation. *Quality Engineering*, 31(4), 596–605.

17

Phi Divergence and Consistent Estimation for Stochastic Block Model

Here, we consider the problem of clustering and inference in stochastic block models, which are notably applied to social networking and biology. For those models of random graphs, most of the literature proposes methods based on the maximization of the likelihood. However, the maximum likelihood approach is known to be non-robust to misspecification. To address this issue, we introduce new criteria. They are based on divergences in the sense of Csiszár. These criteria allow us to estimate the group structure of the graph as well as to estimate the parameters of the model. We show the convergence of the new criteria under the weighted stochastic block model with some assumptions. We also study the robustness properties of our estimators in the presence of misspecification and outliers in edge values. Moreover, we provide simulations to support our theoretical results. Eventually, we present an application on a real dataset.

17.1. Introduction

For several years, there has been great interest in modeling data with random graphs. One of the most popular models is the stochastic block model (SBM). This model is used in various fields such as social networking and biology (see, for example, Girvan and Newman (2002) and Newman (2006)). Because of its many applications, inference under this model has been studied by many. Only recently, has there been interest in the question of whether or not the data really comes from an SBM. Cai and Li (2015) proposed a model robust to the presence of "outliers" nodes, i.e. nodes that does not belong to the block structure of the model. Makarychev et al. (2016) show some robustness properties of the classification in the presence of outliers node and misspecification in the distribution of the SBM model.

The majority of the literature is still based on maximum likelihood estimators. However, it is well known that while this estimation method does very well under the

Chapter written by Cyprien FERRARIS.

model, in case of misspecifications (e.g. in the presence of outliers), this method can produce a highly biased estimator of the true parameter of interest.

To solve this problem, we offer using estimation based on divergences. Indeed, they are known to be robust to misspecification (see, for example, Donoho and Liu (1988)). We study from a theoretical point of view the convergence properties of the estimators based on our criteria. In addition, we provide simulations to show the gain in robustness by using divergence instead of likelihood.

17.2. Statement of the problem

Before looking at the definition of the weighted stochastic block model, we define the following weighted random graph generation approach. Assume that we have n nodes with a partition c in K classes and a family of distributions $(X_{k,l})_{1 \leq k \leq l \leq K}$. Then, we can generate a random graph by assigning at random a weight A_{ij} to the edge between two nodes: for $1 \leq i \leq j \leq n$ sample, independently, $A_{ij} \sim X_{c_i,c_j}$ and $A_{ji} = A_{ij}$.

Now we can define the weighted stochastic block model. It is simply the previous block model, but we consider that the partition of the graph is itself random.

Therefore, the weighted stochastic block model with K groups is generated in the following way. Let n be the number of nodes in the network, π a probability distribution on $\{1, \ldots K\}$ and $(X_{k,l})_{1 \leq k \leq l \leq K}$ be a collection of $K(K + 1)/2$ distributions.

1) For $1 \leq i \leq n$ sample, the class c_i of node i, iid with distribution such that $\mathbb{P}(c_i^* = k) = \pi_k$.

2) For $1 \leq i \leq j \leq n$ sample, independently, $A_{ij} \sim X_{c_i^* c_j^*}$ and $A_{ji} = A_{ij}$.

This means that the distribution of weights A_{ij} depends only on the block of node i and the block of node j.

REMARK 17.1.– *In the literature, it is common to allow K to grow as n grows. Nevertheless, with the model described above, it is not clear how to deal with this setting. So another way to see the stochastic block model is to see it as an infinite mixture model instead of a generative SBM (for more details, see Bickel and Chen (2009)).*

In our formulation, we make no assumptions on the number of communities K. The value can depend on n.

REMARK 17.2.– *Here, all the distance or difference between partitions are considered for the equivalence class and not only the partition itself. For example, we consider* *the partition $c = ((1,2),(3,4))$, i.e. $c_1 = c_2 = 1$ and $c_3 = c_4 = 2$. We consider that it is equal to the partition $c' = ((3,4),(1,2))$, i.e. $c'_1 = c'_2 = 2$ and $c'_3 = c'_4 = 1$.*

We can then define a measure of distance between two partitions c and c':

$$|c - c'| = \frac{1}{n}\sum_{i=1}^{n} I(c_i \neq c'_i)$$

Now we consider the case where the distributions of the weights belong to a set of parametric distributions, $(P_\theta)_{\theta \in \Theta}$, i.e. $P_{kl} = P_{\theta_{kl}}, 1 \leq k, l \leq K$. We assume that the distributions are all discrete and take T values. Without loss of generality, we can assume that their support is $\{1, \ldots, T\}$.

REMARK 17.3.– *The classical SBM corresponds to the case where* $(P_\theta)_\theta = Bernoulli(\theta)_{\theta \in [0,1]}$.

When dealing with those random graphs, there are two main tasks. The first one is to recover the partition c, and the second is to estimate the parameters $(\theta)_{kl}$. A classical way to achieve this is to maximize the (log) likelihood (Choi et al. 2012), which is defined by:

$$\frac{n(n-1)}{2}\ell(c,\theta) = \sum_{i \leq j} log(P_{\theta_{ij}}(A_{ij})) \qquad [17.1]$$

This can be rewritten in order to split each block of the model:

$$\frac{n(n-1)}{2}\ell(c,\theta) = \sum_{i \leq j} log(P_{\theta_{ij}}(A_{ij}))$$
$$= \sum_{k \leq l} n_{kl}(c)\ell((A_{i,j})_{c_i=k,c_j=l}) \qquad [17.2]$$

with $n_{kl}(c) = n_k(c)n_l(c)$ and $n_{kk}(c) = \frac{n_k(c)(n_k(c)+1)}{2}$ and $n_k(c)$ the number of nodes in the group k.

This approach depends on the fact that the distribution of the real data belongs to the model. In real life, it is not unlikely for the distribution to be different. For example, there may be outliers, or some error when collecting the data. And in this case, the likelihood estimator does not converge to the true value of the parameter anymore (see, for example, Huber (1972) in the case of outliers in distribution). Therefore, it is important to look for procedures that are robust to small deviation from the model.

From equation [17.2], we see that the likelihood of the model can be rewritten in terms of the likelihood of each block. Therefore, an idea may be to replace the likelihood in each block by a more suitable criterion in order to be more robust to misspecifications.

One way to produce robust estimators is the ϕ-divergence estimation (Donoho and Liu 1988; Basu and Lindsay 1994).

DEFINITION 17.1 (ϕ-DIVERGENCE).– *A ϕ-divergence (in the sense of Csiszár (1967)) is defined through a function φ, i.e. a convex proper closed function such that $\varphi(1) = 0$. Then, the ϕ divergence between two distributions P and Q, absolutely continuous with respect to a same measure λ, is given by*

$$D_\varphi(P, Q) = \int \varphi \left(\frac{dP}{dQ} \right) dQ$$

In particular, for two distributions p, q, with support $\{1, \ldots, T\}$, the φ-divergence is defined by

$$D_\varphi(P, Q) = \sum_{t=1}^{T} q(t)\varphi \left(\frac{p(t)}{q(t)} \right).$$ [17.3]

REMARK 17.4.– *This class of differences between distributions include many classical distributions, for example Kullback–Leibler (KL), L1, Hellinger, Chi2.*

Therefore, returning to the likelihood of the model, which is a sum of likelihood by block, a completely natural approach to using divergences in the estimation would be to replace the likelihood with a divergence of KL (between the empirical distribution and the parametric distribution) because the two criteria are equivalent in classical parameter estimation (not here). Moreover, more generally, we propose to replace the likelihood in each block by a divergence. Then, we propose the following criterion:

$$\hat{Q}(c, \theta) = \hat{Q}_\varphi(c, \theta) = \sum_{k \leq l} r_{kl} D_\varphi(P_n^{(k,l)}, P_{\theta_{kl}})$$ [17.4]

where $P_n^{(k,l)}(t) = P_n^{(k,l)}(c; t) = \frac{1}{n_{kl}(c)} \sum_{i \in c_k, j \in c_l} I(A_{ij} = t)$ is an estimator of the distribution in the block k, l, and $r_{kl} = r_{kl}(c) = \frac{2n_{kl}(c)}{n(n+1)}$.

It corresponds to a weighted sum for each block of the partition c of the divergence between the empirical distribution of the weights in the block and the parametric distribution with model $(P_\theta)_{\theta \in \Theta}$. The weight of each term is the proportion of edges in the block with respect to the total number of edges in the graph.

Before showing the properties of this criterion, we shall first give some intuition about it. We expect it to work well to estimate the classification if we assume that any mixture of our model is not part of the model. Graphically, assume that the data comes from a two-class SBM. If we compute the criteria for some partition c which is different from the true one c^*, then there is at least a distribution of one block that is not part of our model. Therefore, in Figure 17.1, if we look at the partition c, we note that in the lower right block, there is a mixture between the different distributions of the model. Then, the value of the associated divergence will be large, while if the partition is close to the true one, the divergences will be close to 0.

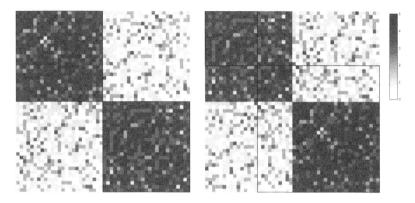

Figure 17.1. *Example of weights of a realization of an SBM with two blocks, i.e. the matrix of $(A_{ij})_{1 \leq i,j \leq n}$, where $X_{kk} \sim B(5, 0.8)$ and $X_{k,l} \sim B(5, 0.2)$, $k \neq l$. On the left, the true partition c^* of the model is highlighted. On the right, another partition c of the nodes is proposed. For a color version of this figure, see www.iste.co.uk/ dimotikalis/data3.zip*

17.3. Results

Now we can state our results on the properties of our estimator.

We denote by $P^{(k,l)}(e)$ the expectation distribution on $\{1, \ldots, T\}$ such that

$$P^{(k,l)}(c; t) = E[P_n^{(k,l)}(c; t)] \tag{17.5}$$

It represents the distribution in the block k, l of the partition c if the true distribution of each weight is known.

We write $P^{(k,l)}(t)$ (respectively $E[P_n^{(k,l)}(t)]$) instead of $P^{(k,l)}(c; t)$ (respectively $E[P_n^{(k,l)}(c; t)]$) when there is no possible confusion on the partition c.

Moreover, we denote

$$\overline{Q}(c, \theta) = \sum_{k \leq l} r_{kl}(c) D_\varphi(P^{(k,l)}(c), P_{\theta_{k,l}}) \tag{17.6}$$

We write $\hat{Q}(c)$ (respectively $\overline{Q}(c)$), for $\inf_{\theta} Q(c, \theta)$ (respectively $\inf_{\theta} \overline{Q}(c, \theta)$).

We formulate the following hypotheses:

- (H.1) The function $\overline{Q}(c)$ has a unique maximum in c^*.

- (H.2) $\min_k n_k(c) = O(\frac{n}{K})$, where K is the number of communities.

- (H.3) The function φ is continuous on $[0, 1]$.

- (H.4) $\min\left(\frac{n}{K^2 log(K) T^2}, \frac{n^2}{K^2 T^2 log(T)}\right) \xrightarrow[n \to \infty]{} +\infty$.

- (H.5) $\|P^{(k,l)}(c) - P^{(k,l)}(c^*)\| = 0$ implies that $c = c^*$.

THEOREM 17.1 (CONSISTENCY OF THE PARTITIONING).– *Assume that the graph is generated from a weighted stochastic block model with K classes such that the distribution in each block k, l is denoted by $X_{k,l}$. Under assumptions H.1–H.5, let $\hat{c}$ be $\arg\min_c \hat{Q}(c)$. Then, for all $\eta > 0$,*

$$\mathbb{P}(|\hat{c} - c^*| > \eta) \xrightarrow[n \to \infty]{} 0 \qquad [17.7]$$

REMARK 17.5.– *H.1 and H.5 are used in order to show that minimizing the criterion allows us to recover the true partition. H.2 and H.4 ensure that in each block, we can accurately evaluate the divergence and H.3 is a regularity assumption used for the consistency of divergence estimation.*

We also demonstrate the consistency of the parameter estimates.

THEOREM 17.2 (CONSISTENCY OF PARAMETERS ESTIMATES).– *Let $\hat{\theta}_{kl} = \arg\min_{\theta} D_{\varphi}(P_n^{(k,l)}, P_\theta)$, and denote $\theta_{k,l}^T = \arg\min_{\theta} D_{\varphi}(P^{(k,l)}, P_\theta)$. If for any $\epsilon > 0$,*

$$\min_{\{\theta : |\theta - \theta_T| > \epsilon\}} D_{\varphi}(P^{(k,l)}, P_\theta) > D_{\varphi}(P^{(k,l)}, P_{\theta_T}),$$ *then under the hypotheses of the previous theorem, we have that*

$$\hat{\theta}_{kl} \xrightarrow{\mathbb{P}} \theta_{kl}^T \qquad [17.8]$$

PROPOSITION 17.1.– *In the case of discrete distribution on finite support, hypothesis H.5 is always verified.*

17.4. Simulations

Since optimizing over all partitions is impossible in practice, we use some heuristic methods in order to explore a part of the partitions.

According to the comparison of Funke and Becker (2019), one of the simplest ways to do this is the Metropolis–Hastings approach. The idea is the following: first, we select an initial partition $c^{(0)}$, a number of iterations M and a temperature parameter β. Then, we iterate from 1 to M, and at each step, we select at random one of the n nodes in the graph and change again at random its class. Then, we obtain a new partition $c^{(i)}$. And with probability $1 - exp(-\beta(\hat{Q}(c^{(i)}) - Q(c^{(i-1)})))$, we undo the change, i.e. $c^{(i)} = c^{(i-1)}$, and perform the next iteration.

For the sake of simplicity, we only compare the likelihood to our proposed method with $\gamma = 0.5$. Indeed, taking another value of $\gamma < 1$ gives the same kind of results.

We compare the partition and the estimation of the parameters between the log likelihood and our approach with different parameters γ.

First, we consider a planted graph with two groups. We assume $\mathbb{P}(c_i^* = 1) = 0.5$ and $A_{ij} \sim Binomial(10, \theta_{c_i^*, c_j^*})$, where $\theta_{kl} = 0.8I(k = l) + 0.6I(k \neq l)$. We run 100 replications of a simulation under this model, and shall report the result of the simulation in Figure 17.2. In this figure, we show for the different values of the number of nodes the percentage of missclassified nodes in the x-axis and the y-axis, the L1-norm of parameters error $\|\hat{\theta} - \theta\|_1$. The estimation with our method is shown in orange and the likelihood is shown in green.

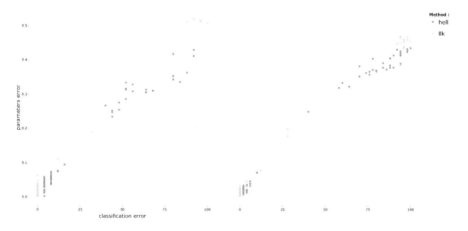

Figure 17.2. *Plot of L_1 error of parameters estimation (y-axis) with respect to the percentage of error of classification (x-axis) for $n = 50$, 100 (from left to right) for an SBM with fixed number of groups. For a color version of this figure, see www.iste.co.uk/dimotikalis/data3.zip*

In both cases, we see that the error of classification and the error of estimation are quite similar (even of the likelihood performs a bit better). This is not surprising since under the model, we expected the likelihood and the Hellinger to be equivalent (Beran 1977). So any of the two methods seems adapted in order to estimate the partition and the parameters under a well-specified parametric SBM. Since this is a simple example, it is easy to estimate the partition and the method produces results close or equal to the true partition even for a small number of nodes. In addition, looking at the scale of the y-axis, we can see that the estimation precision for our parameter increase.

Now, we study the effect of misspecification on the result of estimation. Here, we consider a binomial SBM with two groups. We set $\mathbb{P}(c_i = 1) = 0.5$ and $A_{ij} \sim 0.5 Binomial(10, \theta_{c_i, c_j}) + 0.5\delta_0$, where $\theta_{kl} = 0.8I(k = l) + 0.6I(k \neq l)$. Then, we sample 50 graph for $n = 50, 100, 250$ and run our algorithm on it. The results are presented in Figure 17.3.

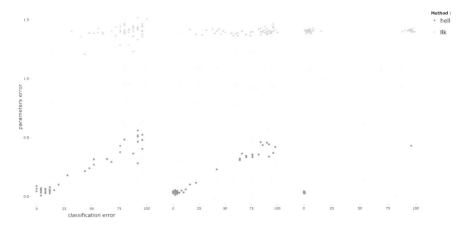

Figure 17.3. *Plot of L_1 error of parameters estimation (y-axis) with respect to the percentage of error of classification (x-axis) for $n = 50, 100, 250$ (from left to right). For a color version of this figure, see www.iste.co.uk/dimotikalis/data3.zip*

We see clearly that our proposed method (in orange) outperforms the likelihood. First, our method converges faster for the problem of estimating the partition. And second, we see in the case where $n = 250$ that even when the likelihood finds a partition close to the true one, the estimation of parameters is wrong. This is not surprising since here, we are looking for θ_{kl} and since we look at a binomial SBM, the likelihood estimator is the empirical mean divided by T, so it is an unbiased estimator of $\theta_{kl}/2$.

17.5. Study of real dataset: email-Enron

Eventually, we apply our method to the email-Enron dataset. The Enron Corporation was an energy commodities and services firm, which declared bankruptcy at the end of 2001. As a result, an investigation began leading to a trial, where several employees were convicted of fraud. From this, a dataset with the emails of the company's employees was made available (Benson et al. 2018). Here, we focus on a weighted network with as nodes almost 150 people working at Enron and as weights for the edges the number of emails sent between two people (here, we consider an undirected graph by counting sent and received emails). To simplify the analysis of the graph, we apply, as in Ludkin (2020), a log transformation to the weights so that we look at the rounding of $[log(1 + \text{number of emails})]$. It gives a graph with weights from 0 to 8. Applying our method for the Hellinger divergence with a binomial model with 8 trials, for $K = 10$, it gives the graph in Figure 17.4.

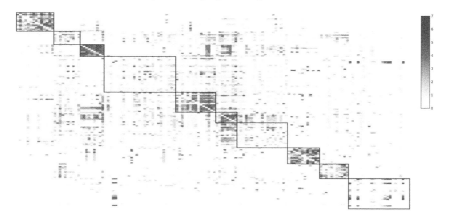

Figure 17.4. *Plot of weighted matrix of the email-Enron network after classification. For a color version of this figure, see www.iste.co.uk/dimotikalis/data3.zip*

We clearly see a block structure in the graph thanks to the method. An interesting thing about this dataset is that we know most of the posts in the company of the people in the graph (Creamer et al. 2022). So we can look at it in each block. We see that in blocks 1 and 3, the blocks are named from left to right and are mainly managers, directors and vice-president. In block 5, it is mainly traders: 11 of the 15 people have trades in their jobs names. Block 6 contains the CEO, president and vice-president. In group 8, there are jobs linked to the law and counsel. Therefore, the groups found by the method produce a partition that highlights the different categories of jobs in the firm.

17.6. Summary and discussion

In this chapter, we offer a novel estimator based on divergences. We show that this estimator has asymptotic properties close to the case of the likelihood when the assumed model corresponds to the true model. However, our methods produce estimators robust to misspecification in the model when the classical approach with the likelihood estimation does not.

In our analysis, we assume that the graph is undirected because it is the classical setting of SBM. Nevertheless, we can also apply our method to the case of directed graphs. In this case, we just have K^2 parameters instead of $K(K+1)/2$.

There are two things that would make this approach as truly concurrent as the likelihood one. First, we have to extend our analysis to include the case of continuous distribution. This is different since to have a good divergence estimate, it is recommended in the literature not to use the empirical probability density function, but a smooth density function (see Basu and Lindsay (1994) and Mohamad (2018)).

Then, we have to look for the asymptotic distribution of the parameter and of its estimates. This would allow us to construct test for parameters, model adequation or even model selection, for example, for selecting the number of groups.

17.7. Acknowledgment

We would like to thank Michel Broniatowski and Frédéric Guilloux for the interesting discussions and comments that helped us to improve this chapter.

17.8. Appendix

PROOF (OF THEOREM 17.1).– For this proof, we process as in Zhao et al. (2012). First, we show that the criterion and a mean version of it are asymptotically close. Then, we show that this implies that the argmax of the criterion is close to the true partition of the data.

Step 1: From H.2, we can focus on partitions c that verify this hypothesis. So let c be a partition of the n nodes in K classes satisfying H.2.

$$
\begin{aligned}
|\hat{Q}(c) - \overline{Q}(c)| &= \left| \sum_{k \le l} r_{kl} \left(\inf_{\theta_{kl}} D_\varphi(P_n^{(k,l)}, P_{\theta_{kl}}) - \sum_{k \le l} \inf_{\theta_{kl}} D_\varphi(P^{(k,l)}, P_{\theta_{kl}}) \right) \right| \\
&\le \sum_{k \le l} r_{kl} \left| \inf_{\theta_{kl}} D_\varphi(P_n^{(k,l)}, P_{\theta_{kl}}) - \inf_{\theta_{kl}} D_\varphi(P^{(k,l)}, P_{\theta_{kl}}) \right| \\
&\le \sum_{k \le l} r_{kl} \sup_{\theta_{kl}} \left| D_\varphi(P_n^{(k,l)}, P_{\theta_{kl}}) - D_\varphi(P^{(k,l)}, P_{\theta_{kl}}) \right| \\
&\le \max_{k \le l} \sup_{\theta_{kl}} \left| D_\varphi(P_n^{(k,l)}, P_{\theta_{kl}}) - D_\varphi(P^{(k,l)}, P_{\theta_{kl}}) \right|
\end{aligned}
$$

So using a union bound, it gives for all $\epsilon > 0$

$$\mathbb{P}\left(\max_c|\hat{Q}(c) - \overline{Q}(c)| > \epsilon\right)$$

$$\leq \sum_c\sum_{k\leq l}\mathbb{P}\left(\sup_{\theta_{kl}}\left|D_\varphi(P_n^{(k,l)}, P_{\theta_{kl}}) - D_\varphi(P^{(k,l)}, P_{\theta_{kl}})\right| > \epsilon\right) \qquad [17.9]$$

Since in hypothesis H.3 the function $x \mapsto \varphi(x/p_{\theta_{kl}}(t))p_{\theta_{kl}}(t)$ is continuous for all $t \in \{1,\ldots,T\}$, it is uniformly continuous. Then, for all $\epsilon > 0$, all k, l and all θ_{kl}, there is $\delta_\epsilon > 0$ such that if $|x - y| \leq \delta_\epsilon$, then $|\varphi(x/p_{\theta_{kl}}(t))p_{\theta_{kl}}(t) - \varphi(xy/p_{\theta_{kl}}(t))p_{\theta_{kl}}(t)| \leq \epsilon$. So

$$\mathbb{P}\left(\sum_{t=1}^T|\varphi(x/p_{\theta_{kl}}(t))p_{\theta_{kl}}(t) - \varphi(y/p_{\theta_{kl}}(t))p_{\theta_{kl}}(t)| > \epsilon\right)$$

$$\leq \sum_{t=1}^T\mathbb{P}\left(|\varphi(x/p_{\theta_{kl}}(t))p_{\theta_{kl}}(t) - \varphi(y/p_{\theta_{kl}}(t))p_{\theta_{kl}}(t)| > \epsilon/T\right)$$

Using $x = p_n^{(k,l)}(c;t)$, $y = p^{(k,l)}(c;t)$. And with this setting, $\mathbb{P}(|x - y| > \delta_\epsilon) \leq 2exp(-2n_{kl}\delta_\epsilon^2)$ by convergence of the empirical probability function.

So we have

$$\mathbb{P}\left(\sup_{\theta_{kl}}\left|D_\varphi(P_n^{(k,l)}(c), P_{\theta_{kl}}(c)) - D_\varphi(P^{(k,l)}(c), P_{\theta_{kl}}(c))\right| > \epsilon\right)$$

$$\leq \sum_{t=1}^T\mathbb{P}(|p_n^{(k,l)}(t) - p^{(k,l)}(t)| > \delta_\epsilon/T)$$

And finally by hypothesis H.2,

$$\mathbb{P}\left(\sup_{\theta_{kl}}\left|D_\varphi(P_n^{(k,l)}(c), P_{\theta_{kl}}(c)) - D_\varphi(P^{(k,l)}(c), P_{\theta_{kl}}(c))\right| > \epsilon\right)$$

$$\leq 2Texp(-2\frac{n^2\delta_\epsilon^2}{K^2T^2})$$

and

$$\mathbb{P}\left(\max_c|\hat{Q}(c) - \overline{Q}(c)| > \epsilon\right)2 \leq TK^{n+2}exp(-2\frac{n^2\delta_\epsilon^2}{K^2T^2})$$

which goes to zero by hypothesis H.4.

Now that we have bounded the distance between the empirical criterion and its mean version, we can study the properties of the optimal partition.

Step 2:

Now by hypothesis H.1 and continuity for all $\delta > 0$, for all e such that there exists (k, l) such that $\|P^{(k,l)}(c) - P^{(k,l)}(c^*)\| > \delta$, there exists $\epsilon > 0$ such that

$$\overline{Q}(c) > \overline{Q}(c^*) + 2\epsilon$$

Moreover, by step 1, we have

$$\mathbb{P}\left(\min_{\{c|\|P(c)-P(c^*)\|>\delta\}} \hat{Q}(c) > \hat{Q}(c^*)\right)$$

$$\geq \mathbb{P}\left(\left|\min_{\{c|\|P(c)-P(c^*)\|>\delta\}} \hat{Q}(c) - \min_{\{c|\|P(c)-P(c^*)\|>\delta\}} \overline{Q}(c)\right| < \epsilon,\right.$$

$$\left.\left|\hat{Q}(c^*) - \overline{Q}(c^*)\right| < \epsilon\right)$$

$$\geq 1 - 2TK^{n+2}\exp(-2\epsilon^2\frac{n^2}{K^2T^2})$$

The first inequality comes from the fact that when $\min_{\{c|\|P(c)-P(c^*)\|>\delta\}} \overline{Q}(c) > \overline{Q}(c^*) + 2\epsilon$ and $\left|\min_{\{c|\|P(c)-P(c^*)\|>\delta\}} \hat{Q}(c) - \min_{\{c|\|P(c)-P(c^*)\|>\delta\}} \overline{Q}(c)\right| < \epsilon$, we have $\min_{\{c|\|P(c)-P(c^*)\|>\delta\}} \hat{Q}(c) > \overline{Q}(c^*) + \epsilon$ and with $\left|\hat{Q}(c^*) - \overline{Q}(c^*)\right| < \epsilon$, we have $\min_{\{c|\|P(c)-P(c^*)\|>\delta\}} \hat{Q}(c) > \hat{Q}(c^*)$.

For the second inequality, we use $\mathbb{P}(A \cap B) = 1 - \mathbb{P}(A^c \cup B^c) \geq 1 - \mathbb{P}(A^c) - \mathbb{P}(B^c)$, with the result of step 1.

Moreover, from hypothesis H.5, for all $\eta > 0$, for all e such that $|e - c| > \eta$, there exists $\delta > 0$ such that $\|P(c) - P(c^*)\| > \delta$. This implies $\mathbb{P}(|c - c^*| > \eta) \leq \mathbb{P}(\|P(c) - P(c^*)\| > \delta)$.

So we have, with probability going to 1, that for all $\eta > 0$,

$$|\hat{c} - c^*| < \eta$$

The proof is complete.

PROOF (OF THEOREM 17.2).– We will proceed as in Theorem 5.7 of Van der Vaart (1998).

First assume that $\sup_\theta|\hat{Q}(\hat{c}, \theta) - \overline{Q}(c^*, \theta)| \overset{\mathbb{P}}{\to} 0$. Then, in particular, $\hat{Q}(\hat{c}, \theta_T) \overset{\mathbb{P}}{\to} \overline{Q}(c^*, \theta_T)$. And we have that $\hat{Q}(\hat{c}, \hat{\theta}) \leq \overline{Q}(c^*, \theta_T) + o_{\mathbb{P}}(1)$.

So, $\overline{Q}(c^*, \hat{\theta}) - \overline{Q}(c^*, \theta_T) \leq \overline{Q}(c^*, \hat{\theta}) - \hat{Q}(\hat{c}, \hat{\theta}) + o_{\mathbb{P}}(1)$ and $\leq sup_\theta |\hat{Q}(\hat{c}, \theta) - \overline{Q}(c^*, \theta)| + o_{\mathbb{P}}(1) \xrightarrow{\mathbb{P}} 0$

Moreover, by hypothesis, we have that for any $\epsilon > 0$, there is $\eta > 0$ such that $M(\theta) > M(\theta_T) - \eta$ for all θ with $d(\theta, \theta_T) \geq \epsilon$. So the event $\{d(\hat{\theta}, \theta_T) \geq \epsilon\}$ is included in the event $\{\overline{Q}(c^*, \hat{\theta}) < \overline{Q}(c^*, \theta_T) - \eta\}$. And we have the convergence in probability.

Now we have to prove $sup_\theta |\hat{Q}(\hat{c}, \theta) - \overline{Q}(c^*, \theta)| \xrightarrow{\mathbb{P}} 0$.

By step 1 of the Proof of Theorem 17.1, we have that $\sup_\theta |\hat{Q}(\hat{c}, \theta) - \overline{Q}(\hat{c}, \theta)|$ goes to 0 in probability. So we have to show that this is also the case for $sup_\theta |\overline{Q}(\hat{c}, \theta) - \overline{Q}(c^*, \theta)|$.

From Theorem 17.1, we have that $|\hat{c} - c^*|$ goes to zero in probability. So we have $n_{kl}(\hat{c}) \xrightarrow{\mathbb{P}} n_{kl}(c^*)$ for all k, l and for all t, $p_n^{(k,l)}(\hat{c}; t) \xrightarrow{\mathbb{P}} p^{(k,l)}(c^*; t)$.

We have

$$|\overline{Q}(\hat{c}, \theta) - \overline{Q}(c^*, \theta)| = |\sum_{kl} r_{kl}(\hat{c}) D_\varphi(P^{(k,l)}(\hat{c}), P_{\theta_{kl}}) - \sum_{kl} r_{kl}(c^*) D_\varphi(P^{(k,l)}(c^*), P_{\theta_{kl}})|$$

$$\leq |\sum_{kl} r_{kl}(\hat{c}) D_\varphi(P^{(k,l)}(\hat{c}), P_{\theta_{kl}}) - \sum_{kl} r_{kl}(\hat{c}) D_\varphi(P^{(k,l)}(c^*), P_{\theta_{kl}})$$

$$+ \sum_{kl} r_{kl}(\hat{c}) D_\varphi(P^{(k,l)}(c^*), P_{\theta_{kl}}) - \sum_{kl} r_{kl}(c^*) D_\varphi(P^{(k,l)}(c^*), P_{\theta_{kl}})|$$

$$\leq |\sum_{kl} r_{kl}(\hat{c}) D_\varphi(P^{(k,l)}(\hat{c}), P_{\theta_{kl}}) - \sum_{kl} r_{kl}(\hat{c}) D_\varphi(P^{(k,l)}(c^*), P_{\theta_{kl}})|$$

$$+ |\sum_{kl} r_{kl}(\hat{c}) D_\varphi(P^{(k,l)}(c^*), P_{\theta_{kl}}) - \sum_{kl} r_{kl}(c^*) D_\varphi(P^{(k,l)}(c^*), P_{\theta_{kl}})|$$

$$\leq |\sum_{kl} r_{kl}(\hat{c})(D_\varphi(P^{(k,l)}(\hat{c}), P_\theta) - D_\varphi(P^{(k,l)}(c^*), P_\theta))|$$

$$+ |\sum_{k,l} D_\varphi(P^{(k,l)}(c^*), P_{\theta_{kl}})(r_{kl}(\hat{c}) - r_{kl}(c))|$$

$$\leq max_{kl} |D_\varphi(P^{(k,l)}(\hat{c}), P_\theta) - D_\varphi(P^{(k,l)}(c^*), P_\theta)|$$

$$+ max_{k,l} D_\varphi(P^{(k,l)}(c^*), P_{\theta_{kl}})| \sum_{kl}(r_{kl}(\hat{c}) - r_{kl}(c^*))|$$

$$= max_{kl} |D_\varphi(P^{(k,l)}(\hat{c}), P_\theta) - D_\varphi(P^{(k,l)}(c^*), P_\theta)|$$

Now since we have $P^{(k,l)}(\hat{c}) = \pi_{kl} P^{(k,l)}(c^*) + (1 - \pi_{kl}) Q^{(k,l)}$, we have $\|P^{(k,l)}(\hat{c}) - P^{(k,l)}(c^*)\| \leq (1 - \pi_{kl}) \|Q^{(k,l)} - P^{(k,l)}(c^*)\|$.

And by hypothesis, $\|P^{(k,l)}(\hat{c}) - P^{(k,l)}(c^*)\| \leq (1 - \pi_{kl}) D$.

In addition, $max_{kl}(1 - \pi_{kl}) \leq |\hat{c} - c^*|$. So $\|P^{(k,l)}(\hat{c}) - P^{(k,l)}(c^*)\|$ goes to zero in probability.

Then, by uniform continuity of $\cdot \mapsto D_\varphi(\cdot, P_\theta)$ for discrete distributions, $max_{kl} \sup_\theta |D_\varphi(P^{(k,l)}(\hat{c}), P_\theta) - D_\varphi(P^{(k,l)}(c^*), P_\theta)|$ goes to zero in probability.

Then, it is also the case for $|\overline{Q}(\hat{c}, \theta) - \overline{Q}(c^*, \theta)|$, which concludes the proof.

Before showing Proposition 17.1, we need additional notations. Let $s_{k,a}(c) = \sum_i \frac{I(c_i = k, c_i^* = a)}{n_k(c)}$. Then

$$P^{(k,l)}(c)(t) = \frac{1}{n_k n_l} \sum_{c_i = k, c_j = l} \mathbb{P}(A_{ij} = t)$$

$$= \sum_{i,j} \frac{I(c_i = k, c_j = l)}{n_k n_l} \mathbb{P}(A_{ij} = t)$$

$$= \sum_{i,j} \sum_{a,b} \frac{I(c_i = k, c_j = l, c_i^* = a, c_j^* = b)}{n_k n_l} \mathbb{P}(A_{ij} = t)$$

$$= \sum_{i,j} \sum_{a,b} \frac{I(c_i = k, c_j = l, c_i^* = a, c_j^* = b)}{n_k n_l} \mathbb{P}(X_{ab} = t)$$

$$= \sum_{a,b} \sum_i \frac{I(c_i = k, c_i^* = a)}{n_k} \sum_j \frac{I(c_j = l, c_j^* = b)}{n_l} \mathbb{P}(X_{ab} = t)$$

$$= \sum_{a,b} s_{ka} s_{lb} \mathbb{P}(X_{ab} = t)$$

[17.10]

PROOF (OF PROPOSITION 17.1).– It is clear that when $|c - c^*| = 0$, $\|P^{(k,l)}(c) - P^{(k,l)}(c^*)\|_\infty = 0$.

So assume that $\|P^{(k,l)}(c) - P^{(k,l)}(c^*)\|_\infty = 0$. It implies that for all t, $\sum_{a,b}(s_{k,a}(c)s_{l,b}(c) - s_{k,a}(c^*)s_{l,b}(c^*))P_{ab}(t) = 0$.

And $s_{k,a}(c^*) = \delta_{k,a}$ so $\sum_{a,b}(s_{k,a}s_{l,b} - \delta_{k,a}(c^*)\delta_{l,b}(c^*))P_{ab}(t) = 0$, where we omit the (c) to simplify the notation.

Moreover,

$$0 = \sum_{a,b}(s_{k,a}s_{l,b} - \delta_{k,a}(c^*)\delta_{l,b}(c^*)) P_{ab}(t)$$

$$\iff \sum_{a,b} s_{k,a}s_{l,b}P_{ab}(t) = P_{kl}(t)$$

Now let (k, l, t) such that $max_{a,b;l} P_{a,b}(l) = P_{kl}(t)$. And let $A_t = \{(a, b)|P_{ab}(t) = P_{kl}(t)\}$, we have that

$$0 = \sum_{a,b} (s_{k,a} s_{l,b} - \delta_{k,a}(c^*)\delta_{l,b}(c^*)) P_{ab}(t)$$

$$\Longleftrightarrow \sum_{a,b} s_{k,a} s_{l,b} P_{ab}(t) = P_{kl}(t)$$

$$\Longleftrightarrow \sum_{a,b \in A_t^c} s_{k,a} s_{l,b} P_{ab}(t) + \sum_{a,b \in A_t} s_{k,a} s_{l,b} P_{ab}(t) = P_{kl}(t)$$

$$\Longleftrightarrow \sum_{a,b \in A_t^c} s_{k,a} s_{l,b} P_{ab}(t) = P_{kl}(t) - \sum_{a,b \in A_t} s_{k,a} s_{l,b} P_{ab}(t)$$

$$\Longleftrightarrow \sum_{a,b \in A_t^c} s_{k,a} s_{l,b} P_{ab}(t) = P_{kl}(t) \left(1 - \sum_{a,b \in A_t} s_{k,a} s_{l,b} \right)$$

If $\sum_{a,b \in A_t^c} s_{k,a} s_{l,b} \neq 0$, then there is one $s_{k,a} s_{l,b} > 0$ since all $P_{ab}(t) > 0$ (discrete distribution over a finite support). And because, for all $a, b \in A_t^c$ $P_{ab}(t) < P_{kl}(t)$,

$$P_{kl}(t) \left(1 - \sum_{a,b \in A_t} s_{k,a} s_{l,b} \right) = \sum_{a,b \in A_t^c} s_{k,a} s_{l,b} P_{ab}(t) < \sum_{a,b \in A_t^c} s_{k,a} s_{l,b} P_{kl}(t)$$

This is impossible, so $\sum_{a,b \in A_t^c} n_{k,a} n_{l,b} = 0$, which is equivalent to $1 = \sum_{a,b \in A_t} s_{k,a} s_{l,b}$ so $s_{k,k} s_{l,l} = 1$.

If we now consider the model without blocks k and l, we can apply the same procedure and show that two other blocks are perfectly classified. Therefore, using this recursively will give the desired results.

17.9. References

Basu, A. and Lindsay, B. (1994). Minimum disparity estimation for continuous models: Efficiency, distributions and robustness. *Annals of the Institute of Statistical Mathematics*, 46, 683–705.

Benson, A., Abebe, R., Schaub, M., Jadbabaie, A., Kleinberg, J. (2018). Simplicial closure and higher-order link prediction. *Proceedings of the National Academy of Sciences*, 115, E11221–E11230.

Beran, R. (1977). Minimum Hellinger distance estimates for parametric models. *The Annals of Statistics*, 5, 445–463.

Bickel, P. and Chen, A. (2009). A nonparametric view of network models and Newman–Girvan and other modularities. *Proceedings of the National Academy of Sciences*, 106, 21068–21073.

Cai, T. and Li, X. (2015). Robust and computationally feasible community detection in the presence of arbitrary outlier nodes. *The Annals of Statistics*, 43, 1027–1059.

Choi, D., Wolfe, P., Airoldi, E. (2012). Stochastic blockmodels with a growing number of classes. *Biometrika*, 99, 273–284.

Creamer, G., Stolfo, S., Creamer, M., Hershkop, S., Rowe, R. (2022). Discovering organizational hierarchy through a corporate ranking algorithm: The Enron case. *Complexity*, 1–18.

Csiszár, I. (1967). Information-type measures of difference of probability distributions and indirect observation. *Studia Scientiarum Mathematicarum Hungarica*, 2, 229–318.

Daudin, J., Picard, F., Robin, S. (2008). A mixture model for random graphs. *Statistics and Computing*, 18, 173–183.

Donoho, D. and Liu, R. (1988). The "automatic" robustness of minimum distance functionals. *The Annals of Statistics*, 16, 552–586.

Funke, T. and Becker, T. (2019). Stochastic block models: A comparison of variants and inference methods. *PLOS ONE*, 14, e0215296.

Girvan, M. and Newman, M. (2002). Community structure in social and biological networks. *Proceedings of the National Academy of Sciences*, 99, 7821–7826.

Huber, P. (1972). The 1972 Wald lecture robust statistics: A review. *The Annals of Mathematical Statistics*, 43, 1041–1067.

Ludkin, M. (2020). Inference for a generalised stochastic block model with unknown number of blocks and non-conjugate edge models. *Computational Statistics & Data Analysis*, 152, 107051.

Makarychev, K., Makarychev, Y., Vijayaraghavan, A. (2016). Learning communities in the presence of errors. *Conference on Learning Theory*, 1258–1291.

Mohamad, D. (2018). Towards a better understanding of the dual representation of phi divergences. *Statistical Papers*, 59, 1205–1253.

Newman, M. (2006). Finding community structure in networks using the eigenvectors of matrices. *Physical Review E*, 74, 036104.

Newman, M. and Girvan, M. (2004). Finding and evaluating community structure in networks. *Physical Review E*, 69, 026113.

Rohe, K., Chatterjee, S., Yu, B. (2011). Spectral clustering and the high-dimensional stochastic blockmodel. *The Annals of Statistics*, 39, 1878–1915.

Van der Vaart, A. (1998). *Asymptotic Statistics*. Cambridge University Press, Cambridge.

Zhao, Y., Levina, E., Zhu, J. (2012). Consistency of community detection in networks under degree-corrected stochastic block models. *The Annals of Statistics*, 40, 2266–2292.

List of Authors

Mohammed Albuhayri
Division of Mathematics and Physics
Mälardalen University
Västeraås
Sweden

Narayanaswamy Balakrishnan
Department of Mathematics and
Statistics
McMaster University
Ontario
Canada

Samuel Bonello
Department of Statistics and
Operations Research
Faculty of Science
University of Malta
Msida
Malta

Monique Borg Inguanez
Department of Statistics and
Operations Research
Faculty of Science
University of Malta
Msida
Malta

Frederico Caeiro
NOVA School of Science and
Technology
Centro de Matemática e Aplicações
(CMA)
NOVA University Lisbon
Portugal

Mark Anthony Caruana
Department of Statistics and
Operations Research
Faculty of Science
University of Malta
Msida
Malta

Marko Dimitrov
Division of Mathematics and Physics
Mälardalen University
Västeraås
Sweden

Yiannis Dimotikalis
Department of Management Science
and Technology
Hellenic Mediterranean University
Heraklion
Crete
Greece

Cyprien FERRARIS
LPSM
Sorbonne Université
Paris
and
Safran Aircraft Engines
Corbeil-Essonnes
France

Adelaide FIGUEIREDO
Faculdade de Economiada
Universidade do Porto
and
LIAAD-INESCTEC
Portugal

Fernanda Otilia FIGUEIREDO
Faculdade de Economiada
Universidade do Porto
and
CEAUL
Portugal

George FILANDRIANOS
School of Electrical and Computer
Engineering
National Technical University of
Athens
Greece

Jim FREEMAN
Alliance Manchester Business School
University of Manchester
United Kingdom

Eleni GENITSARIDI
Hellenic Open University
Patra
Greece

Oladapo T. IBITOYE
Department of Electrical, Electronics
and Computer Engineering
Afe Babalola University
Ado-Ekiti
Nigeria

María JAENADA
Department of Statistics and O.R.
Complutense University of Madrid
Spain

Lu JIN
Department of Informatics
University of
Electro-Communications
Tokyo
Japan

Aggeliki KAZANI
Department of Social Policy
Panteion University of Social and
Political Sciences
Athens
Greece

Hlabishi I. KOBO
Council for Scientific and Industrial
Research (CSIR)
Pretoria
South Africa

Gabriele LENTINI
Department of Statistics and
Operations Research
Faculty of Science
University of Malta
Msida
Malta

Anatoliy MALYARENKO
Division of Mathematics and Physics
Mälardalen University
Västeraås
Sweden

George MATALLIOTAKIS
Hellenic Open University
Patra
Greece

Ayana MATEUS
NOVA School of Science and
Technology
Centro de Matemática e Aplicações
(CMA)
NOVA University Lisbon
Portugal

Haoyu MIAO
Alliance Manchester Business School
University of Manchester
United Kingdom

Ying NI
Division of Mathematics and Physics
Mälardalen University
Västeraås
Sweden

Hossein NOHROUZIAN
Division of Mathematics and Physics
Mälardalen University
Västeraås
Sweden

Leandro PARDO
Department of Statistics and O.R.
Complutense University of Madrid
Spain

Dimitrios PARSANOGLOU
Department of Sociology
National and Kapodistrian University
of Athens
Greece

Lincoln S. PETER
Department of Electronic
Engineering
Howard College
University of KwaZulu-Natal
Durban
and
Council for Scientific and Industrial
Research (CSIR)
Pretoria
South Africa

Maria SACHINIDOU
Hellenic Open University
Patra
Greece

Christos H. SKIADAS
Technical University of Crete
Chania
Greece
and
ISAST
Athens
Greece

Viranjay M. SRIVASTAVA
Department of Electronic
Engineering
Howard College
University of KwaZulu-Natal
Durban
South Africa

Giorgos STAMOU
School of Electrical and Computer
Engineering
National Technical University of
Athens
Greece

David SUDA
Department of Statistics and
Operations Research
Faculty of Science
University of Malta
Msida
Malta

Maria SYMEONAKI
Department of Social Policy
Panteion University of Social and
Political Sciences
Athens
Greece

Kouki TAKADA
Department of Informatics
University of
Electro-Communications
Tokyo
Japan

Konstantinos A. TASIAS
Department of Science and
Technology
Hellenic Open University
Patras
and
Department of Mechanical
Engineering
University of Western Macedonia
Kozani
Greece

Sofia TRIKALLIOTI
Hellenic Open University
Patra
Greece

Konstantina TSIOTA
R.T. Vanderbilt Global Services LLC
Department of Quality
Norwalk
Connecticut
USA
and
Department of Science and
Technology
Hellenic Open University
Patras
Greece

Index

K, L

Kelly criterion, 46, 48
lean management, 167–172, 176, 177, 179
link failure, 198, 205
liquidity, 13, 147, 149, 150, 152, 156
log-logistic distribution, 53–56, 58, 60

M, N

machine learning, 29, 209, 212
Magnesia, 183, 189
Markov chain, 225, 227, 232–234, 237, 238
maximum likelihood, 64, 243
mean reversion property, 98
measuring/measure risk, 131–133, 135, 137, 142, 144
Monte Carlo simulation, 43, 97, 102, 105
multiple assignable causes, 225, 235, 242
multivariate kernel density estimation, 13–15, 25
neural network(s), 25, 209–213

O, P

one-shot devices, 63–70, 73, 75
ontology, 29–41
OpenFlow switches, 198, 199, 202, 205
open-source, 29, 31, 32, 39, 41, 211, 216
optimal exercise region, 79–81, 83, 89, 90
P4 protocol, 197, 201, 203, 205

policy,
  collateral life, 19, 24, 25
  credit, 163
  health, 188
  optimal, 80
  threshold type, 81, 89
principal component analysis, 7
  double, 3, 6, 7
  dynamic, 131, 132

R, S

restricted minimum density power divergence estimator (restricted MDPDE), 63–75
robust estimators, 64, 68, 246
semi-Markov decision process, 79–82, 93
severe pandemic, 147
shape parameter, 53, 55–57, 60, 84
Software Defined Network (SDN), 197–203
Statistical Process Control (SPC), 225–227, 230–234, 236, 237, 239, 241
stochastic
  block models, 243
  process, 116, 117, 119, 121, 123
Stratonovich integrals, 109

T, W

transition probability matrix, 79, 81, 83, 86–88, 91–93
Wiener space, 109–111, 113, 129

Other titles from

in

Innovation, Entrepreneurship and Management

2023

BOLLINGER Sophie
Management Control and Creativity: Challenges of Managing Innovation Processes
(Smart Innovation Set – Volume 41)

BOUVIER-PATRON Paul
Frugal Innovation and Innovative Creation
(Smart Innovation Set – Volume 40)

BRASSEUR Martine, BARTOLI Annie, CHABAUD Didier, GROUIEZ Pascal, ROUET Gilles
Inclusive Territories 1: Role of Enterprises and Organizations
(Territorial Entrepreneurship and Innovation Set – Volume 1)

CASADELLA Vanessa, UZUNIDIS Dimitri
Agri-Innovations and Development Challenges: Engineering, Value Chains and Socio-economic Models
(Innovation in Engineering and Technology Set – Volume 8)

VAYRE Emilie
Digitalization of Work: New Spaces and New Working Times
(Technological Changes and Human Resources Set – Volume 5)

ZAFEIRIS Konstantinos N, SKIADIS Christos H, DIMOTIKALIS Yannis,
KARAGRIGORIOU Alex, KARAGRIGORIOU-VONTA Christina
Data Analysis and Related Applications 1: Computational, Algorithmic and
Applied Economic Data Analysis
(Big Data, Artificial Intelligence and Data Analysis Set – Volume 9)
Data Analysis and Related Applications 2: Multivariate, Health and
Demographic Data Analysis
(Big Data, Artificial Intelligence and Data Analysis Set – Volume 10)

2021

ACH Yves-Alain, RMADI-SAÏD Sandra
Financial Information and Brand Value: Reflections, Challenges and
Limitations

ARCADE Jacques
Strategic Engineering
(Innovation and Technology Set – Volume 11)

BÉRANGER Jérôme, RIZOULIÈRES Roland
The Digital Revolution in Health
(Health and Innovation Set – Volume 2)

BOBILLIER CHAUMON Marc-Eric
Digital Transformations in the Challenge of Activity and Work:
Understanding and Supporting Technological Changes
(Technological Changes and Human Resources Set – Volume 3)

BUCLET Nicolas
Territorial Ecology and Socio-ecological Transition
(Smart Innovation Set – Volume 34)

DIMOTIKALIS Yannis, KARAGRIGORIOU Alex, PARPOULA Christina, SKIADIS Christos H
Applied Modeling Techniques and Data Analysis 1: Computational Data Analysis Methods and Tools
(Big Data, Artificial Intelligence and Data Analysis Set - Volume 7)
Applied Modeling Techniques and Data Analysis 2: Financial, Demographic, Stochastic and Statistical Models and Methods
(Big Data, Artificial Intelligence and Data Analysis Set – Volume 8)

DISPAS Christophe, KAYANAKIS Georges, SERVEL Nicolas, STRIUKOVA Ludmila
Innovation and Financial Markets
(Innovation between Risk and Reward Set – Volume 7)

GAUDIN Thierry, MAUREL Marie-Christine, POMEROL Jean-Charles
Chance, Calculation and Life

GASMI Nacer
Corporate Innovation Strategies: Corporate Social Responsibility and Shared Value Creation
(Smart Innovation Set – Volume 33)

GIORGINI Pierre
The Contributory Revolution
(Innovation and Technology Set – Volume 13)

GOGLIN Christian
Emotions and Values in Equity Crowdfunding Investment Choices 2: Modeling and Empirical Study
Emotions and Values in Equity Crowdfunding Investment Choices 1: Transdisciplinary Theoretical Approach

GRENIER Corinne, OIRY Ewan
Altering Frontiers: Organizational Innovations in Healthcare
(Health and Innovation Set – Volume 1)

GUERRIER Claudine
Security and Its Challenges in the 21st Century
(Innovation and Technology Set – Volume 12)

HELLER David
Performance of Valuation Methods in Financial Transactions
(Modern Finance, Management Innovation and Economic Growth Set –
Volume 4)

LEHMANN Paul-Jacques
Liberalism and Capitalism Today

LIMA Marcos
Entrepreneurship and Innovation Education: Frameworks and Tools
(Smart Innovation Set – Volume 32)

MACHADO Carolina, DAVIM J. Paulo
Sustainable Management for Managers and Engineers

MEUNIER François-Xavier
Dual Innovation Systems: Concepts, Tools and Methods
(Smart Innovation Set – Volume 31)

UZUNIDIS Dimitri, KASMI Fedoua, ADATTO Laurent
Innovation Economics, Engineering and Management Handbook 1:
Main Themes
Innovation Economics, Engineering and Management Handbook 2:
Special Themes

2020

ANDREOSSO-O'CALLAGHAN Bernadette, DZEVER Sam, JAUSSAUD Jacques,
TAYLOR Robert
Sustainable Development and Energy Transition in Europe and Asia
(Innovation and Technology Set – Volume 9)

BEN SLIMANE Sonia, M'HENNI Hatem
Entrepreneurship and Development: Realities and Future Prospects
(Smart Innovation Set – Volume 30)

CHOUTEAU Marianne, FOREST Joëlle, NGUYEN Céline
Innovation for Society: The P.S.I. Approach
(Smart Innovation Set – Volume 28)

DOU Henri, JUILLET Alain, CLERC Philippe
Strategic Intelligence for the Future 1: A New Strategic and Operational Approach
Strategic Intelligence for the Future 2: A New Information Function Approach

FRIKHA Azza
Measurement in Marketing: Operationalization of Latent Constructs

FRIMOUSSE Soufyane
Innovation and Agility in the Digital Age
(Human Resources Management Set – Volume 2)

GAY Claudine, SZOSTAK Bérangère L.
Innovation and Creativity in SMEs: Challenges, Evolutions and Prospects
(Smart Innovation Set – Volume 21)

GORIA Stéphane, HUMBERT Pierre, ROUSSEL Benoît
Information, Knowledge and Agile Creativity
(Smart Innovation Set – Volume 22)

HELLER David
Investment Decision-making Using Optional Models
(Economic Growth Set – Volume 2)

HELLER David, DE CHADIRAC Sylvain, HALAOUI Lana, JOUVET Camille
The Emergence of Start-ups
(Economic Growth Set – Volume 1)

HÉRAUD Jean-Alain, KERR Fiona, BURGER-HELMCHEN Thierry
Creative Management of Complex Systems
(Smart Innovation Set – Volume 19)

LATOUCHE Pascal
Open Innovation: Corporate Incubator
(Innovation and Technology Set – Volume 7)

LEHMANN Paul-Jacques
The Future of the Euro Currency

SERVAJEAN-HILST Romaric
Co-innovation Dynamics: The Management of Client-Supplier Interactions for Open Innovation
(Smart Innovation Set – Volume 20)

SKIADAS Christos H., BOZEMAN James R.
Data Analysis and Applications 1: Clustering and Regression, Modeling-estimating, Forecasting and Data Mining
(Big Data, Artificial Intelligence and Data Analysis Set – Volume 2)
Data Analysis and Applications 2: Utilization of Results in Europe and Other Topics
(Big Data, Artificial Intelligence and Data Analysis Set – Volume 3)

VIGEZZI Michel
World Industrialization: Shared Inventions, Competitive Innovations and Social Dynamics
(Smart Innovation Set – Volume 24)

2018

BURKHARDT Kirsten
Private Equity Firms: Their Role in the Formation of Strategic Alliances

CALLENS Stéphane
Creative Globalization
(Smart Innovation Set – Volume 16)

CASADELLA Vanessa
Innovation Systems in Emerging Economies: MINT – Mexico, Indonesia, Nigeria, Turkey
(Smart Innovation Set – Volume 18)

CHOUTEAU Marianne, FOREST Joëlle, NGUYEN Céline
Science, Technology and Innovation Culture
(Innovation in Engineering and Technology Set – Volume 3)

CORLOSQUET-HABART Marine, JANSSEN Jacques
Big Data for Insurance Companies
(Big Data, Artificial Intelligence and Data Analysis Set – Volume 1)

MILLOT Michel
Embarrassment of Product Choices 1: How to Consume Differently

PANSERA Mario, OWEN Richard
Innovation and Development: The Politics at the Bottom of the Pyramid
(Innovation and Responsibility Set – Volume 2)

RICHEZ Yves
Corporate Talent Detection and Development

SACHETTI Philippe, ZUPPINGER Thibaud
New Technologies and Branding
(Innovation and Technology Set – Volume 4)

SAMIER Henri
Intuition, Creativity, Innovation

TEMPLE Ludovic, COMPAORÉ SAWADOGO Eveline M.F.W.
Innovation Processes in Agro-Ecological Transitions in Developing
Countries
(Innovation in Engineering and Technology Set – Volume 2)

UZUNIDIS Dimitri
Collective Innovation Processes: Principles and Practices
(Innovation in Engineering and Technology Set – Volume 4)

2017

AÏT-EL-HADJ Smaïl
The Ongoing Technological System
(Smart Innovation Set – Volume 11)

D'ANDRIA Aude, GABARRET Inés
Building 21st Century Entrepreneurship
(Innovation and Technology Set – Volume 2)

BAUDRY Marc, DUMONT Béatrice
Patents: Prompting or Restricting Innovation?
(Smart Innovation Set – Volume 12)

BÉRARD Céline, TEYSSIER Christine
Risk Management: Lever for SME Development and Stakeholder Value Creation

CHALENÇON Ludivine
Location Strategies and Value Creation of International Mergers and Acquisitions

CHAUVEL Danièle, BORZILLO Stefano
The Innovative Company: An Ill-defined Object
(Innovation between Risk and Reward Set – Volume 1)

CORSI Patrick
Going Past Limits To Growth

DAIDJ Nabyla
Cooperation, Coopetition and Innovation
(Innovation and Technology Set – Volume 3)

FERNEZ-WALCH Sandrine
The Multiple Facets of Innovation Project Management
(Innovation between Risk and Reward Set – Volume 4)

FOREST Joëlle
Creative Rationality and Innovation
(Smart Innovation Set – Volume 14)

GUILHON Bernard
Innovation and Production Ecosystems
(Innovation between Risk and Reward Set – Volume 2)

HAMMOUDI Abdelhakim, DAIDJ Nabyla
Game Theory Approach to Managerial Strategies and Value Creation
(Diverse and Global Perspectives on Value Creation Set – Volume 3)

LALLEMENT Rémi
Intellectual Property and Innovation Protection: New Practices and New Policy Issues
(Innovation between Risk and Reward Set – Volume 3)

UZUNIDIS Dimitri, SAULAIS Pierre
Innovation Engines: Entrepreneurs and Enterprises in a Turbulent World
(Innovation in Engineering and Technology Set – Volume 1)

2016

BARBAROUX Pierre, ATTOUR Amel, SCHENK Eric
Knowledge Management and Innovation
(Smart Innovation Set – Volume 6)

BEN BOUHENI Faten, AMMI Chantal, LEVY Aldo
*Banking Governance, Performance And Risk-Taking: Conventional Banks
Vs Islamic Banks*

BOUTILLIER Sophie, CARRÉ Denis, LEVRATTO Nadine
Entrepreneurial Ecosystems
(Smart Innovation Set – Volume 2)

BOUTILLIER Sophie, UZUNIDIS Dimitri
The Entrepreneur
(Smart Innovation Set – Volume 8)

BOUVARD Patricia, SUZANNE Hervé
Collective Intelligence Development in Business

GALLAUD Delphine, LAPERCHE Blandine
Circular Economy, Industrial Ecology and Short Supply Chains
(Smart Innovation Set – Volume 4)

GUERRIER Claudine
Security and Privacy in the Digital Era
(Innovation and Technology Set – Volume 1)

MEGHOUAR Hicham
Corporate Takeover Targets

MONINO Jean-Louis, SEDKAOUI Soraya
Big Data, Open Data and Data Development
(Smart Innovation Set – Volume 3)

MOREL Laure, LE ROUX Serge
Fab Labs: Innovative User
(Smart Innovation Set – Volume 5)

PICARD Fabienne, TANGUY Corinne
Innovations and Techno-ecological Transition
(Smart Innovation Set – Volume 7)

2015

CASADELLA Vanessa, LIU Zeting, DIMITRI Uzunidis
Innovation Capabilities and Economic Development in Open Economies
(Smart Innovation Set – Volume 1)

CORLOSQUET-HABART Marine, GEHIN William, JANSSEN Jaques,
MANCA Raimondo
Asset and Liabilities Management for Banks and Insurance Companies

CORSI Patrick, MORIN Dominique
Sequencing Apple's DNA

CORSI Patrick, NEAU Erwan
Innovation Capability Maturity Model

FAIVRE-TAVIGNOT Bénédicte
Social Business and Base of the Pyramid

GODÉ Cécile
Team Coordination in Extreme Environments

MAILLARD Pierre
Competitive Quality and Innovation

MASSOTTE Pierre, CORSI Patrick
Operationalizing Sustainability

MASSOTTE Pierre, CORSI Patrick
Sustainability Calling

2014

DUBÉ Jean, LEGROS Diègo
Spatial Econometrics Using Microdata

LESCA Humbert, LESCA Nicolas
Strategic Decisions and Weak Signals

2013

HABART-CORLOSQUET Marine, JANSSEN Jacques, MANCA Raimondo
VaR Methodology for Non-Gaussian Finance

2012

DAL PONT Jean-Pierre
Process Engineering and Industrial Management

MAILLARD Pierre
Competitive Quality Strategies

POMEROL Jean-Charles
Decision-Making and Action

SZYLAR Christian
UCITS Handbook

2011

LESCA Nicolas
Environmental Scanning and Sustainable Development

LESCA Nicolas, LESCA Humbert
Weak Signals for Strategic Intelligence: Anticipation Tool for Managers

MERCIER-LAURENT Eunika
Innovation Ecosystems

2010

SZYLAR Christian
Risk Management under UCITS III/IV

2009

COHEN Corine
Business Intelligence

ZANINETTI Jean-Marc
Sustainable Development in the USA

2008

CORSI Patrick, DULIEU Mike
The Marketing of Technology Intensive Products and Services

DZEVER Sam, JAUSSAUD Jacques, ANDREOSSO Bernadette
Evolving Corporate Structures and Cultures in Asia: Impact of Globalization

2007

AMMI Chantal
Global Consumer Behavior

2006

BOUGHZALA Imed, ERMINE Jean-Louis
Trends in Enterprise Knowledge Management

CORSI Patrick, CHRISTOFOL Hervé, RICHIR Simon, SAMIER Henri
Innovation Engineering: the power of intangible networks

.

Printed and bound by CPI Group (UK) Ltd, Croydon, CR0 4YY

27/10/2024

14580731-0004